RECLAIMING MEN

WHAT HAPPENED TO AMERICA'S BOYS AND HOW WE FIX IT

RUSSELL STUART

RSE

TABLE OF CONTENTS

PRAISE FOR RECLAIMING MEN

"Finally, someone is calling out what we've all been observing for the last decade. I spent years training, assessing, and selecting military candidates to become the toughest men on earth. And while I saw an uptick in physical performance, there was a complete recession in the grit and resilience in our young candidates.

Reclaiming Men is a call to action for parents and mentors to trust their gut instincts and raise their son's to be mentally and physically strong and not kowtow to societal pressures to adopt weakness. We need messages like this, now more than ever."

— *Mike O'Dowd, Navy SEAL & Founder, Defense Strategies Group*

"Russell Stuart's book speaks to every parent and educator who still believes schools should build strength, not suppress it. His words are a wake-up call to restore purpose, structure, and pride in our classrooms."

— *Leandra Blades, Trustee, Placentia-Yorba Linda Unified School District & Former Police Officer*

"Russell Stuart has written a book that speaks to the men who still work, stand guard, provide and protect, whether in uniform or in the home.

Reclaiming Men is not about apology or softness; it's about taking ownership again of what a man truly is meant to be. In an age of distractions and drifting values this book reminds us that strength, purpose and discipline aren't optional, they're foundational. Every man who wants to lead, not follow, should read this."

— *Mark Walters, Host, Armed American Radio & Founder, CCW Broadcast Media*

"Hard hitting and on-point. In both uniform and civilian life, what matters is the bond between purpose and integrity. Russell Stuart's *Reclaiming Men* cuts straight to the heart, reminding men what they were built for and refusing the narrative that strength must be suppressed.

This book doesn't just point out the problems, it arms the reader with truths that demand action. If you serve, lead, provide, or protect in any capacity, read this. Then step into the role you were made for."

— *Joe Wildman, Colonel (ret.), US Air Force*

"On tour, I've seen what it takes each night to get a massive show on-stage and it's the men behind the scenes who make it happen: dependable, hard-working, committed. *Reclaiming Men* speaks to those men. It reminds them, and all of us, that effort, responsibility, and reliability still matter. Whether you're loading trucks, building sets, or leading a crew, this book is a call to show up, stand firm, and lead by example."

— *Matt Peloquin, Tour Manager (various major artists)*

"As a father, musician and business owner, I know how rare it is to find reliable, motivated men who take real ownership. In *Reclaiming Men*, Russell Stuart doesn't just issue a challenge, he gives a roadmap for how every man can rise up. If you want a book that talks about competence, character, and commitment, not just idealism, read this. We need men we can trust with our businesses, our families, and our daughters."

— *Bobby Alt, Co-founder, Street Drum Corps & Owner, Bobby's Pizzeria*

DISCLAIMER

This book reflects the personal observations, experiences, and opinions of the author. While every effort has been made to ensure the accuracy of information and statistics cited herein, the author and publisher make no representations or warranties regarding the completeness or accuracy of the contents. The information provided is not intended as professional, medical, legal, or therapeutic advice.

The views and opinions expressed in this book are those of the author and do not necessarily reflect the official policy or position of any organization, institution, or agency with which the author is or has been affiliated, including but not limited to the Beverly Hills Unified School District or any other entity.

Some names and identifying details have been changed to protect the privacy of individuals. This book discusses controversial social and cultural topics. Readers are encouraged to conduct their own research and form their own conclusions.

The author and RSE Publishing shall have neither liability nor responsibility to any person or entity with respect to any loss or damage caused, or alleged to have been caused, directly or indirectly, by the information contained in this book.

For Lisa,
my wife, my twin-flame, and the calm that keeps me steady. You've carried
more than anyone should, yet you never stopped believing in me. I love you
aafaad.

For Arabelle,
my daughter and my purpose. You remind me what all of this is for. I fight so
your generation will know strong, honorable men again.

For my mother,
whose love demanded strength, not excuses. You taught me how to stand tall
when life pushes back.

For my father,
whose lessons still guide me long after he's gone.

And for Rudy,
my loyal companions and reminder that love doesn't need words.

Everything I build, I build for you.

"Hard times create strong men.
Strong men create good times.
Good times create weak men.
Weak men create hard times."
— G. Michael Hopf

ACKNOWLEDGMENTS

This book exists because of people I'll never meet.

To the fathers sitting alone at kitchen tables at 2 AM, wondering if they're failing their sons, you're not. You're the last line of defense. *Keep fighting.*

To the mothers raising boys without a roadmap, terrified the world will destroy them before you can armor them, you see what's happening. Trust your instincts. Your sons need you to be ferocious.

To the single moms doing the work of two parents because the father walked away, you're building men in impossible conditions. That makes you a warrior. Don't let anyone tell you otherwise.

To the young men reading this who feel completely lost... good. Lost means you're looking. That's more than most are willing to do. You're not broken. You're not the problem. You're the solution. But you have to choose it.

To the teachers who still believe boys need structure, competition, and standards, not medication and apologies, you're fighting a rigged system. Keep teaching. We need you.

To the coaches who refuse to hand out participation trophies and still make kids earn respect, you're doing God's work. Boys don't need more friends. They need men who demand excellence.

To the first responders, the tradesmen, the veterans, the blue-collar guys who still believe work matters, you're proof this isn't theory. You're living it. You're the standard.

To the neighbors who step in when fathers fail, the grandfathers who teach boys how to use their hands, the mentors who show up when no one else will, you're the invisible army rebuilding manhood one kid at a time. You won't get credit. Do it anyway.

To the strangers on the internet who shared their stories, their scars, their failures, your honesty made this book real. Men don't heal in silence. Thank you for speaking up.

To the men who told me to make this book harder, not softer, to stop apologizing and start swinging, you were right. The world doesn't need another polite conversation. It needs a wakeup call. And to the young man reading this right now, the one everyone has written off, the one who's been told he's toxic, dangerous, unnecessary, listen carefully:

They lied to you.

You are not the problem. Masculinity is not the disease. Strength is not oppression. Your instinct to protect, to build, to lead, that's not something to apologize for. That's what the world needs most.

This book is your permission to stop pretending you're something you're not.

Reclaim who you are. Reject the lies. Rebuild what they tore down.

This fight isn't over. It's just beginning

And you're not alone.

INTRODUCTION

THE LOST GENERATION OF BOYS

Something is wrong with young men in America. Anyone who pays attention can see it.

Boys who should be confident and curious are anxious and unsure. Men who should be building, leading, and protecting are disappearing into screens, pills, and excuses. Look around. The modern young man is lost. He's medicated, distracted, disconnected, and unsure of who he's supposed to be. He's told that masculinity is dangerous, that ambition is selfish, and that being proud to be a man makes him part of the problem. He scrolls endlessly, argues online, avoids risk, and measures worth by validation instead of results. He'll spend three hours debating strangers on Reddit but won't spend three minutes introducing himself to a woman in real life.

We've taken the men who built, fought, invented, and protected, and convinced them their instincts are flaws. The result is a generation of boys without a clear map to manhood.

I'm not a psychologist or an academic. My name is Russell Stuart, and I'm an elected member of the Beverly Hills Unified School District Board of Education. I'm not observing this crisis from a distance; I'm IN the system, making decisions, and facing the consequences. I served as a Captain in the California State Guard for nearly a decade. I'm the CEO of Force Protection Agency, a private security firm built on the principles of discipline, vigilance, and responsibility. But more importantly, I'm a father raising a daughter in a world that desperately needs strong men.

I've seen what happens when men stop leading, and I've seen what happens when they remember how. I'm not speaking from theory or research papers. I'm speaking from the trenches of a cultural battle being waged for the future of young men in our schools, our homes, and our communities.

For decades, we've been told that men are the root of violence, war, and oppression. Every generation has its slogans such as *"toxic masculinity," "male privilege,"* and *"patriarchy."*

But the message underneath is always the same.

Men are the problem.

That message has consequences. It's no coincidence that suicide among young men is at record highs *(CDC data shows male suicide rates are nearly 4 times higher than females),* that more women than men are graduating college *(currently 58% of bachelor's degrees go to women),* that testosterone levels have dropped, or that fewer men are marrying, having children, or joining the workforce *(prime-age male labor force participation has dropped from 98% in the 1950s to 89% today).*

Let me put that in perspective: your grandfather's generation had higher testosterone levels, fought in wars, built the suburbs, and raised families on a single income. You're struggling to move out of your parents' house.

These aren't isolated statistics; they're warning lights on the dashboard of a dying engine. When a society convinces its men that they're expendable, the society collapses.

We've replaced courage with compliance, conviction with apology, and leadership with silence. We've built classrooms that punish risk-taking, workplaces that reward inoffensiveness, and media that portrays fathers as fools.

Turn on any sitcom and watch Dad struggle to operate the washing machine while his 10-year-old explains it to him.

Hilarious, right?

Except your son is watching, learning that being a father means being incompetent.

We've trained men to filter every action through the fear of being labeled wrong, offensive, or outdated. The result isn't progress; it's paralysis.

I see boys who can't look people in the eye. I see men afraid to date, afraid to speak, afraid to lead. They're told they're either potential predators or emotionally unavailable, depending on which day it is. So they do nothing. They swipe right 500 times and wonder why they can't connect. They avoid eye contact because someone might call it aggressive. They stay silent in meetings because disagreement could cost them their job. They've been broken down, not by failure, but by constant accusation.

We tell boys to open up, then shame them for not being emotional enough. We tell men to lead, then accuse them of being controlling. We teach them that their instincts to compete, protect, and push forward are outdated. Eventually, they stop trying altogether.

It didn't happen overnight. It started when schools stopped rewarding discipline and started rewarding compliance. It got worse when fathers were removed from homes. And it reached full speed when social media began teaching young men that being a man means being loud, rich, or angry. Now your son's role model is a 22-year-old on TikTok flexing in front of a rented Lamborghini, selling a course on "alpha male mindset" for $997. That's who's raising him because you're not.

This book isn't about nostalgia for the 1950s or today's political divides. It's about facts. It's about the recognition that the pendulum swung too far, from discipline to dysfunction and from strength to shame. It's about understanding how we arrived here, who pushed the shift, and how we start rebuilding the men this country desperately needs.

This isn't theory. It's a field report.

We'll trace the timeline:

- When schools stopped rewarding male energy and started medicating it (today, 12.9% of boys are diagnosed with ADHD compared to 5.6% of girls).
- When fathers were pushed out of homes in the name of liberation.
- When masculinity became a punchline instead of a goal.
- When digital culture gave boys screens instead of purpose.

You'll see how it all connects and how policy, education, entertainment, and ideology worked together to neuter what used to be called "being a man."

But this book isn't just about the fall. *It's about the rebuild.*
Because the truth is simple. Masculinity isn't toxic.

Weakness is.
Cowardice is.
Aimlessness is.

Masculinity at its best means discipline, courage, protection, and sacrifice. That's what keeps the world turning. Every bridge, law, family, and freedom we depend on exists because some man chose responsibility over comfort. Your house has electricity because a man climbed a pole in a storm. Your Wi-Fi works because a technician showed up at 6 AM. Your trash gets picked up because men do the jobs no one else wants. And yet we've raised a culture that mocks that same instinct while depending on it for survival.

This book is for the men who still feel the weight of duty and don't apologize for it. It's for the fathers raising sons in a world that tells them their instincts are wrong. It's for the young men who want to be strong without being labeled dangerous, assertive without being called oppressive, and proud without being told they're problematic.

It's also for the mothers, wives, and daughters who miss what real men used to be, not perfect, but grounded, protective, and reliable.

The goal here isn't to blame. It's to rebuild. We'll face the data honestly. We'll follow the history. We'll name the forces that broke our boys, and we'll lay out what needs to be done to bring them back.

There's still time. The decline didn't happen overnight, and the fix won't either. But it starts by saying the one thing too few people are willing to say anymore.

Men matter. Masculinity matters. And it's time we stop apologizing for it.

This isn't a complaint. It's a call to stand up for our sons, for our daughters, and for a country that cannot survive without strong men.

PART ONE

THE COLLAPSE

1

GROUND ZERO

We have destroyed an entire generation of boys... not through violence or war, but through slow confusion. Over time we dismantled everything that once gave men a sense of identity and direction. We told them they were the problem, that masculinity itself was something to fear, and then we acted surprised when they stopped showing up for life.

This isn't hyperbole. This is the reality young men and boys are living in right now.

While you're reading this, there's a fifteen-year-old boy sitting in a classroom being told his natural energy is a disorder. There's a twenty-two-year-old man living in his parents' basement wondering why he can't get out of bed. There's a father who hasn't heard from his son in six months because the boy doesn't know what to say anymore.

These aren't edge cases. This is the new normal. And if we don't act now, if we keep pretending this is just a phase or a trend, we will lose an entire generation before they ever get the chance to become men.

Walk through any school, college campus, or workplace and you can see it. Boys who used to compete now hesitate. Young men who once wanted to build or lead are unsure of whether they're even allowed to try.

They're medicated to sit still, distracted into silence, and too tired to fight back." They spend more time staring into screens than looking people in the eye. They've been trained to believe that confidence is arrogance, that leadership is domination, that ambition is selfish, and that masculinity is inherently toxic.

We didn't reach this point by accident. It happened one small shift at a time. You'll see it most clearly in schools, where risk-taking has been replaced by rule-following. Television turned fathers into punchlines. Politicians sold victimhood as virtue. And when these boys looked for guidance, they found algorithms and influencers instead of mentors and fathers.

Today's statistics don't lie. Fewer men graduate from college. Fewer men marry or become fathers. Male suicide rates rise each year while male labor participation keeps falling.

Behind every number is a story of disconnection, boys who no longer know who they are or where they fit.

This isn't longing for some past version of America. It's recognition that our culture has stopped producing strong men, and that the cost is showing up everywhere: in families, in classrooms, and in our national spirit. When men lose purpose, everything built on their shoulders begins to shake.

You can see it in schools first. Boys once pushed to compete and explore now sit through classrooms built to reward quiet obedience. They're expected to learn like girls, behave like girls, and think like girls. When they can't, they're labeled with attention disorders or anger issues. Instead of channeling energy into discipline or strength, we dull it with medication and apology.

We see it again in work. Forty years ago, men defined themselves by providing and producing. Today, many are told those instincts are outdated. The decline in trade education has left millions of young men without a clear path to skilled work, while universities push degrees that teach theory but not purpose. A man without a skill is a man without direction, and a society full of men without direction will always fall behind.

Relationships tell the same story. Dating has become digital, impersonal, and disposable. Men approach women with hesitation, afraid that confidence will be misread as aggression. Many stop trying at all, retreating into isolation or online fantasy. Marriage rates are at record lows, births are declining, and children are growing up without fathers in the home. Every missing father creates a new cycle of instability that no government program can replace.

Mental health is collapsing along with it. According to the *CDC*, men account for approximately 79% of suicide deaths in America *(CDC WISQARS, 2022)*. The average young man spends more than eight hours a day consuming digital media and less than one hour in physical activity *(Common Sense Media, 2021)*. Let me translate that: your son spends more time watching other people live their lives on TikTok than he spends actually living his own. He'll scroll through 800 videos of strangers doing stupid dances, but he won't walk around the block. And we wonder why he's depressed. Therapy and self-help can't fill the void created by the loss of purpose, duty, and connection. You can't therapize your way out of a life with no meaning.

This isn't just a crisis of the individual male. It's a national crisis. A country that stops producing strong men doesn't stay strong for long. We're already seeing it in our workforce participation, military readiness, and civic engagement. The very qualities that once built America, such as discipline, competition, risk, and leadership, are being stripped from our culture in real time.

They Knew What They Were Doing

The truth is uncomfortable, but it's simple. We created a culture that no longer respects men, and we did it while pretending that progress was the goal. We told ourselves that breaking traditional gender roles would free everyone, yet the result has been confusion and resentment on both sides. The modern man is unsure of what he is supposed to be, and the modern woman often cannot find a man who meets the standards she still quietly hopes for. That gap between expectation and reality is growing wider every year.

You see it in classrooms where girls outperform boys in nearly every subject, not because boys have become less intelligent, but because we built an education system that no longer fits the way they learn. Boys are built for action. They learn through structure, challenge, and movement. Yet schools today have turned learning into endless discussion and emotional reflection. A boy who fidgets is treated like a patient. A boy who questions authority is labeled defiant. Instead of being guided toward purpose, he's medicated into compliance. We are training boys to suppress the very instincts that once made them exceptional.

> *We built an education system that no longer fits the way boys learn and the damage didn't stop at the classroom door.*

We can't be shocked that these boys are confused. Imagine being told from the time you're young that everything masculine is suspect, then being asked to lead, protect, and provide once you reach adulthood. It's an impossible contradiction. No one can build confidence when the culture around them treats their nature like a flaw.

And here's the part that should make you furious: they did this on purpose. Not with malice, maybe, but with certainty. Every policy that feminized schools, every curriculum that pathologized male behavior, every media campaign that mocked fathers, it was all deliberate. They knew exactly what would happen when you strip boys of competition, discipline, and purpose. They knew, and they did it anyway. Because weak men are easier to manage, easier to sell to, and easier to control.

Mission: Control

A generation of uncertain, dependent men doesn't threaten the system. It feeds it. That's not conspiracy theory. That's just business. And your sons are the product.

The damage shows up in ways most people don't even recognize. Boys now fall behind girls in reading by nearly a full grade level on average by the end of elementary school, and the gap widens as they age *(NAEP, 2022)*. High school graduation rates for boys lag several percentage points behind girls nationwide *(National Center for Education Statistics, 2023)*. At the college level, the imbalance is now so extreme that some universities quietly worry about how to attract male applicants at all. In 2024, women made up almost 60 percent of college students in the United States *(NCES, 2024)*. That's not equality. That's imbalance.

Workforce numbers tell the same story. Millions of working-age men have left the labor force altogether. Some are out of work due to automation or economic shifts, but many simply gave up trying. They drift between part-time jobs or stay home entirely, disconnected from the sense of pride that comes with producing something of value. This isn't laziness. It's learned helplessness. It's what happens when a man's effort no longer feels necessary or appreciated.

It also changes the structure of families. A man without direction rarely becomes a husband or a father. Why would he? He's been told he isn't needed. Meanwhile, women are told they can do everything alone. The result isn't empowerment. It's loneliness on both sides. Marriage rates have fallen to historic lows, and nearly forty percent of American children are born outside of marriage *(CDC National Vital Statistics, 2023)*. Those numbers have consequences that no slogan can cover up. Children raised without fathers are more likely to drop out of school, more likely to experience poverty, and more likely to end up in the criminal justice system *(U.S. Department of Health and Human Services, 2020)*. That isn't ideology; it's data.

Mental health is the other part of the collapse. Men are less likely to seek therapy or medication, not because they don't feel pain, but because they've been taught that admitting pain will be used against them. At the same time, the culture pushes self-indulgence as healing.

Young men drown in screens, gaming, and porn because it's easier than facing the emptiness of a world that doesn't expect anything from them. We told them *"self-care"* means smoking weed and playing video games until 3 AM. Turns out, that's not healing. That's just slow-motion suicide with better graphics. Purpose has been replaced by comfort, and comfort is a slow killer.

If you talk to young men honestly, many will admit they feel invisible. They don't feel valued in school, respected at work, or wanted at home. Some respond by withdrawing. Others lash out. A few become extreme, convinced that anger is the only form of power they have left. Every one of those outcomes is a failure of culture, not of character.

Yet even with all of this decline, the message from many institutions remains the same: men are the problem. The conversation rarely asks what happens to a society when men stop believing they matter. We see it already. Declining male participation in the economy drags down productivity. Declining male participation in families increases welfare dependency. Declining male participation in civic life weakens communities and leaves leadership voids that no bureaucracy can fill.

Their Mischaracterized Role

Strong societies need strong men, not in the outdated sense of dominance, but in the moral sense of stability. A good man is not a threat to women or to progress. He's the foundation of both. When we erase that truth, everything else falls apart.

We can debate politics all day, but the cultural evidence doesn't lie. The further we move from traditional values of responsibility, discipline, and faith, the more unstable life becomes for everyone. These aren't conservative talking points; they are the conditions that make civilization possible. Without them, we drift toward disorder.

What we're facing now is not a temporary downturn. It's a generational unraveling. Boys who grow up without clear expectations turn into men who avoid responsibility. Men who avoid responsibility create weak families. Weak families create unstable communities, and unstable communities create the kind of society we see on the news every night. Violence, addiction, and despair are symptoms, not causes.

The question isn't whether this decline is happening. The evidence is overwhelming. The question is whether we have the courage to name it out loud and start reversing it. That begins by restoring honor to being a man again.

Raised by Algorithms

When you strip a generation of boys of purpose, they don't disappear. They find purpose in other places, often in ways that society doesn't like. Some bury themselves in digital worlds where strength and victory still mean something. Others attach themselves to extreme ideologies or influencers who promise the confidence that schools, parents, and leaders failed to give them. That's not a coincidence; it's the predictable outcome of neglect. If you refuse to guide young men toward honor, someone else will guide them toward chaos.

The internet is filled with voices claiming to represent masculinity. Some are harmless, encouraging discipline and physical fitness. Others cross the line into resentment and contempt.

But we should be honest: *these figures wouldn't have influence if mainstream culture hadn't abandoned the job of forming men.*

Boys are searching for someone who speaks directly to them, who doesn't treat them like potential criminals or broken projects. When the only people doing that are loud, angry, or extreme, it tells us where the real vacuum lies.

The Crisis Of Meaning

This is where leadership failed most. Our institutions used to produce men who carried themselves with quiet authority. Teachers, coaches, pastors, and fathers worked together to shape boys into men who understood duty. Now most of those institutions are gone, and the few that remain are afraid to talk about masculinity at all. We replaced the word *"man"* with *"person,"* as if pretending gender doesn't exist would solve anything. The result is a generation that doesn't know how to balance strength with kindness because no one ever showed them what that looks like in practice.

We are not just facing a crisis of men; we are facing a crisis of meaning. A man without meaning will look for stimulation. He'll chase pleasure instead of purpose. He'll substitute short-term reward for long-term fulfillment. That's what we see now: endless consumption, no creation.

Men are not lazy by nature. They're designed to pursue, to build, to overcome. Take away those outlets and you don't get peace; you get addiction and apathy.

Economic trends only make it worse. Over the last fifty years, manufacturing and trade jobs, the backbone of working-class male identity, have collapsed *(Bureau of Labor Statistics, 2023)*. Your grandfather built cars, fixed machines, and went home knowing he made something real. You push spreadsheets and attend Zoom meetings where nothing ever gets decided.

The modern service economy doesn't value the traits that once defined a good man: physical strength, endurance, and reliability. Instead, it values flexibility and emotional labor, qualities that align more closely with how women tend to communicate.

Translation: the economy wants you to be good at PowerPoint presentations and *"circling back"* on emails, not actually building or fixing anything.

There's nothing wrong with that, but pretending it's the same thing as masculine purpose is dishonest.

Not every man wants to be a social media strategist. Some want to build, weld, or fix things, and there's nothing regressive about that. Yet we keep treating those men as if they're relics from a primitive past.

You can't measure the loss of pride that comes from being told your natural instincts are outdated. When a man no longer feels useful, he stops growing. When millions of men stop growing, the country stops advancing. We talk endlessly about innovation, but innovation requires builders.

We celebrate freedom, but freedom requires defenders. We glorify progress, but progress requires families strong enough to raise the next generation. Men play central roles in all three, and yet we've spent decades minimizing them.

The Problem Download

The media doesn't help. Every advertisement, movie, and television show seems obsessed with tearing down the idea of a competent man. The father is the fool. The husband is the obstacle. The male leader is corrupt. Boys absorb that message from a young age, long before they can articulate what it's doing to them. By the time they reach adulthood, many already believe that being male means being wrong by default.

That's not equality; it's indoctrination.

Even the language around men has turned hostile. *"Toxic masculinity"* became a casual insult, used to describe anything traditionally male, such as confidence, competitiveness, or assertiveness. There are toxic people, sure, but masculinity itself is not toxic. It's protective, productive, and necessary.

Every civilization that survived long enough to build something lasting relied on men who were strong and disciplined. We've forgotten that because we've become too comfortable. And comfort is dangerous.

Removing The Protectors

Comfort convinces us that security is permanent, that the world will stay safe even if we stop doing the hard things that keep it that way. History proves otherwise. The societies that reject their men always collapse from within. They grow cynical, indulgent, and weak. Their enemies don't need to defeat them. They defeat themselves.

We are walking that same path right now. We celebrate fragility instead of resilience. We promote self-expression without self-control. We encourage men to *"get in touch with their feelings,"* but not with their duties. We've built a culture that rewards the appearance of virtue over the practice of it. We post slogans about mental health but remove every structure that gives mental health meaning: faith, family, and purpose.

And what do we have to show for it? Boys who can't speak to girls without anxiety. Men who can't lead families. A generation that can't handle criticism without calling it trauma. We are producing men who can identify every microaggression but can't change a tire. That's not progress; it's decay.

None of this is inevitable. It's the result of choices, made slowly and quietly, in boardrooms, classrooms, and newsrooms. Each decision was sold as compassion or equality, but together they created confusion. We made masculinity a problem to be solved instead of a strength to be shaped. And now we are living with the results.

The Return is Possible

The good news is that nature doesn't disappear; it only waits. The same qualities that built this country, such as courage, discipline, and risk-taking, still exist in men. They're buried under shame and neglect, but they're there. Every man still has that fire inside him. What he needs is permission to use it again.

If we want to rebuild, we need to stop apologizing for being male. We need to stop pretending that traditional manhood and equality are enemies. They're not. They depend on each other. A society with weak men cannot protect women or children. A society that treats masculinity as evil cannot produce virtue. The balance between strength and compassion is what made Western civilization possible. Losing that balance is what's destroying it.

This chapter isn't about despair. It's about clarity.

We have to see where we are before we can move forward. Every number and every story points to the same truth: we've built a culture that undermines men at every stage of life. The cost is showing up in our schools, our homes, our streets, and our headlines. It's time to stop pretending it's normal.

If you're a young man reading this and you've felt like something fundamental was stolen from you, like you were set up to fail before you even started, you're not paranoid. You're right. They took the roadmap, burned the bridge, and then called you lost. But here's what they don't want you to know: you can rebuild it. Every man who figures out who he is and what he's for becomes a threat to the system that profits from your confusion. That's why this book exists. Not to make you comfortable, but to make you dangerous in the best possible way. Dangerous to mediocrity. Dangerous to the lie that men don't matter. Dangerous to every force that wants you weak, silent, and compliant.

The next few chapters will trace how this all started, when the cultural foundation shifted, who pushed it, and why so many people were too afraid to speak up. But before we go there, we have to admit the reality in front of us. America doesn't have a man problem. America has a purpose problem, and men are paying the price for it.

We Stopped Asking

We've started to accept dysfunction as ordinary life. We see broken families, fatherless homes, and unmotivated young men, and we shrug. We call it modern times. We blame technology, politics, or economics, but we rarely look at the deeper cause. The truth is that we stopped believing that men have a distinct and necessary role. Once that belief vanished, everything that depended on it began to crumble.

Look at education. A century ago, schools were designed to toughen minds. They expected discipline, competition, and mastery. Today they focus on self-esteem, identity, and comfort. We measure feelings instead of results. We reward cooperation more than achievement. None of this is evil on its own but taken together it punishes the very instincts that drive boys to become capable men. They learn to avoid risk. They learn to apologize for confidence. By the time they reach adulthood, the habit of hesitation is already set.

We do the same thing in households. Parents fear letting boys face struggle. Every scraped knee is treated like a crisis. Every failure brings an excuse. But growth doesn't happen without friction. Boys who are protected from discomfort grow into men who can't handle conflict. Then society calls them weak, without admitting that it trained them to be that way.

Popular culture repeats the same pattern. When men are portrayed at all, they're mocked. The dependable father is boring. The masculine hero is rewritten as a joke or a villain. We rarely see portrayals of men who are disciplined, loyal, and quietly strong. That absence matters.

Culture teaches by example. When every example of manhood is either comic relief or moral failure, boys internalize it.

The breakdown of the family amplifies it further. Single-parent homes now make up almost one-quarter of American households with children *(U.S. Census Bureau, 2023)*. Most of those homes are led by mothers doing their best, but even the strongest mother can't replace the influence of a present father. Boys need to watch how men handle pressure. They need to see restraint, integrity, and sacrifice lived out in front of them. Without that, they try to piece together an idea of manhood from whatever fragments the culture gives them. Too often those fragments are violent, sexualized, or empty.

Economics adds another layer. For decades, the conversation about equality has centered on getting more women into boardrooms and politics. That's fine. But we rarely talk about the men who were left behind. Blue-collar jobs vanished, trade programs closed, and entire towns built around physical labor collapsed. We told those men to "learn to code," as if identity and pride could be switched out like software. The result is visible in opioid addiction, suicide, and chronic unemployment across rural America. Those aren't failures of intelligence. They're failures of belonging.

Meanwhile, in urban areas, young men drift between low-wage jobs, entertainment, and the false validation of social media. They perform for likes instead of working for respect. It's performance without purpose, expression without consequence. We created an economy that rewards attention more than contribution, and young men fell into that trap faster than anyone else.

Even religion, which once grounded men in duty and humility, has weakened. Churches that used to challenge men to lead and serve now worry about sounding offensive. Faith communities that once called men to discipline and sacrifice now talk about comfort and affirmation. The spiritual backbone that sustained generations of men has softened, leaving another vacuum where purpose used to live.

What ties all of this together is a quiet lie: that men are optional. That they can be replaced by programs, policies, or new definitions. But there's no substitute for what a good man provides. You can automate labor and digitize communication, but you can't replicate presence, courage, or moral authority. Those are human qualities, and they're learned from other men.

Every civilization that forgot that truth eventually relearned it the hard way. Rome, Britain, every empire that grew too comfortable eventually fell for the same reason: the next generation stopped believing that strength mattered. They became spectators instead of builders.

They confused comfort with progress. We are not different.

We still have time to correct course, but only if we're willing to tell the truth. The state of men today is not a mystery. It's the logical result of the choices we've made about education, family, faith, and culture. We can't fix what we refuse to name.

If we start valuing men again, not the image of men but real men who take responsibility, everything else will begin to recover. Families will stabilize. Schools will regain discipline. Communities will regain safety. The country will regain direction. But none of that happens until we admit that the crisis is real.

That's where we are today: a nation living off the momentum of the men who came before us, unsure if we still believe in the same virtues that built what we have. The numbers prove the decline, but the solution will come from something deeper than data.

It will come from remembering what we used to ask of men: to protect, to provide, to lead, and to serve, and having the courage to ask it again.

What Happens Next

We stand at a crossroads. Every generation before us faced hardship that tested its character, but ours faces something different: a crisis of identity. We have technology our grandparents could never imagine, comfort they could never afford, and yet a spiritual emptiness they would never understand. That emptiness has settled deepest in our young men, who look around and see no clear path forward, no code to live by, and no one telling them what it means to be good at being a man.

They've inherited a world built by strong fathers and grandfathers, but they were raised

to believe that strength itself is suspect. So they retreat, they numb, they quit. Many of them don't even realize what they've lost because they've never seen it modeled. They grew up without rites of passage, without mentors, without meaningful responsibility. A culture that no longer respects men cannot produce them.

The results are everywhere, but most people are too distracted to notice. A country cannot function when half its population feels unwanted and directionless. The numbers are not just statistics; they are alarm bells. Men are lonelier than ever recorded. They're less likely to work, to marry, to raise families, or to belong to any organization at all. These trends are not isolated; they're connected. They show what happens when a nation forgets that manhood isn't an idea, it's an obligation.

We used to understand this instinctively. Men had duties, women had expectations, and children grew up watching that partnership in action. It wasn't perfect, but it was functional.

Everyone knew their role, and society moved forward. Then we started believing that equality meant sameness. We decided that masculinity itself was a threat instead of a resource. We taught boys to feel instead of act, to doubt instead of decide, and we congratulated ourselves for being enlightened. Now we're living in the aftermath.

What we see today is not liberation. It's disorientation. The pendulum didn't just swing; it snapped. The push to soften men didn't create balance, it created weakness. And weakness always leads to instability. You can see it in the streets, in the classrooms, and online. A generation of men desperate for meaning is being told that meaning doesn't exist. That's how civilizations fade, not through invasion or disaster, but through the slow erosion of purpose. The good news is that men can be rebuilt. They always can. History proves that masculine strength, once lost, can return, but only if we stop lying about it. We don't need to invent new definitions of manhood. We need to return to the truths that have always worked. Men are at their best when they serve, when they protect, when they build, when they lead. These are not outdated concepts.

They are timeless realities. Every man, no matter his age or back-ground, can start living them again.

But to do that, we have to admit what went wrong. We have to trace the path that brought us here, from the cultural revolutions that redefined gender to the policies that weakened family and faith. None of this happened overnight. It happened step by step, generation by generation, through the choices of people who thought they were improving the world.

Before we can rebuild, we must understand the destruction. We must see how our institutions, our entertainment, and our leadership slowly turned against the very values that held this country together. Only then can we begin the work of reclaiming what was lost.

This book is not about blame. It's about restoration. It's about telling the truth even when it's uncomfortable. Because until we tell that truth, until we stop pretending that this crisis doesn't exist, the decline will continue quietly, invisibly, and completely avoidable.

The question is whether we have the courage to face it. Whether we can look at the state of men today and say, honestly and without apology, that this is not who we were meant to be.

That courage starts with understanding how we got here.

2

WHEN THE FOUNDATION CRACKED

Every collapse starts quietly. No one wakes up one morning to find that a civilization's values have vanished; they erode one habit, one policy, one belief at a time. That's what happened to American manhood. The foundation didn't fall overnight. It was chipped away, decade by decade, until the structure that once held boys upright started to tilt.

Your grandfather didn't see it coming. He couldn't have imagined a world where his grandsons would grow up afraid to be men. He fought in wars, built with his hands, raised kids on a single income, and died knowing he mattered. His generation handed down a stable country, and in two generations we burned it to the ground. Not through malice, but through cowardice. We let activists, academics, and corporations rewrite the rules of manhood, and we stayed silent because speaking up wasn't worth the cost. That silence has a price. Your sons are paying it right now.

The first cracks appeared in the mid-1960s. America was prosperous, powerful, and restless. After two world wars and a Depression, the country had survived by relying on discipline and duty, traits that were undeniably masculine. But by the sixties, a new generation was tired of rules. The culture shifted from obligation to self-expression. The message was simple: authority is bad, tradition is oppressive, and freedom means doing what feels right. It sounded harmless. It wasn't.

At the same time, the family itself began to change. Divorce rates doubled between 1965 and 1975 *(U.S. Census Bureau, Historical Statistics)*. Fathers who had been anchors in their homes were suddenly outsiders. The feminist movement, which began as a call for fairness and opportunity, gradually blurred into an ideology that treated men as competitors rather than partners. Many women simply wanted respect, but activists and academics pushed something else, the idea that masculinity and patriarchy were the same thing. In their version of history, every success a man had came at a woman's expense.

That theory made its way into universities first, then media, and eventually public schools.

Policy followed culture. Welfare programs introduced in the late sixties often punished marriage instead of rewarding it. The *"War on Poverty"* made it easier for single-parent households to survive without fathers present. That was never the intent, but it became the effect. The number of children growing up without a father figure rose steadily, and with each decade the pattern deepened. We replaced family accountability with government dependency, and generations of boys paid the price.

By the seventies, television became the new teacher. Sitcoms replaced sermons, and the family man turned into a caricature, lazy, clueless, always in need of correction from his wife or children. It seemed funny at the time. It wasn't. Homer Simpson became the template for an entire generation of fathers. We laughed at the bumbling dad who can't figure out how to work the dishwasher, and then we wondered why sons stopped respecting their fathers. Culture teaches through repetition. When you watch thousands of hours of stories where men are buffoons, you stop expecting men to be anything more.

In the eighties the shift spread to education. The rise of standardized testing and behavioral management rewarded compliance over initiative. Classrooms became quieter, not better. The natural energy that once fueled competition, shop class, and physical education was pushed out to make room for sensitivity training and conflict-avoidance programs. Boys who couldn't sit still were labeled hyperactive. Teachers, most of them female and under pressure to control classrooms, relied on medication to manage behavior.

The message was clear: boyhood itself was a problem to be solved.

Through the nineties and early 2000s, academia sealed the narrative. Entire departments formed around *"gender studies,"* built on the belief that traditional masculinity was a social construct designed for dominance. Professors taught that the path to equality required dismantling every system built by men, family leadership, religious authority, and even objective truth. That thinking spread far beyond college campuses. It entered corporate training, media hiring, and government diversity initiatives. No one dared question it publicly, because to question it was to invite accusation.

Technology finished what ideology started. The smartphone gave every boy an escape hatch. Reality became optional. Porn and social media offered reward without effort, intimacy without vulnerability, status without responsibility. Each swipe dulled his drive a little more. For the first time in human history, a young man could simulate success without ever earning it. He gets dopamine hits from likes, validation from strangers, and fake intimacy from pixels on a screen. His great-grandfather stormed a beach in Normandy. He can't order a pizza without using an app.

We can't pretend that all of this just *"happened."* It was built on ideas, some well-intentioned, others poisonous. The well-intentioned part came from people who wanted fairness, peace, and self-expression. The poisonous part came from those who saw family, faith, and masculine order as obstacles to power. Together they created a culture that dismantled the scaffolding of manhood and replaced it with therapy, entertainment, and shame.

Every decade since has inherited the same broken story: men are dangerous, strength is oppression, leadership is privilege. Schools still teach it, media still sells it, and corporations still echo it in slogans about *"redefining masculinity."* Yet no one stops to ask why redefining something that worked for thousands of years was necessary in the first place.

That's where we stand now, a nation that remembers the benefits of strong men but has forgotten how to make them. The cultural foundation that once trained boys to serve and sacrifice was replaced with one that trains them to apologize and conform.

The result isn't equality; it's emptiness.

The People Who Did This

When we look back, it's easy to think these changes were random or cultural *"evolution."* They weren't. They were driven by specific groups and philosophies that believed the traditional man stood in the way of progress. They didn't attack men directly at first. They attacked the systems that built them. Once those systems weakened, men followed.

Universities led the charge. What started as legitimate academic inquiry into gender became an ideological project.

> **The idea was simple but corrosive: society is an ongoing power struggle between oppressors and oppressed.**

In that model, men were cast as the permanent oppressor. Every institution built or led by men, family, business, religion, was treated as proof of their guilt. By the 1990s, this worldview dominated the humanities and social sciences. Students carried it into journalism, entertainment, and government. Many believed they were fighting injustice. In practice, they were rewriting the story of what men were allowed to be.

Media turned those theories into emotion. Films and television began portraying strong men as dangerous or broken, and weak men as noble victims. In the news, stories about male violence or misconduct became proof that masculinity itself was flawed. Nuance vanished. Good men disappeared from the narrative because complexity doesn't sell. What sells is outrage. Every industry followed that formula. The entertainment business stopped celebrating builders and heroes and started rewarding confession, vulnerability, and chaos.

The old archetype of the steady, reliable man was replaced by one of two extremes: the predator or the fool. Both were easier to mock than to admire.

It Didn't Happen Overnight

Politics played its part too. The social revolutions of the 1960s and 1970s brought real benefits, civil rights, workplace equality, but they also created a permanent activist class that thrives on division. Those movements needed a villain to stay alive, and the "patriarchy" filled that role. Policy and public messaging began to frame traditional families as outdated. Fathers were no longer seen as anchors; they were painted as obstacles to independence. Tax structures and welfare laws made fatherless homes more common, not less. Every generation since has grown up thinking men are expendable because the laws quietly treated them that way.

The corporate world soon followed. As public relations replaced purpose, companies realized that appealing to grievance sold products. Ads began targeting women by mocking men.

"You don't need him," became both slogan and strategy.

In the process, the idea of mutual respect between the sexes disappeared. The marketplace started treating men not as customers, but as problems to be fixed. The psychological effect of being told you're unnecessary seeps into everything, from how men work to how they love. It turns confidence into silence.

Meanwhile, public education absorbed these ideas almost without debate. Guidance counselors began telling girls to chase leadership and boys to check their privilege. Career days glorified every field that symbolized compassion or creativity, while hands-on, practical paths, mechanic, builder, soldier, were treated as last resorts. We told every kid they needed to go to college to be successful, then wondered why plumbers make more than social workers with $80,000 in student debt.

Vocational training programs vanished. By 2010, most American high schools offered little or no shop or trade instruction *(Association for Career and Technical Education, 2013).*

We erased the natural route through which millions of working-class boys had once found pride and independence.

Technology magnified the damage. The same decades that softened male identity also connected the world through digital networks. That combination, moral confusion and unlimited access, was deadly. Boys grew up bombarded with sexualized images, false status, and algorithmic dopamine hits. They learned that gratification is instant and effort is optional. A father used to teach patience. A screen teaches consumption. We shouldn't be surprised that attention spans collapsed along with discipline.

Through all of this, one message remained constant: *masculinity must evolve.* But evolve into what? No one ever defined it. They just kept dismantling the old model without replacing it. The result was a vacuum.

Men stopped knowing what role they were supposed to play, and women grew frustrated that men weren't playing any role at all. Both sides were right, and both were victims of the same confusion.

There were people who tried to warn us. In the late 1980s, writers such as *George Gilder (Men and Marriage, 1986) and Robert Bly (Iron John, 1990)* warned that the erosion of masculine purpose posed a serious threat to both social stability and individual well-being.They were ridiculed as reactionaries. Politicians ignored them. Universities mocked them. Yet three decades later, everything they predicted is visible. The data matches the warning: declining male wages, declining marriage rates, rising depression, and the slow disappearance of fatherhood.

Facts don't care about feelings; they just record the fallout.

We should be clear about what really changed. It wasn't just women entering the workforce or social norms adjusting. The deeper shift was philosophical. We replaced moral frameworks that demanded discipline and sacrifice with ones that worship self-expression. We began to measure virtue by emotion instead of action. In that system, stoic men looked cold, decisive men looked oppressive, and protective men looked controlling. Once you label virtue as vice, you make vice inevitable.

The damage spread across class lines. In elite circles, men were told to be soft and nonthreatening. In working-class neighborhoods, men were told they were obsolete. Both messages led to withdrawal. Some men tried to prove their worth through money or status; others gave up altogether. The result is the same emptiness at both ends of society, loneliness, addiction, and confusion wrapped in different packaging.

We can't move forward without acknowledging how deep this shift runs. It's not just about changing laws or media portrayals. It's about redefining what we expect from men at every level. A century ago, young men were told they were the backbone of civilization. Today they're told civilization is a burden they didn't build and don't deserve. No group can thrive under that message for long.

The foundation shifted because we stopped teaching that strength and virtue are linked. Strength without virtue becomes cruelty. Virtue without strength becomes impotence. We need both. Every healthy culture finds that balance. Ours lost it on purpose. The people who pushed

this change didn't understand that they weren't just dismantling patriarchy, they were dismantling stability.

The Damage Becomes Measurable

As the twenty-first century began, the consequences of these cultural shifts started to harden into daily life. We were no longer debating ideas about men; we were living with the results of decades spent undermining them. Boys entered schools where no one looked like them in authority. They turned on screens that told them masculinity was either comic or criminal. They watched families collapse around them and were told that "a family can be anything." And for the first time in our history, a generation grew up with no clear picture of what a good man actually looks like.

In schools, the damage became measurable. By 2010, girls outperformed boys in reading, writing, and overall GPA across almost every state. The *National Assessment of Educational Progress (NAEP, 2011)* reported a gap of more than 10 points in literacy by the end of middle school. Teachers, often unintentionally, reinforced this imbalance. They praised traits more common in girls, verbal expression, cooperation, and emotional awareness, while discouraging traits more common in boys, assertiveness, competitiveness, and risk-taking. What used to be considered normal male behavior became pathology.

The new educational dogma was that equality meant sameness. Instead of meeting boys where they are, we tried to turn them into girls who happen to be male. We gave them coloring books when they needed wrestling mats. We asked them to journal their feelings when they needed to build something with their hands. And when they couldn't sit still for six hours discussing emotions, we called it a disorder. The cost of that mistake is enormous. Boys who don't fit the system learn early that they are defective. Some rebel and get punished for it. Others withdraw and fade quietly into mediocrity. Either way, the lesson sticks: they don't belong.

At home, fathers were vanishing in slow motion. Divorce normalized single parenting. The rise of social media replaced time once spent mentoring children with scrolling and distraction. Even men who stayed in the home were often emotionally absent, drained by work or buried in digital escape. A boy without a present father learns what it means to be a man from the culture around him, and that culture, by now, despised men.

Religion, once a counterweight to these forces, began to retreat as well. Churches that had once called men to leadership and service softened their message to avoid controversy. Sermons about duty and discipline became sermons about self-care. Many congregations feminized their worship, both in tone and structure, and men quietly stopped showing up. Surveys from *Pew Research (2020)* show that church attendance in the United States has fallen sharply over the past few decades, with men remaining consistently less likely than women to attend. In 2020, only about one-third of U.S. adults said they attended services at least once a month. Without faith or mentorship to anchor them, many boys instead turned to peers and online personalities in search of meaning. The results speak for themselves.

Meanwhile, the entertainment industry fully embraced the new narrative. Superheroes became neurotic. Action heroes turned into self-parodies. The *"strong male lead"* was replaced by the *"reluctant antihero"* or the bumbling fool. Commercials began depicting fathers as overgrown children who needed their wives or daughters to fix their mistakes. Dad can't figure out how to work the dishwasher. Dad forgot to pick up the kids.

These messages might seem harmless, but they accumulate.

When every cultural image of manhood is negative, the subconscious message becomes permanent: men can't be trusted.

Corporate marketing joined the crusade. The same companies that once sold products with aspirational masculine imagery, strength, mastery, competence, shifted to campaigns that apologized for those traits. In 2019, *Gillette* released the controversial *"We Believe"* ad lecturing men about *"toxic behavior."* It wasn't just tone-deaf; it was a public scolding of the company's own customers. The backlash should have been predictable. Millions of men were tired of being told they were the problem for simply existing.

At the policy level, the bias continued. Legal systems still treated fathers as secondary parents. In custody disputes, mothers were awarded primary custody nearly 80 percent of the time *(U.S. Census Bureau, Custodial Mothers and Fathers, 2020)*. Family courts often presumed men guilty in cases of domestic conflict before evidence was presented. These realities rarely made the news, but they shaped how men saw themselves: disposable, distrusted, and easily replaced.

All of this created a feedback loop. Young men disengaged from the systems that insulted them. Schools lost male teachers. Churches lost male members. Families lost fathers. Each loss made the next one more inevitable. The absence of men became both the cause and the symptom of the decline.

And nobody stopped it. The people who saw what was happening, the fathers, the coaches, the pastors, the teachers who remembered what boys used to be, they stayed quiet. They watched their sons medicated into compliance and said nothing. They watched masculinity turned into a slur and nodded along. They were afraid of being called sexist, outdated, or toxic. So they surrendered without a fight. That cowardice cost us everything. Because when good men go silent, bad ideas win by default. The cultural engineers who wanted to feminize boys and domesticate men didn't need a majority. They just needed the decent people to shut up and look away. And that's exactly what happened.

Technology poured fuel on the fire. Social media rewarded outrage, sarcasm, and emotional confession, traits that fit better with female communication styles. Men, less verbal by nature, either withdrew or mimicked the behavior to stay visible. The result was a generation of men communicating like reality-show contestants: dramatic, impulsive, reactive. The more they tried to fit the new model of *"open"* masculinity, the less stable they became. Recent research shows that adult men in the U.S. are experiencing increases in depression-symptom prevalence, though the rise has been greater among women and younger populations *(NIMH, 2022; CDC, 2023).*

The collapse of traditional courtship followed. Dating apps turned relationships into markets. Algorithms replaced human introductions. Attraction became a numbers game dominated by appearance and instant gratification. In that world, average men vanished. A small percentage of high-status men gained all the attention while the rest gave up trying. *Pew Research Center (2023)* found that nearly two-thirds of men under thirty are now single, up sharply from just over half in 2019.

While dating app use among young adults remains high, men report far less success and satisfaction on these platforms than women, leading many to disengage from dating altogether. These men aren't celibate by choice, they've been removed from the mating pool by a culture that devalues ordinary masculine traits like reliability, courage, and modest confidence.

Every one of these trends feeds into the same truth: a society cannot function without men who believe they matter. We can't build families, defend freedom, or maintain order if men are afraid of being men. The cultural engineers who reshaped masculinity never understood that what they were really dismantling was civilization itself.

By the late 2010s, even mainstream commentators began to notice the pattern. The *"boy crisis"* became a topic of study, but most discussions treated it like a curiosity rather than an emergency. Panels were hosted, papers were written, and nothing changed. Politicians avoided the subject entirely. Helping men is not a popular cause in a society addicted to victim hierarchies. There's no grant money in masculine responsibility.

But ignoring a crisis doesn't erase it. The data kept coming, year after year, painting the same bleak picture. Workforce participation for men hit record lows. Fertility rates dropped below replacement level. Testosterone levels fell kept falling. These are not abstract trends; they are biological and cultural warning signs. The very engine of human continuity is slowing down, and the people in charge act as if it's progress.

That is how the foundation shifted: not through revolution, but through erosion.

Every system that once produced capable men was reprogrammed to neutralize them instead. The shift was slow enough that most people never noticed. By the time we did, the old structure of family, faith, and community had already been hollowed out.

Living in the Wreckage

By the start of the 2020s, the collapse was no longer cultural theory, it was daily life. Every indicator that measures the health of men was flashing red. Marriage rates at record lows.

Birth rates below replacement. Suicide climbing every year. College campuses two-thirds female. Millions of men leaving the workforce permanently. And behind the numbers, a quiet sadness that no one wants to name: millions of boys growing up without purpose.

We built a society that forgot how to challenge men and then pretended to be surprised when they stopped rising to the challenge. The system didn't just stop producing strong men, it stopped believing they were needed at all. The few who still carried themselves with confidence were labeled as relics or threats. The rest learned to shrink.

If you talk to men privately, you'll hear it. They feel invisible, mistrusted, and blamed. They censor themselves at work to avoid conflict. They second-guess their instincts in relationships. They watch the culture celebrate every other group's identity while treating theirs as something shameful. Even the word *"man"* is used less, replaced with neutral terms like *"person"* or *"partner."* Language itself is being cleaned of masculinity, as though removing the word will remove the need.

What's left is confusion. We tell men to be strong but sensitive, confident but not assertive, protective but never possessive, successful but never proud. These contradictions don't create balance, they create paralysis. The modern man lives under constant contradiction: encouraged to lead yet punished for doing it, told to express himself yet mocked when he does. A generation raised in that tension will either collapse inward or lash out. We see both happening.

The most tragic part is that this was all avoidable.

The problem isn't that men changed, it's that society redefined the rules without telling them why. We traded discipline for comfort, tradition for novelty, and responsibility for self-expression. We called it progress, but progress that produces weaker people isn't progress at all. It's regression with better branding.

The past had its flaws, but it had clarity. Men knew what was expected of them. They were taught to protect their families, serve their communities, and find dignity in labor. They might not have always been gentle, but they were grounded. Today's men have endless comfort and no compass. They can stream a thousand opinions but can't decide who they are.

The loss of male leadership has consequences that go far beyond individual lives. It reshapes the moral structure of a nation. When men no longer lead with integrity, chaos fills the void. We see it in rising crime, political extremism, and moral confusion. Strength without virtue turns violent; virtue without strength turns cowardly. Right now, we are living through both.

The same society that attacks masculinity still depends on it every time disaster strikes. When the grid fails, when war breaks out, when danger appears, it's men who rush forward. The very instincts we label *"toxic"* are the same ones that keep civilization alive. The firefighter, the soldier, the builder, the police officer, all the men whose courage makes safety possible, are living proof that masculinity isn't the problem. The absence of it is.

But we've created generations of boys who don't see those men as role models. They see them as stereotypes. Schools rarely invite veterans to speak. Media rarely celebrates builders or fathers. Instead, we flood screens with influencers who confuse narcissism for confidence. Boys learn early that fame beats service, emotion beats reason, and comfort beats commitment. It's no wonder they crumble under pressure. We trained them for weakness.

The culture won't admit this, because admitting it would mean confronting its own hypocrisy. It would mean admitting that the social experiments of the last sixty years, designed to liberate everyone, actually enslaved a generation to confusion. The data is undeniable: fewer marriages, fewer children, lower life satisfaction, higher depression. The promise of a world without gender roles was that everyone would be free. The result is a world where no one knows who they are.

What We Do About It

So where do we go from here? We start by being honest about who did this and why. These shifts didn't emerge naturally. They were shaped by movements, thinkers, and industries that saw traditional manhood as competition. They dismantled it deliberately, piece by piece, until even men themselves stopped defending it. That's not conspiracy, it's history.

In the next chapter, we'll name those forces clearly: the ideological movements that reframed masculinity as oppression, the media machines that profited from its destruction, and the political systems that kept it in decline. We'll separate the genuine pursuit of equality from the calculated campaign to erase the masculine identity altogether.

The purpose isn't revenge. It's understanding. We can't rebuild what we don't understand, and we can't defend what we're afraid to name. If we want to restore balance, we have to see how it was lost. Only by tracing the roots of this collapse can we begin to grow something strong again.

The foundation shifted because we stopped guarding it. The task now is to rebuild it, stone by stone, truth by truth, until men once again know who they are, and the nation once again remembers why that matters.

But rebuilding requires rage first. Not reckless anger, but righteous fury at what was done. You should be angry that an entire generation of boys was used as a social experiment. You should be furious that policies designed to "liberate" women ended up destroying families and abandoning sons. You should be livid that the people who caused this damage, the academics, the activists, the corporate marketers, they got rich and famous while your sons paid the price.

That anger is useful. It's fuel. Because men who are comfortable with the status quo will never change it. Only men angry enough to fight back can rebuild what was destroyed.

The question is: are you angry enough yet?

If we want to fix the nation, we have to fix our men. That starts with being honest about how we got here, who pushed it, and why.

The next chapter begins that story.

3

WHO PUSHED IT AND WHY

Cultural collapse doesn't happen by accident. Someone always benefits from confusion. When men doubt who they are, they're easier to control, easier to sell to, and easier to replace. The destruction of manhood wasn't spontaneous, it was engineered through ideology, profit, and politics.

This isn't conspiracy; it's incentives. No secret meetings in smoke-filled rooms, just people acting in their own interests.

Universities profit from endless grievance studies. Universities feed on grievance. Corporations cash in on insecurity. Politicians harvest dependency. Media sells outrage.

Every major institution discovered that weak, confused men are better for business than strong, confident ones.

They didn't coordinate the attack. They just all attacked at once because it served their interests. Your sons weren't casualties. They were the target.

But money wasn't the only motive. The ideology came first, the profits followed.

The first force was intellectual. The second was financial. The third was political. Together, they formed an unholy alliance that rewired how the Western world sees masculinity.

The intellectual attack began in universities in the mid-twentieth century, led by a group of postmodern thinkers who believed that all truth was subjective. They argued that there were no moral absolutes, only power structures. In that worldview, men represented *"the system."* Masculinity wasn't virtue; it was oppression. Every traditional institution, the church, the family, the military, was reinterpreted as a mechanism for male dominance.

These ideas came from theorists who may have never built anything tangible in their lives, but who held enormous influence over the students they taught. Think about that: people who never started a business, never raised a family, never served in the military, never fixed a car, decided they were qualified to tell the world that masculinity was the problem. They questioned whether objective truth even existed, and once you remove truth, you remove standards. Without standards, morality becomes politics. And in politics, power replaces character.

Students raised on those theories entered media, education, and government, carrying their professors' skepticism toward anything traditional. They didn't think they were destroying culture; they thought they were improving it. They believed that tearing down the *"patriarchy"* would make the world fairer. What they never understood was that removing structure doesn't create freedom, it creates chaos.

The financial incentive followed soon after. Corporations realized that social revolution sells. A population that's uncertain of its identity is a perfect consumer base. Men who no longer find pride in family or craftsmanship start looking for status in possessions. Women who distrust men buy more products marketed as independence. Companies figured out how to monetize division. They turned your identity crisis into a revenue stream. Can't figure out how to be a man? Buy this watch. This cologne. This car. This lifestyle subscription service. It wasn't personal. It was business.

Advertising stopped appealing to virtue, hard work, loyalty, honor, and started appealing to insecurity. Every campaign told you that you weren't enough unless you bought something. The economy shifted from production to consumption, from building to branding. It was a slow transformation, but by the 1980s and 1990s, the masculine role of the provider was being replaced with that of the customer. A man who measures his worth in purchases, not principles, is easy to manage.

The political side was even more calculated. As Western nations grew more bureaucratic, government programs began replacing the roles once filled by men. Welfare replaced fathers. Regulation replaced local leadership. Safety nets turned into webs. Every new dependency made citizens less self-reliant, and self-reliant men are the hardest people to govern. Politicians discovered that promoting victimhood wins votes. A man who can provide for his family, fix his own problems, and doesn't need government assistance? That's a voter they can't control. Strong, confident men don't need saving, and that makes them inconvenient.

Over time, these three forces, academia, commerce, and politics, built an ecosystem that rewarded weakness and punished strength. Men who questioned it were labeled bigots or extremists. Institutions that once trained men to be disciplined started training them to be compliant. The cultural elite didn't have to ban masculinity; they just had to make it unfashionable.

By the 2000s, the message was clear across every platform: *traditional manhood is outdated.* Movies mocked it, universities dismantled it, corporations lectured it, and governments ignored it. The average man who resisted this shift didn't feel rebellious, he felt alone.

There's a reason movements like "men's rights" or "traditional masculinity" never gain mainstream support. They don't fit the narrative.

Talking about men's decline threatens too many interests, the academic class that profits from endless social theory, the corporations that profit from perpetual insecurity, and the political machines that profit from dependence.

The pattern isn't hard to see. Every time men begin to recover confidence or unity, another crisis or controversy appears to put them back in their place. When fathers ask for custody reform, they're accused of sexism. When veterans talk about discipline, they're accused of toxic behavior. When young men push for fitness or competition, they're called aggressive.

The Goal Isn't Equality, It's Control

None of this means there's a shadowy conspiracy. It's more subtle than that. It's an alignment of incentives. Every major cultural institution found a reason to undermine masculine virtue, some for ideology, some for money, some for power. The result is the same: *a society where the average man feels unwelcome in his own skin.*

You can measure that outcome in every statistic that matters. Male wages stagnate while consumer debt rises. Men own fewer homes. They marry later, if at all. Their physical health declines while their digital consumption explodes. The system doesn't need strong men, it needs obedient ones. And obedience is easiest to maintain when people have nothing solid to stand on.

What's remarkable is how few people admit this openly. Even many conservatives, terrified of being labeled misogynists, tiptoe around the issue. They talk about *"family values"* or *"faith-based solutions,"* but rarely confront the source of the problem: decades of cultural engineering designed to remove men from leadership.

When men stop leading, they don't disappear, someone else takes their place.

That's what happened. Bureaucrats, activists, and corporations filled the gap once occupied by fathers, teachers, and builders. They run the culture now, and they have no intention of giving it back.

This chapter isn't about conspiracy theories. It's about cause and effect.

When the people in charge of information, education, and economics all benefit from a population that doubts itself, masculinity becomes collateral damage.

Weak men make easy subjects. Strong men ask questions.

And so, we arrive at the present moment, a time when the very qualities that built the modern world are treated as liabilities. Hard work is exploitation. Discipline is oppression. Leadership is privilege. Men didn't invent those accusations, but they live with the consequences.

The campaign against masculinity didn't come from a single source. It evolved from overlapping movements that shared one goal: dismantling the social order built on masculine virtues. Each group claimed to be fighting for progress, but together they built a culture that taught men to doubt their own worth.

The most influential was radical feminism. It's important to separate this from classical feminism, which fought for legal equality, equal pay, voting rights, education, opportunity. Those goals were just and necessary. But in the 1970s and 1980s, a new strain emerged inside universities that saw men not as partners but as oppressors. It wasn't about fairness anymore; it was about power.

Thinkers like *Andrea Dworkin (Pornography: Men Possessing Women, 1981) and Catharine MacKinnon (Toward a Feminist Theory of the State, 1989)* argued that under patriarchy, masculinity had become inseparable from dominance and violence. They saw male power as the organizing force of society, a system in which aggression wasn't an exception, but the expectation. To them, the family structure was a prison, sexual relations were political acts, and male authority was always abuse in disguise. These ideas sounded extreme, but they spread quickly through academic departments, then into media.

Within a decade, the word "patriarchy" became shorthand for everything wrong with the world. It was the perfect villain, faceless, vast, and impossible to defend without being accused of guilt.

The media amplified it because outrage sells.

Newsrooms learned that conflict draws attention, and nothing fuels conflict like gender politics. Stories about men behaving badly became daily entertainment. A single high-profile scandal could be used to smear an entire gender. The nuances of human nature, virtue, temptation, redemption, were erased. Every story had to fit a moral binary: *women good, men bad.*

Opportunity in Division

The entertainment industry has always reflected social values, but in this era, it began shaping them outright. Screenwriters and producers, many educated in those same ideological universities, used movies and television to rewrite cultural norms. The dependable father became a joke. The confident leader became the villain. The male hero had to be broken or apologetic before the story could end. By the 2000s, the formula was standard: *men were obstacles, women were saviors, and traditional families were outdated relics.*

Corporations saw opportunity in this divide. They hired marketing firms fluent in identity politics. The message was simple: *empowerment sells.* A woman told she doesn't need a man becomes a lifelong consumer. A man told he's defective becomes a repeat customer for anything that promises confidence, cars, supplements, distractions. The system doesn't care about ideology; it cares about keeping people insecure. Every billboard and ad reinforces the same message: you're not enough as you are.

Meanwhile, politicians realized that every social divide can be turned into votes. In the 1990s and 2000s, entire political platforms were built on grievance rather than growth.

The more divided the sexes became, the easier it was to mobilize fear and resentment.

Policies that rewarded single-parent homes, that penalized male custody, that framed gender as conflict rather than cooperation, all were sold as compassion. But behind every law labeled "equality," another layer of dependency formed. The bigger the government grows, the smaller the man becomes.

Education, too, became a front line. Activist groups pressured schools to teach gender theory, not as discussion, but as doctrine.

Textbooks and trainings taught that gender is fluid, that masculinity is a performance, and that traditional male behavior is a potential threat. Boys heard those lessons long before they understood them. By high school, many already believed there was something wrong with wanting to be strong, assertive, or protective. Teachers who questioned the material risked losing their jobs. Parents who objected were labeled intolerant.

Ideology Became Policy, Then Culture

The final and perhaps most powerful push came from technology. Social media didn't invent narcissism, but it gave it a platform. Algorithms reward emotion, not truth. The louder and angrier a message, the more it spreads. That's why outrage over masculinity became a permanent trend. Every viral post or clip that mocked men or framed gender as conflict earned clicks, money, and attention. The truth didn't matter, engagement did.

Influencers built careers by attacking traditional gender roles. They mocked fathers, ridiculed marriage, and framed masculinity as insecurity. Major media outlets boosted them because it aligned with their brand of social activism. The more unstable the public became, the more content there was to sell.

It's a perfect economy of dysfunction.

Through all of this, ordinary men and women were caught in the middle. Most women don't hate men. Most men don't resent women. But both sides are manipulated by institutions that profit from division. If men and women worked together again, the entire outrage economy would collapse overnight. There is too much money and power invested in keeping the genders suspicious of each other.

That's the *"why"* behind the collapse. It wasn't just ideology, it was economics. An ungrounded population is easier to influence. When men no longer build, they consume. When families fall apart, everyone becomes a client of the state. When fathers vanish, government programs multiply. The loss of manhood feeds the system that profits from dependence.

This is why the attack on masculinity has never stopped, even when its results are obvious. Broken homes, failing schools, depressed men, anxious women, these aren't glitches. They're the outcomes of a design that rewards instability.

> *A stable society built on strong families, faith, and male virtue doesn't need endless intervention. A fractured one does.*

The saddest part is that many people pushing this agenda truly believe they're helping. Teachers think they're protecting children. Journalists think they're fighting injustice. Executives think they're promoting fairness. They don't see the long game. They see only the trend in front of them, not the damage behind it. The architects of confusion rarely live long enough to see what they built.

But we can see it now. We live inside the experiment. The result is a generation of men disconnected from themselves, and a nation disconnected from reality. The people who pushed this may never admit responsibility, but their fingerprints are everywhere, in policy, in education, in media, and in the hollow eyes of the boys they claimed to be liberating.

They Changed the Words, Not the Goal

The system that dismantled masculinity didn't vanish when people began to notice it. It adapted. Institutions learned to use new language to keep the same agenda alive. Instead of *"patriarchy,"* they began talking about *"equity."* Instead of *"toxic masculinity,"* they spoke of *"inclusive behavior."* The words softened, but the goal remained the same: to reshape men into something passive and dependent.

Corporate boardrooms became the front line of this rebranding. Diversity initiatives, once aimed at fair opportunity, evolved into loyalty tests. Men were expected to apologize for their existence before they could participate. Hiring decisions started to favor ideology over competence. Promotions required compliance with whatever social narrative was trending. Even the most capable professionals learned to keep quiet rather than risk being labeled outdated.

It's not equality that offends men, it's hypocrisy.

The same culture that claims to reject gender stereotypes now rewards them in reverse. Assertive women are celebrated. Assertive men are scolded. Companies that push *"empowerment"* slogans still exploit both sexes for profit. What matters isn't fairness; *it's optics.* The people running these campaigns know exactly what they're doing. They understand that moral posturing sells products and silences criticism at the same time.

Universities kept the ideological machine running. In the classroom, masculinity is discussed not as a natural trait but as a social illness. Research papers are funded to *"deconstruct gender norms,"* not to understand them.

Professors teach young men that their instincts, ambition, competition, strength, are symptoms of privilege. Then they grade them on how well they repent.

The result is predictable: *fewer male students, lower confidence, and growing resentment among those who remain.*

This culture rewards self-denial. Men are told to *"listen"* and *"learn"* while everyone else is encouraged to "speak their truth." But if only one side is allowed to speak, it isn't truth, it's propaganda. The irony is that the same society that demands men express vulnerability ridicules them when they do. We've created an emotional trap: silence is guilt, honesty is aggression, and confidence is arrogance.

Technology amplified this trap. Social media created a public arena where every word can be misinterpreted. Men learned to self-censor to survive. They share less, build less, risk less. They live in quiet suspicion that everything they do could be weaponized against them. And yet, these same platforms flood their feeds with messages about *"authenticity"* and *"mental health."* The contradiction is deliberate. Conflicted people stay online longer. The algorithm feeds on insecurity, and insecure men are perfect content consumers.

The academic and corporate sectors work hand in hand with media to enforce this new order. You can see the pattern in how scandals are handled. When a man misbehaves, his gender is blamed. When a woman does, she's an individual. Every major news outlet uses this double standard. It's not journalism, it's cultural conditioning. It teaches the audience what to think before they can process what they've seen.

The government, too, benefits from this imbalance. When men are portrayed as threats or failures, the state gains moral authority. Each social crisis justifies new laws, new programs, and new bureaucracies. But government cannot replace fathers, mentors, or discipline. It can only regulate what's left after those things disappear. Bureaucracy is not compassion, it's control wearing a friendly mask.

This machine isn't sustained by evil people; it's sustained by cowardly ones. Most men in positions of influence see what's happening. They just won't say it. They know that defending masculinity publicly can end careers. They watch as younger men flounder and hope someone else will fix it. Silence, in this case, is complicity. Every time a good man avoids the subject out of fear, the narrative grows stronger.

Yet, there's a reason the narrative keeps cracking. Reality always wins. No matter how many headlines declare masculinity obsolete, men are still the ones who build, protect, and endure. They're still the ones who run toward danger when others run away. They still form the backbone of every functioning community. That truth can't be erased, only ignored.

And it's being ignored on purpose. A generation raised to doubt men has trouble admitting that they're still essential. It's easier to rewrite history than to confront the consequences of tearing down the people who keep society standing. The same universities that mock masculinity rely on male engineers to keep their lights on. The same journalists who attack traditional men rely on male soldiers to defend their right to publish.

The hypocrisy is constant and complete.

The modern campaign against men has become self-sustaining. Academia supplies the theory, media supplies the narrative, corporations fund the message, and politics enforces it. Each piece feeds the others.

The more confused the population becomes, the more these systems thrive. It's not a conspiracy; it's an ecosystem of incentives.

But every ecosystem has limits. Eventually, the disconnect between ideology and reality becomes too obvious to ignore. We're approaching that point now. The data is too overwhelming, the frustration too widespread. People are beginning to ask questions again, questions that institutions can't answer without exposing their own contradictions. Why are boys failing? Why are men depressed? Why is the most prosperous society in history producing the least fulfilled generation of males?

Those questions terrify the people in charge because the answers lead back to them. They reveal that the problem isn't men at all, it's the systems that humiliated them. The people who built this mess want men docile, distracted, and apologetic. The only thing they can't control is a man who knows who he is.

That's the point of this chapter. The collapse wasn't random. It was built and maintained by people who believed that dismantling masculinity would make society kinder and safer. It didn't. It made it weaker and angrier. The evidence is all around us: broken homes, medicated boys, disengaged fathers, confused women. This isn't evolution. It's decay.

The first step to reversing it is simple but hard: *we have to tell the truth out loud.* We have to name the people, institutions, and ideologies that profited from the destruction of manhood. Not to hate them, but to stop them from doing it again. If we don't, our sons will inherit a world built to keep them small.

Why They'll Never Stop

There's a reason the attack on masculinity feels endless. Weak men are predictable. They don't lead revolutions, start companies, defend borders, or protect families. They comply. A culture built on compliance is easier to manage, and every institution that profits from control understands this. When men lose their backbone, the people in power gain freedom to act without resistance.

That's why the campaign never ends, not because it's true, but because it works. Every generation of uncertain men produces a new generation of dependent citizens. Dependence keeps systems alive. If you can convince men that their strength is shameful, you can convince them to hand it over.

The proof is visible in the way institutions react to masculine resurgence. Whenever a cultural moment arises that celebrates strength, discipline, or male leadership, it's immediately smeared as extremist. Words like *"patriarchy"* and *"fascism"* are thrown around not because they apply, but because they're useful. They shut down conversation before facts can surface. It's not logic, it's strategy.

But the truth has a way of returning. Even the loudest campaigns can't erase the realities of biology and human nature. Men are designed to build, compete, protect, and pursue meaning. When those drives are suppressed, the results are always the same: anxiety, addiction, resentment, and collapse. The proof isn't theoretical; it's statistical. The nations that treat masculinity as strength have higher birth rates, stronger economies, and more stable families.

The real victims of this war on men aren't just the men. They're the women and children left to live in a world without dependable partners, protectors, or fathers.

Feminism promised liberation but delivered loneliness. It told women they didn't need men, and it told men they weren't wanted. The result isn't equality, it's alienation. Two generations of broken families and confused relationships prove it.

Still, the same institutions that caused this damage keep doubling down. They push "men's mental health campaigns" that treat sadness as the disease instead of rootlessness. They sponsor panels about "positive masculinity" hosted by people who have no respect for men.

They create slogans instead of solutions.

It's not help; it's containment. They want men quiet, not better.

How to Break Free

So, what can be done? The answer begins with awareness. Once you see the system, you can't unsee it. Men need to start recognizing manipulation for what it is: a sales pitch dressed as morality. Every commercial, curriculum, and speech that tells you to be ashamed of your strength is selling something, control, dependence, or distraction. Rejecting that doesn't make you radical. It makes you free.

Freedom starts small. It starts with personal discipline, the one thing no system can fake. A man who gets up early, trains his body, master's a trade, and keeps his word is immune to propaganda. You can't control a man who controls himself. That's why self-mastery terrifies those who profit from weakness. Every strong, grounded man is a living threat to the machine that feeds on insecurity.

But this isn't just about men. Women have been misled too. They were told that independence means isolation, that strength means hardness, and that happiness comes from rejecting the very partnership that sustained humanity for thousands of years. They were promised empowerment and given exhaustion. They were promised freedom and handed fear. The lie hurt both sexes. The cure must involve both as well.

Rebuilding trust between men and women starts with honesty. We need to stop pretending that competition between the sexes is progress. It isn't. The modern gender war produces no winners, only lonely individuals fighting for validation. Real equality isn't sameness; it's mutual respect built on difference. Strong women need strong men, and strong men need strong women. Both thrive when they know who they are.

The system that pushed this division knows how powerful unity can be. That's why it works so hard to keep us apart. When men and women cooperate, families thrive. When families thrive, children grow up confident. Confident children don't need government programs, activist ideologies, or social media therapy. They grow into adults who can think for themselves. That's the one outcome the system can't afford.

This is why naming what happened matters. We can't rebuild manhood if we can't describe what destroyed it. The people and institutions responsible for this cultural collapse aren't unstoppable; they're just unchallenged. Their power depends on our silence. The moment men start speaking with clarity, the narrative begins to fall apart.

Every movement in history that restored sanity started with people refusing to repeat lies.

It doesn't take a mob; it takes a few honest voices. When those voices belong to disciplined, articulate, grounded men, the effect multiplies. That's how revival begins, not from politicians or think tanks, but from individual men reclaiming their purpose one choice at a time.

That's what the next chapters are about. We've covered what happened and who caused it. Now we need to face what it cost. The cost of weak men is written across every headline and every broken home in this country. It's the silent crisis that defines our era, and it's the reason this conversation can't stay polite anymore.

They Didn't Expect This

Because the truth is simple: when men fail, civilizations fail. When men rise, civilizations recover. Every empire that fell, fell first through its men. And every society that rebuilt itself did so through men who remembered what they were made for.

The people who pushed this cultural collapse wanted to erase that memory. It's our job to restore it.

And here's the part they never expected: men are waking up. Slowly at first, but it's happening. Young men are realizing they've been lied to. Fathers are realizing their sons were sacrificed for an ideology that hates them. The system thought it could keep men docile forever, but nature doesn't disappear, it only waits. Every man who breaks free from the programming, who rejects the narrative and reclaims his purpose, becomes a crack in their foundation. They can't stop you from becoming who you were meant to be. They can only hope you stay asleep long enough not to try. *Don't give them that satisfaction.*

4

THE FATHERLESS NATION

If you want to know why boys are lost, look for where the fathers went. You'll find the answer in empty dinner tables, court orders, and silent phone calls. You'll find it in classrooms full of restless boys who have never been told by a man that they matter. You'll find it in prisons packed with men who never had one to follow.

There's a specific moment when a boy realizes his father isn't coming back. Not physically, maybe he never left, but emotionally. The moment when he stops asking, *"Dad, can you help me?"* because he's learned the answer is always no. That moment destroys something fundamental.

It doesn't make headlines. It doesn't trend on social media. But it creates the man, or the broken version of one, that he'll become for the rest of his life.

We've had that moment happen to tens of millions of boys over the last fifty years. That's not a crisis. That's a massacre. And we did it to ourselves.

We didn't just lose fathers. We forgot what they were for.

Unfortunately, many of the fathers who are present are distracted or exhausted. Technology has replaced time. Screens have replaced mentorship. A generation of boys is learning manhood from video clips and influencers because no one real is there to show them what responsibility looks like.

So your son's learning how to be a man from a 19-year-old on YouTube who made $2 million selling a course on "alpha male mindset" while still living in your basement at 26.

That's his role model. Not you. Not his grandfather. Some kid with a ring light and a crypto scam. The message they absorb from the world around them is that men are either useless or dangerous.

There is no middle ground offered to them.

For most of history, a father's role was simple and sacred. He provided, he protected, and he prepared his sons to do the same. He was the bridge between childhood and manhood, the one who taught a boy how to take hits, how to work, how to lead. When that bridge broke, boys stopped crossing.

Today, that bridge is gone for millions. The numbers are staggering. In the United States, nearly one in four children grow up without a father in the home *(U.S. Census Bureau, 2023)*. Among certain communities, it's more than half. Studies from the *U.S. Census Bureau, the Department of Justice, and multiple universities* all show the same outcome: *when fathers disappear, everything else collapses.*

Crime rises. Grades fall. Depression climbs.

Boys who grow up without fathers are twice as likely to drop out, four times more likely to end up in poverty *(National Fatherhood Initiative, 2021)*, and five times more likely to commit suicide *(U.S. Department of Health and Human Services, 2020)*. *Those numbers aren't talking points. They're tombstones.*

We have built an entire culture that treats fathers as optional, a nice bonus, not a necessity. Television turned them into jokes. Courts turned them into visitors. Bureaucracies replaced them with programs. Feminists said they were oppressive. Corporations said they were replaceable. And now, decades later, we are reaping what we've sown.

When you remove the father, you remove the structure. The home loses its balance. The mother carries a weight she was never meant to carry alone. The son grows up without a model of manhood, and the daughter grows up without an example of how a good man loves a woman.

That's not progress. That's decay dressed as freedom.

Every society that has collapsed shared the same early symptom, the breakdown of the family. Rome had it. Babylon had it. America has it now. The family isn't just a social unit. It's the first government, the first school, the first church. And the father is its cornerstone.

A strong father is more than a paycheck. He's a compass. He's the man who teaches a boy that feelings aren't facts, that respect must be earned, and that failure isn't fatal. He's the one who turns chaos into order by setting limits and enforcing standards.

When that guidance disappears, boys go looking for it anywhere they can find it, gangs, influencers, video games, pornography. All of those become counterfeit fathers.

They give a sense of belonging without responsibility, approval without accountability. So your son's father figure is now a 23-year-old millionaire on YouTube who made his money selling fitness courses while flexing in front of rented Lamborghinis. That's who's teaching him what it means to be a man. But counterfeit love always leads to real destruction.

Schools can't replace fathers. *Teachers can educate, but they can't initiate.* You can't grade a boy into manhood. You can only guide him there. You can't fill out a worksheet titled *"How to Be a Man"* and expect results.

The same goes for therapy. It can help a man process his pain, but it can't give him a model to imitate. A therapist can tell him it's okay to cry. They can't show him how to carry 200 pounds up a flight of stairs or how to look another man in the eye when things get heated. Boys don't just need support. They need example.

The tragedy is that many men who grew up without fathers now don't know how to become them. They were never shown how. They were told to "be better," but not how to begin. You can't pass down what you never received. That's why this crisis repeats generation after generation, until someone breaks the cycle. *Breaking that cycle starts with truth.*

We have to stop pretending fathers are interchangeable. They aren't. Every boy needs to hear from a man who's been there: *that he's capable, that he's needed, and that he's expected to grow up.* No program or policy can replace that sentence.

A boy who grows up with a strong father learns that rules aren't restrictions, they're protection.

He learns that emotions aren't enemies, they're signals to master. He learns that failure isn't shame, it's instruction. That kind of boy becomes a man who doesn't crumble when life gets hard.

But a boy without that example learns something else. He learns that power is control, that love is weakness, that attention is validation. He builds an identity out of pain because no one showed him purpose. That boy grows into the kind of man we see everywhere today, reactive, uncertain, hungry for affirmation, angry at the world.

We can't fix that with slogans about empowerment or mental health hashtags. We fix it by rebuilding the role of the father. Not just biologically, but culturally.

We need to bring back the expectation that men will lead their homes, not just visit them. That they will train their sons, not outsource it. That they will stay, protect, and guide, even when it's hard.

The absence of fathers is not a small wound. It's the fracture line running through everything, crime, addiction, education, politics, relationships. We can trace nearly every major social problem back to the same missing piece: *the man who was supposed to be there, but wasn't.*

That's why rebuilding masculinity starts with rebuilding fatherhood.

Because until we bring fathers back into homes, we'll keep sending broken boys into the world and calling it progress.

They Destroyed Fatherhood on Purpose

The collapse of fatherhood didn't happen overnight. It was engineered, not by one law or one movement, but by a steady combination of policy, culture, and ideology that all shared one blind spot: the belief that men don't matter.

It began with government welfare programs in the 1960s. The goal was to help struggling families. The result was to punish fathers who stayed. Under the structure of the *Great Society*, families received more assistance if there was no working man in the home. Millions of women were told, *often by social workers*, that they'd lose benefits if the father lived with them. It didn't take long for that incentive to destroy generations of family stability.

The numbers tell the story. Before the welfare reforms of the mid-60s, about 8 percent of children in America were born to unmarried mothers *(Ventura & Bachrach, National Vital Statistics, 2000)*. By the 1980s, that number tripled. By 2020, it had reached over 40 percent nationwide *(CDC National Vital Statistics, 2023)*, with some communities surpassing 70 percent.

> *No society in human history has ever remained stable with that level of father absence.*

Read that again. *No society in history.*

This isn't a social experiment we're running. *This is civilizational suicide in slow motion.*

We took the most fundamental building block of human society, the father-led family, and we demolished it with government money and good intentions.

The architects of this disaster are still celebrated. The politicians who designed these policies got reelected. The academics who cheered it on got tenure. The boys who paid the price? They got prison, poverty, and despair. And we're still pretending it was all an accident. It wasn't.

Every step of this collapse was deliberate, documented, and defended. The only question left is: *are we going to keep doing it, or are we finally going to admit we were catastrophically wrong?*

The Celebration of Weakness

While policy stripped men from homes, media stripped them from respect. Sitcoms in the 70s and 80s turned fathers into punchlines, out of touch, lazy, clueless. Homer Simpson, Al Bundy, and countless others became the cultural image of fatherhood:

foolish men saved by smarter wives and precocious children.

Every sitcom dad became the same character: *the idiot who can't cook, can't remember anniversaries, can't be trusted with basic household tasks.* The 10-year-old daughter had to explain how to use the microwave. The dog was smarter than Dad. It seemed funny at first. But over time, those portrayals reshaped expectations. When you laugh at something long enough, you start believing it's normal.

At the same time, academia began rebranding masculinity itself as a social illness. Gender studies programs framed the traditional father as a relic of *"patriarchal oppression."* The new message was that families didn't need hierarchy or leadership, they needed equality, which in practice meant removing masculine authority altogether.

The feminist movement of the 1970s had noble beginnings. It fought for fairness and opportunity. But a radical wing within it became something else, a campaign not for balance, but for dominance. It began teaching that dependence on men was inherently degrading and that the nuclear family was a form of female captivity. Fathers were no longer seen as protectors but as obstacles.

The courtroom soon followed the classroom. Divorce laws shifted to *"no-fault"* systems, making it easy to dissolve marriages without proving wrongdoing. Custody rulings overwhelmingly favored mothers. Decades later, the family court system still treats fathers as visitors in their own children's lives. Many men simply give up after years of legal defeat, worn down by the financial and emotional toll.

The message to the next generation was clear: *fathers are replaceable.*

But fathers aren't just providers of money, they're providers of meaning. They set the moral tone of the household. They give boys the discipline and structure that mothers can't replicate alone. They show daughters what respect feels like so they can recognize love that's real. You can't replace that with a monthly check or a government counselor.

As fatherhood declined, the effects rippled through every corner of society. Crime exploded in the 1980s, driven largely by boys who grew up without fathers. Decades of federal and academic research have shown that father absence is one of the strongest predictors of youth risk. Studies have linked it to higher rates of suicide, school dropout, and incarceration. For example, a *U.S. Department of Justice report* in the late 1990s found that roughly 70 percent of juveniles in state institutions came from fatherless homes, and other studies have shown similar patterns in youth suicide and dropout data *(U.S. Department of Justice, 1998; U.S. Census Bureau, 2017).*

The reports showed what culture already knew instinctively...

the absence of fathers was tied to nearly every measure of collapse among boys.

The pattern hasn't changed. Kids growing up without fathers *still make up most of the dropouts, the addicts, and the inmates.* You don't need a think tank to see it, just walk through a juvenile detention center. Every generation proves the same point: *take the father out of the home, and the foundation cracks. The National Center for Fathering (2023)* and the *National Fatherhood Initiative (2015)* both found that children from father-absent homes are far more likely to face behavioral disorders, substance abuse, and long-term unemployment *(U.S. Department of Justice, 1998; National Fatherhood Initiative, 2015).*

When you remove the father, you remove restraint.

Boys grow up without learning how to channel aggression into purpose. That aggression doesn't disappear, it mutates. It becomes violence, addiction, obsession, or apathy. The same energy that once built civilizations now burns them down.

But this isn't just a poor or urban problem. It's everywhere. In upper-class suburbs, fathers are present but absent, physically home, emotionally gone. They work nonstop to provide but fail to connect. Their sons grow up starved for affirmation, drowning in comfort but starving for guidance. Affluence hides the same wound that poverty exposes.

Technology widened the gap. When fathers stopped teaching, the internet filled the silence.

Porn became the sex educator. YouTube became the father figure.

Boys learned how to act from influencers who were either angry, nihilistic, or lost themselves. The screen became the new authority.

We now live in a society where boys grow up without initiation, without challenge, and without direction. A boy used to earn manhood through a series of trials, learning to work, to fight, to sacrifice. Now he earns it through nothing. He ages, but he doesn't mature. He becomes legally adult but emotionally unfinished.

The result is a generation of adult boys, physically grown but spiritually unformed. They have muscles but no mission. Opinions but no wisdom. Freedom but no discipline.

And society treats this as progress. We call it equality. We celebrate *"independent parenting"* while ignoring what the data screams:

children raised without fathers suffer in almost every measurable way.

When men are gone, women suffer too. They carry double burdens. They become both nurturer and enforcer. Many of them do heroic work, but even they will tell you, this isn't how it was meant to be.

The cost doesn't end in the home. It spills into schools, workplaces, and politics. A nation full of fatherless boys becomes a nation full of angry men searching for identity. That's how movements built on resentment rise. That's how extremism, both left and right, finds recruits. Because when men don't belong to a family, they'll belong to anything that gives them purpose, even if it destroys them.

That's the tragedy of the fatherless nation. We didn't just lose men from the home. We lost direction from the culture. We replaced leadership with sensitivity, strength with comfort, and accountability with excuse. And the results are written across every headline, every broken home, every lost young man wandering without meaning.

Until we confront this truth, not with slogans, but with courage, nothing will change.

5 Steps to Rebuild What Was Destroyed

The fatherless crisis can be reversed, but not by programs, slogans, or more government money. It can only be reversed by men deciding to step back into their roles. A boy can't learn manhood from a pamphlet. He learns it from watching another man live it.

We rebuild fatherhood the same way we lost it, one decision at a time.

The first step is responsibility. Every man, whether he's a father yet or not, has to understand that fatherhood isn't just biological. It's moral. You don't have to create a child to act like a father. Mentorship, coaching, teaching, these are all forms of fatherhood. They carry the same weight, the same duty to guide, correct, and protect.

Every community should have men who treat fatherhood as a public service. That's how it used to be. The older men of the neighborhood watched over everyone's kids. If a boy got out of line, it wasn't just his dad who corrected him, it was the whole tribe. Those informal systems kept order long before schools or police had to.

We can rebuild that. Start small.

A few men meeting once a week to talk, train, and hold each other accountable. A local coach who teaches discipline along with the game. A neighbor who shows a kid how to fix a flat tire or change oil. These acts look small, but they rebuild what institutions destroyed, the transfer of wisdom from man to boy.

The second step is presence. Too many fathers think providing money is enough. It isn't. A child doesn't need more gifts. He needs time. He needs correction. He needs affection. Those things can't be delegated. You can't outsource fatherhood to schools, babysitters, or screens.

Presence means showing up, even when you're tired, even when you fail. It means being there for the boring stuff: *homework, dinner, discipline.* Boys don't remember what you said as much as they remember that you were there.

The third step is strength, not just physical, but moral. Boys learn how to act by watching how men respond to pressure. They watch how you handle anger, how you treat women, how you talk about your boss when he's not in the room. Every moment teaches. You don't get days off from example.

Strength also means consistency. Weak fathers swing between apathy and rage. Strong fathers stay steady. They correct without humiliating, discipline without breaking. A boy who sees controlled power learns to control his own. A boy who only sees chaos grows up to repeat it.

The fourth step is reconciliation. Many men reading this carry guilt, for leaving, for failing, for being absent. That guilt is real, but it doesn't have to be final. You can't rewrite the past, but you can redeem it. You can pick up the phone. You can show up today. Boys don't need perfection; they need effort. The act of returning, of saying, *"I'm here now"*, can change everything.

The fifth step is mentorship for the fatherless. There are millions of boys who will never have a biological father return. They can still have male role models. Churches, schools, and communities need to start seeing mentorship as national security, because it is. Every boy guided by a good man becomes one less man lost to despair.

We also need to start celebrating fatherhood again. Culturally, not commercially. Father's Day shouldn't be an afterthought. It should be national pride. The media should tell the stories of men who stayed, worked, built, and protected, not just the ones who left or failed.

A society that mocks fatherhood will eventually need the kind of men it refused to honor.

We can't rebuild strong nations without strong homes. And we can't have strong homes without strong fathers. It doesn't matter how progressive, wealthy, or educated a society becomes, if the family collapses, the civilization follows.

Rebuilding fatherhood starts with truth-telling. We need to stop pretending this is a private issue. It's not. It's a national emergency. Every statistic on crime, suicide, and addiction is a siren warning that something deeper has broken. Until we treat fatherlessness with the urgency it deserves, nothing else we fix will hold.

That means changing how we talk about men. Instead of scolding them, challenge them. Instead of mocking them, invite them. Men rise when they're called to something greater than themselves. Tell a man he's useless and he'll give you proof. Tell him he's needed and he'll give you miracles.

We also have to bring back the dignity of the word "patriarch." It's been twisted into an insult, but it used to mean "head of the family", a man who led with love and strength. The healthy patriarch doesn't dominate. He anchors. He sacrifices first and takes last. We need that image back. Boys need to see what authority guided by love looks like.

If we want the next generation to respect women, we must show them men who do. If we want them to value family, we must show them fathers who stay. If we want them to believe in themselves, we must show them men who believe in duty more than comfort.

Rebuilding fatherhood isn't nostalgia. It's survival. A culture that loses its fathers loses its direction. The map to meaning disappears. And what fills the vacuum isn't freedom, it's chaos.

The world doesn't need more perfect men. It needs more present men. More steady men.

More men who get up when they're knocked down, who show up when they're tired, who lead even when no one says thank you.

That's how we rebuild the foundation. One home at a time. One son at a time. One man deciding that enough is enough.

What The Data Won't Let Us Ignore

Rebuilding fatherhood isn't about politics. It's about survival. Nations don't collapse because of economics or enemies. They collapse when men stop leading families. When fathers disappear, order disappears with them.

That's the truth nobody wants to say out loud. Politicians talk about poverty, violence, and education, but almost never about fathers. It's too uncomfortable. It forces responsibility instead of sympathy. It forces people to admit that freedom comes with duty.

But the numbers don't care about comfort. They keep shouting what culture keeps whispering, that fatherless homes are the common thread in every major crisis we face. You can't fix a country by ignoring the people who raise it.

Fatherhood is not optional. It's the foundation of everything else. Every school, every law, every dream sits on top of what happens inside the home.

And yet we act like the role of father can be replaced by feelings, therapy, or social programs. It can't. The State can feed a child. It can't form his character. It can pay for his housing. It can't teach him honor. It can hand him a device. It can't teach him restraint. *Only a father can do that.*

The tragedy is that we've raised generations of boys who don't know what a good father looks like. They think manhood is domination or detachment because that's all they've seen. They don't realize real fatherhood is both tender and tough, firm hands guided by a steady heart.

The cure for fatherlessness begins with men redefining what strength looks like. It isn't distance. It's discipline. It's showing up even when you're hurting. It's giving before taking. It's correcting without cruelty. It's being strong enough to love and humble enough to listen.

We've taught men that emotions are weakness. *That's false.*

The right emotion, in the right place, under control, is power.

The father who can show compassion without surrendering authority teaches his children how to be human and how to stay grounded.

That balance is what makes a man dangerous in the best way. A good father is dangerous to chaos, to despair, to the decay that feeds on broken homes. His strength stops it at the door. His love repairs what it breaks.

We need to build a world where fatherhood is honored again, where men are encouraged to lead, not mocked for it. Where sacrifice is respected. Where staying is celebrated. Where children grow up hearing not just *"you are loved,"* but *"you are expected to become strong."*

That expectation saves lives. It pulls boys out of addiction, gangs, and mediocrity. It calls them to something higher. Boys need to hear *"you have what it takes."* When that sentence is missing, they spend the rest of their lives trying to find it in all the wrong places.

A father's voice is the first authority a child learns to trust. When that voice goes silent, the world gets louder, and none of it loves them back.

Break the Cycle or Become It

We can't go back in time, but we can rebuild what's been lost. It starts with one generation deciding that the excuses end here. Men who grew up without fathers must become the fathers their children deserve. That's redemption. That's strength.

And if you're a young man reading this who grew up without a father,

I need you to hear this clearly: what happened to you was not your fault, but what you do next is your choice.

You can let that absence define you, or you can let it forge you. The world doesn't owe you healing. Your father's failures are not excuses for your own. Every day you wake up is a chance to be the man no one showed you how to be. That's harder than anything else you'll ever do. It's also the only thing that matters. You can break the cycle, or you can become another casualty of it. That's the choice. Make it count.

It doesn't matter if you came from chaos. You can build order now. It doesn't matter if your own father failed. You can end that story. The greatest legacy a man can leave is the one that breaks the cycle.

Start where you are. Lead your home. Mentor a boy who doesn't have a dad. Reconnect with your children. Apologize if you must, but don't disappear. Every step you take toward responsibility ripples farther than you'll ever see.

That's how we rebuild a nation, not with politics or programs, but with fathers who stay and are present.

A strong nation begins with strong homes. Strong homes begin with strong men. And strong men begin with fathers who show their sons how to be both warrior and protector, builder and believer.

That's what the next generation needs, not softer men, not angrier men, but better men.

Men who know that strength isn't about control; it's about stewardship. It's about carrying weight so others don't have to. It's about leading through service and loving through action.

We can have all the technology, wealth, and education in the world, but if boys grow up without fathers, none of it will hold. The cracks are already showing, loneliness, depression, confusion, addiction. Every statistic about men today is a cry for leadership.

Fatherhood is that leadership. It's not glamorous. It won't trend on social media. But it's the only kind that lasts.

We don't need new systems. We need old wisdom. We need men to stand back up, dust themselves off, and remember who they are.

Because every generation either rebuilds manhood or buries it. *The time for rebuilding is now.*

5

THE EDUCATION TRAP

If you wanted to design a system to weaken boys, you couldn't do much better than the modern American school. It's not that teachers hate boys. Most don't. It's that the entire structure has been reshaped around values that reward quiet, passive, compliant behavior. Those are not male instincts. Boys are built to move, to compete, to question. When you train that out of them, you don't get better students. You get broken spirits.

I see this happening across schools every day. We call it *"behavioral intervention"* when boys can't sit still for seven hours straight. The data tell the story: boys are suspended at three times the rate of girls *(U.S. Department of Education Office for Civil Rights, 2021)*, medicated at twice the rate *(CDC, 2022)*, and dropping out in numbers that should alarm every parent in America. These aren't signs of bad kids, they're signs of a broken system.

The problem isn't cruelty; it's confusion. Too often, schools treat masculine energy as a threat to be managed rather than a force to be guided. Policies meant to equalize outcomes end up punishing normal male behavior. The result is predictable: frustrated boys, exhausted teachers, and generations of young men who learn that their nature is a problem to be fixed instead of a strength to be shaped.

Decades ago, school was where boys learned discipline, pride, and skill. They built projects, joined teams, and took risks. Now the same energy that once fueled discovery is labeled a disorder. The boy who can't sit still is medicated. The boy who speaks too bluntly is scolded. The boy who asks why is called *defiant*.

In most classrooms, success comes down to obedience and verbal expression. Sit still. Follow instructions. Talk about your feelings. These are feminine-coded traits. There is nothing wrong with them, but when they become the only traits rewarded, half the student population is punished for being who they are.

That's the quiet crisis in education no one wants to talk about. We built schools for the way girls learn best, then act confused when boys fall behind.

The numbers prove it. Boys are now nearly a full grade level behind girls in reading and writing by the time they reach middle school *(NAEP, 2022)*. They're more likely to be suspended, more likely to drop out, and far less likely to graduate from college. Only about 40 percent of college students in America are male *(National Student Clearinghouse, 2023)*, the lowest in history. That's not an accident. It's the result of policies and attitudes that punish male energy instead of shaping it.

The system rewards compliance over courage. It teaches boys that success means fitting in, not standing out. The problem isn't that boys can't learn. It's that they're being taught in ways that go against their nature.

A boy learns by doing. He learns by testing limits, by failing, by trying again. He learns through physical movement and competition. Remove those elements and his brain disengages. But we've stripped them all out. Physical education is an afterthought. Recess is shortened or removed. Shop class is extinct. In its place, we've added hours of sedentary screen time and emotional workshops.

We tell boys to *"use their words"* instead of their actions. But words don't always fit what boys feel. A boy's first language is movement. When you stop him from using it, his energy has nowhere to go but inward. That's why so many are anxious, angry, or medicated.

The *ADHD explosion* is the clearest symptom of this broken model. Millions of boys are being drugged not because they're sick, but because they don't conform to a classroom built for stillness. A healthy, curious boy who can't sit through a 90-minute lecture is now considered disordered. We teach him that his natural state is wrong.

Let me be brutally clear about what this means: we are chemically castrating the spirits of millions of boys because it's easier than redesigning a broken system.

Every pill prescribed to a seven-year-old who won't sit still is an admission that we'd rather sedate children than challenge ourselves. The pharmaceutical companies are making billions. The school districts avoid lawsuits. The teachers get compliant classrooms.

And your son?

He gets to spend his childhood in a fog, learning that who he is at his core is a problem that needs to be medicated away. When he's twenty-five and can't feel anything, when he has no drive and no passion, remember this moment. Remember that we did this to him on purpose.

And when you tell a boy he's wrong for being himself, he starts to believe it. That belief turns to shame, then resentment, then apathy. By high school, many of these boys have checked out completely. They are not stupid. They're disillusioned.

They sense the system wasn't made for them.

This didn't happen overnight. It started when education turned from preparation to protection. We stopped preparing kids for the world and started protecting them from it. We removed competition because losing might hurt feelings. We removed grading curves because failure might lower self-esteem. We replaced shop class with *"life skills"* courses that teach kids how to talk about stress instead of how to handle it.

Schools once trained young men to take responsibility. Now they train them to avoid risk.

The message is subtle but constant: *stay safe, stay small, stay agreeable.*

Those aren't lessons that produce builders or leaders. They produce employees. They produce dependents.

The irony is that while we talk endlessly about empowering women, we're simultaneously disempowering men. The education system became the first place where that imbalance took root. It's not about blaming teachers. Many are doing the best they can in a broken structure. The blame lies with the ideology that reshaped schools into social-engineering labs instead of places that teach excellence.

We told boys to be sensitive and open, which are fine traits when balanced with discipline. But we forgot the other half of the equation. We stopped teaching toughness, precision, and skill. We told boys to express emotion but never taught them how to control it. So now we have young men who can talk about their feelings but can't manage their lives.

You can't build confident men by eliminating competition. Confidence comes from mastery. You don't give it through praise. You earn it through effort. That's what the education system used to teach. When a boy built a birdhouse, repaired a car engine, or ran a race, he learned that results come from skill and work. That lesson sticks for life.

Now, his biggest achievement might be a group project graded on teamwork. Boys aren't learning to lead anymore. *They're learning to follow instructions.*

But teamwork without leadership is just managed mediocrity.

It's no wonder so many feel lost. They were built to test themselves. When you take that away, they either rebel or retreat. Some act out in anger. Others disappear into online worlds where they can at least feel challenge and reward, even if it's simulated.

We've created a generation of young men who are mentally overstimulated and physically underdeveloped. Their minds are racing, but their bodies are idle. Their confidence has been replaced by self-doubt because the system trained them to see their instincts as defects.

The Education Trap is not just an academic failure. It's a cultural one. It's the moment when society decided that molding character mattered less than managing behavior.

When we stopped teaching boys to push themselves, we stopped teaching them to grow.

A System Is Designed to Break Them

We didn't just fail boys academically. We failed them spiritually. Schools once reinforced the idea that effort mattered, that hardship produced strength, and that rules existed for a reason. Today those messages have been replaced with therapy language and slogans about feelings. Students are encouraged to talk about anxiety, identity, and comfort, but not to face the kind of discomfort that builds resilience.

When you remove challenge from education, you remove growth. Challenge is what turns lessons into wisdom. Without it, learning becomes memorization, facts without foundation.

We replaced discipline with diagnosis. A boy who can't focus is told he has ADHD. A boy who won't sit still is told he's oppositional. A boy who questions authority is labeled defiant.

We medicate into compliance and call it success.

Medication can help in legitimate cases, but we've turned it into a management tool. The problem isn't the child; it's the system. The classroom isn't built for his nature, so instead of fixing the structure, we fix the student. We sedate curiosity. We dull aggression. We chemically erase the very traits that once created inventors, explorers, and leaders.

The result is a generation of young men trained to wait for permission instead of taking initiative. They've been told that action is dangerous, that confidence is toxic, and that masculinity itself needs correction. It's not hard to see where that leads, hesitation, dependency, and confusion about who they're supposed to be.

We Traded Away Skill

The loss of trade education was the final blow. When shop class disappeared, something deeper vanished with it. It wasn't just about teaching kids how to use tools. *It was about teaching cause and effect.* A boy could build something, see it work, and feel the pride of creation. That process wired his brain for problem-solving and persistence.

Here's what that loss looks like in real terms:

an entire generation of men who can't change a tire, can't fix a leaky faucet, can't build a bookshelf.

They're completely dependent on systems they don't understand and people they have to pay to solve basic problems. That's not just inconvenient. *That's emasculating.*

A man who can't fix anything can't protect anything. He becomes a consumer, not a creator. And a generation of consumers who can't create is a generation that's one breakdown away from total helplessness. We didn't just remove shop class. We removed self-sufficiency. We removed dignity. And we wonder why young men feel useless.

Now he builds nothing. He writes reflections on self-esteem or creates digital slideshows about identity. He gets an A for typing his feelings into a Google Doc. Meanwhile, his great-grandfather was rebuilding a carburetor at age 14. Those activities don't connect him to the physical world. They don't teach him that effort produces results. The hands and the mind have to work together to build confidence. You can't get that through a screen.

Trades were once a path to dignity. A skilled welder, carpenter, or mechanic could provide for his family and contribute something real to society. Those jobs haven't disappeared. We've just stopped respecting them. We tell young men that success means sitting behind a desk. Meanwhile, the people who actually build the world are treated as second-class citizens.

And here's the sick irony:

the college-educated progressives who look down on tradesmen can't survive a single day without them.

When the power goes out, when the pipes burst, when the car breaks down, they call a man with rough hands and practical skills to save them. But they still mock him at dinner parties. They still tell their sons not to be like him. They've created an entire class of people they depend on but refuse to respect. That's not just arrogance. That's parasitic. And when those tradesmen finally stop showing up, when there aren't enough electricians or plumbers or mechanics because we told an entire generation those jobs were beneath them, society will collapse in real time.

You can't run a civilization on TikTok influencers and diversity consultants. That's cultural arrogance.

We've built an economy on services instead of substance. When every kid is told to chase a degree instead of a skill, you end up with a shortage of electricians and a surplus of gender-studies graduates. One can keep the lights on. The other can't change a light bulb.

The consequences go far beyond economics. When men don't know how to fix, build, or repair anything, they lose the instinct to solve problems in their own lives. They become dependent on systems they don't understand. That dependence breeds frustration, and frustration turns into resentment.

You can see it in the tone of young men today. They aren't lazy by nature. *They're discouraged.*

They were promised meaning in exchange for obedience. They followed the rules, got the degree, and now sit in cubicles doing work that feels hollow. They were told to find themselves, but no one told them how.

A system that measures worth only by compliance doesn't produce innovators. It produces employees who fear risk. Real education should do the opposite. It should teach risk management, not risk avoidance.

Progressive Stumped Progress

Look at the history of progress. Every major leap came from people who broke convention, who asked why, who failed, who kept pushing anyway.

The modern classroom teaches the opposite. Don't question, don't challenge, don't offend. That's not education. That's indoctrination.

The irony is that the more we've tried to make school *"inclusive,"* the more exclusive it's become for boys. The system works for those who thrive in structured, verbal, emotionally expressive environments, traits that skew female. For boys, that same environment feels suffocating.

Boys need outlets. They need competition, clear goals, and visible results. They need discipline that's consistent, not punitive. They need mentors who understand that masculine energy isn't a disorder. It's a resource.

When those things disappear, boys either withdraw or rebel. They lose trust in the system because it's obvious the system doesn't trust them.

Parents see this every day. They watch their sons go from energetic to apathetic, from curious to cynical. The spark that once made them dream starts to fade around middle school. By high school, many have decided they hate learning, not because they actually hate it, but because it's been turned into something that rejects their nature.

The teachers who manage to reach these boys almost always do it the same way, by reintroducing challenge. The coaches, mechanics, and military instructors who push young men hard are often the first adults to see those boys come alive again. They don't coddle them. They demand more. And the boys respond because deep down they want to be tested. They want to earn respect, not be handed approval. *I've seen it happen.*

I've watched a sixteen-year-old who'd been written off as a lost cause transform under a coach who held him accountable. I've seen boys who hated school light up in a class where they could build something real.

They're not broken. They're starving.

Starving for someone to look them in the eye and say *"you're capable of more, and I won't let you quit."* Every single time we lower expectations to protect their feelings, we tell them they're weak. Every time we challenge them and refuse to accept excuses, we tell them they're strong. The boys know which message is true. That's why they respond to the hard coaches and ignore the soft teachers. They're desperate for someone to believe they're capable of something difficult.

That's the secret everyone in education keeps missing. Boys don't need more sensitivity training. They need structure, discipline, and real expectations.

When they meet those expectations, they feel capable. *That's how confidence is born.*

Confidence built on performance lasts. Confidence built on praise collapses the moment it's challenged.

That's why the education system keeps failing to build real resilience. It focuses on validation instead of mastery. It's safer to give a student a participation ribbon than to let him fail and learn from it. But failure is how you grow. Every successful man learned through failure. Every great discovery came from it. When you eliminate the possibility of failure, you eliminate the possibility of greatness.

We can't keep pretending boys are broken. They're not. The system is. We've created an environment where natural masculinity is incompatible with success. Then we wonder why men are disengaged, angry, and lost.

Reform won't come from policy. It'll come from people, fathers, mentors, teachers, and coaches who decide to stop apologizing for expecting more.

If we want boys to become men, we have to give them reasons to act like men again.

This Is Why Men Are Dying

The collapse of male education is not an isolated problem. It's the root of nearly every social crisis we see today. When men stop learning how to lead, everything downstream begins to fail, families, industries, communities, and even mental health.

Boys who grow up believing they're defective for being masculine don't become calm, empathetic men. They become frustrated men. They know something in them is being restrained, but they can't name it. The more the system tries to "fix" them, the angrier they get. That anger either turns inward into depression or outward into rebellion.

That's why we're seeing record levels of anxiety, addiction, and suicide among young men. According to the *CDC (CDC WISQARS, 2022)*, men now account for almost 80 percent of suicides in America. Most of those deaths come from men under 45, men who should be building, leading, and raising families. *Instead, they're quietly giving up.*

When a man feels useless, he eventually feels hopeless. And that feeling starts in school. If a boy learns early that his instincts are wrong, his energy is unwanted, and his nature is toxic, he spends the rest of his life trying to justify his existence. You can't build a stable man, or nation, on that foundation. *Think about what we're actually doing here.*

We're taking boys at their most formative stage, when their brains are wiring for life, and we're teaching them that everything natural about them is wrong. We're teaching them to sit still when they need to move, to be quiet when they need to shout, to suppress when they need to express. And then we're shocked, absolutely shocked, when they grow up depressed, angry, and lost.

This isn't accidental damage. This is systematic destruction.

We built a machine designed to break boys, and then we blamed the boys when it worked. Every suicide, every dropout, every young man rotting in his parents' basement, that's on us.

That's on every administrator who knew the system was broken and stayed quiet. That's on every politician who chose votes over children. And that's on every parent who saw their son dying inside and didn't pull him out.

Education is supposed to shape character, not erase identity. But we've turned it into a soft political experiment that treats boys like problems to be managed instead of minds to be developed.

The truth is, boys and girls are different. That's not sexist. It's science.

They learn differently, they compete differently, and they respond to feedback differently. Girls tend to mature faster and excel in environments that reward verbal skills and cooperation. Boys thrive under structure, physical activity, and clear goals.

Yet instead of embracing those differences and designing schools that serve both sexes, we built a one-size-fits-all system around the traits that girls naturally excel at. That's why they outperform boys academically in almost every subject except math and science, and even that gap is closing.

We didn't create equality. We created imbalance. And the cost is a generation of boys who have no idea where they fit.

Look at what happens when those boys leave school. They enter an economy that rewards communication, conformity, and social navigation, skills the education system teaches well to girls but poorly to boys.

Meanwhile, trades and manual work, the traditional male strengths, are stigmatized.

So they drift. They move from one short-term job to another. They struggle to find meaning. They fill the gap with entertainment, games, and online validation because it's the only place they can still feel challenge and achievement.

This is why the education crisis is a cultural crisis. When you strip purpose from learning, you strip purpose from life. A young man without purpose is dangerous, not because he's violent, but because he's lost.

The Message Has Changed

The link between education and manhood goes deeper than grades. It's about formation. Schools used to teach virtues, not religious dogma, but moral principles: honesty, effort, courage, respect. Teachers once had authority and weren't afraid to use it. A boy who misbehaved learned boundaries. A boy who showed effort learned pride. Those lessons built men who could lead.

Now, teachers are told to be facilitators instead of leaders. They manage feelings instead of expectations. They walk on eggshells to avoid being called harsh or outdated. And while they're doing that, the boys who need firm direction slip further away.

When you take authority away from teachers and discipline away from schools, you create chaos. The kids who follow rules suffer because their effort doesn't matter. The kids who break them never learn consequence. Both groups lose.

The decline in male education isn't just a symptom of modern softness. It's a warning. It tells us what happens when a society decides that equality means sameness. Real equality means giving every student what they need to thrive, not forcing them to conform to one mold.

Boys don't need pity. They need purpose. They don't need therapy sessions about their emotions. They need challenges that teach them how to master those emotions. They need structure, not sedation. They need teachers who understand that discipline isn't abuse. It's love in a harder form.

And they need schools that restore balance. That means bringing back physical education as a daily requirement. It means reinstating shop and trade programs that teach real-world skills. It means rewarding achievement through merit instead of participation. It means letting boys compete and fail and win again.

Failure is not trauma. Failure is training. A boy who never fails grows up terrified of risk. A boy who fails and learns grows up fearless.

Parents have a role in this too. Too many outsource discipline to schools and expect results from a system that's been stripped of authority. The first lessons of responsibility and self-control must come from home. A father who holds his son accountable does more to prepare him for life than any curriculum ever could.

But schools can reinforce those values. They can reintroduce mentorship programs, pair older students with younger ones, and bring men back into classrooms. Right now, nearly three-quarters of teachers are women *(National Center for Education Statistics, 2023)*. That's not inherently bad, but it means millions of boys go through twelve years of schooling without a single male role model in authority. Then we wonder why they struggle to identify with strength or leadership.

Representation matters. A boy who never sees a strong man teaching him assumes strong men don't belong in education. He learns that knowledge is feminine and that learning isn't for him. That's not progress. That's regression.

Fixing this isn't about favoring one sex over the other. It's about restoring the balance that makes both stronger. A society that raises strong girls and weak boys will eventually have neither. Because when men fall apart, women and children pay the price.

We have to stop pretending that this imbalance will fix itself. It won't. Boys don't need less structure, they need more. They don't need softer schools, they need stronger ones.

Education should forge character, not erase it.

How to Rebuild What We Destroyed

If we want to fix the next generation of men, we have to start where they first lost their way, in the classroom. The solution isn't complicated, but it does require courage. Schools have to stop pretending that discipline and structure are outdated. *They're not oppressive. They're necessary.*

The first step is to rebuild education around truth, not ideology. That means teaching history, math, and science with rigor again, subjects that demand precision and reward effort. It also means removing the layers of politics that have turned classrooms into culture-war battlegrounds. A boy doesn't need to be taught what to think. He needs to be taught how to think.

The second step is to restore movement. Boys learn through motion. Sitting them behind screens for eight hours a day is psychological cruelty. Physical education should be mandatory again, not optional. Recess should be protected, not treated as a privilege. Every boy should sweat, compete, and learn the discipline of controlling his body. A boy who burns energy productively becomes calmer and more focused. One who's forced to sit still all day builds pressure until it explodes.

The third step is to bring back skill. Shop class, mechanics, woodworking, welding, electrical, these are not relics. They are lifelines. Boys need to see tangible proof that effort produces value. There's a deep satisfaction that comes from fixing something with your hands, from seeing a real result. That satisfaction turns into confidence, and confidence turns into ambition.

Every community in America should be rebuilding trade education. It's not just about jobs. It's about dignity. It's about giving young men a place to learn discipline, problem-solving, and pride in their work. There's honor in building things. There's honor in competence.

The fourth step is to restore male mentorship in education. Boys need to see strong, balanced men in authority, men who are demanding but fair, disciplined but compassionate. You can't teach masculinity through lectures. It has to be modeled. When a boy respects a male teacher, coach, or principal, he starts to understand what accountability looks like. He learns that authority isn't something to resent, it's something to aspire to.

Schools also need to rebuild relationships with parents, especially fathers. A boy's education doesn't end when the bell rings. The lessons he learns at home either reinforce or undo what he learns in class. Fathers have to show up, at the table, in the stands, in the conversations that shape his worldview. If a boy only hears his mother's voice, he grows up with half the guidance he needs.

The fifth step is to stop pathologizing masculinity. Boys are not broken girls. Their energy, competitiveness, and risk-taking are not diseases. They are tools that, when guided correctly, become leadership and innovation. Every great man was once a restless boy. The difference between the ones who built civilization and the ones who fell apart was direction.

Instead of medicating energy, channel it. Instead of silencing confidence, sharpen it. Instead of warning boys not to be too aggressive, teach them how to use their strength responsibly. That's what mentorship and challenge are for. You don't fix masculinity by punishing it. You fix it by refining it.

The sixth step is accountability. Schools need to reward effort again, not just attendance. Grades should mean something. Expectations should be high. A boy should know that laziness has a cost, and excellence has a reward. That's how you build respect for achievement. When everyone gets the same prize, prizes lose meaning.

If we want boys to become men who take pride in their work, we have to start by making school something worth taking pride in. Lowering standards doesn't create equity. It creates mediocrity.

Finally, we have to restore meaning to education itself. Learning isn't just about passing tests. It's about preparing for life. It's about equipping young men and women to carry responsibility, serve others, and think critically. Somewhere along the line, we replaced purpose with comfort. We told kids that happiness was the goal instead of contribution. That's why so many of them are miserable, happiness can't be chased. It's the byproduct of living with purpose.

When we rebuild schools around purpose, challenge, and skill, we don't just save boys. We save society. The men those boys become will build stronger families, safer communities, and more productive economies. They'll be the kind of men who show up, who work hard, who protect and provide.

That's the difference between a culture that survives and one that collapses. One invests in its young men. The other apologizes for them.

Education was never supposed to be comfortable. It was supposed to be transformative.

Transformation requires discomfort. It requires failure, frustration, and persistence. That's what turns children into adults.

When we took discomfort out of school, we took manhood out with it.

If you're a parent reading this, you have a choice to make right now. You can keep sending your son into a system that's designed to break him, hoping he'll somehow survive it. Or you can fight back. Demand shop classes. Demand male teachers. Demand physical education. Demand real standards. Show up at school board meetings and make noise. Pull your son out if you have to and teach him yourself. Because I promise you this: the system will not save him. It's not designed to. Every year you wait is another year of damage that might be irreversible. Your son doesn't have time for you to be polite. He needs you to be his advocate, his protector, his warrior. If you won't fight for him, no one will. And in ten years, when he's lost, you'll wish you had acted when it mattered. This is that moment. *Don't waste it.*

Boys don't need more programs about feelings. They need experiences that show them who they are and what they're capable of. They need standards that demand effort, teachers who expect excellence, and mentors who lead with example.

The future of manhood begins at a school desk, not a therapist's office.

If we rebuild the way we educate boys, we rebuild the foundation of America.

Because education doesn't just produce workers. It produces men. And when education forgets how to do that, everything built on those men begins to crumble.

We traded discipline and skill for comfort and self-expression. *It's time to trade them back.*

6

THE WAR ON PURPOSE

The greatest crisis facing men today isn't poverty or politics, it's meaning. We've built a world that gives men everything except a reason to exist.

For generations, men knew their purpose instinctively. They built, fought, protected, and provided. They didn't need therapy to understand why they were here. Their lives were defined by duty. They were raised to believe that their value came from what they contributed, not what they felt.

But sometime in the last fifty years, that clarity disappeared. The culture told men they no longer had to be needed. The problem was, it never gave them something better to be.

We taught boys that being dependable was oppressive, that responsibility was outdated, and that duty was toxic. We told them to *follow their passions*", as if purpose were a hobby instead of a calling.

The result is a generation of men who feel lost, even when they're successful. They have more comfort, more technology, and more freedom than any men in history, and yet they wake up each morning with a quiet sense that none of it matters. Your great-grandfather woke up knowing exactly what he was for. He built things. Fixed things. Protected things. You wake up, check your phone, see that nothing needs you, and go back to sleep.

That's not a just a mental health crisis. That's a generation dying from the inside out.

We stripped men of the one thing they were built for: purpose. And when you take purpose from a man, you take everything.

You can see it everywhere. Men in their twenties drift through life without direction. Men in their thirties chase distraction to avoid silence. Men in their forties look back and realize they've been working hard at all the wrong things. They bought the dream, career, pleasure, approval, only to find it hollow.

That emptiness isn't accidental. It's designed.

The Invisible Battlefield

This is a war, and young men are the target. It's not fought with bullets. It's fought with algorithms, curriculum, and endless distraction. The weapons are engineered to be invisible. A young man doesn't realize he's under attack until he's already been neutralized.

Let me be clear about who the enemy is. It's not women. It's not older generations. It's the systems that profit from male weakness. Social media companies that optimize for addiction. Universities that teach young men their instincts are toxic. Entertainment corporations that flood screens with purposeless antiheroes. A consumer economy that needs young men buying, not building.

Every institution that touches a young man's life has a financial incentive to keep him confused, insecure, and dependent.

Modern society runs on comfort and consumption. It doesn't want men with purpose. It wants men who buy things, obey rules, and stay quiet. A man with purpose is hard to manipulate.

A man without it will do whatever it takes to feel alive, even if it destroys him.

A 2023 study by the *National Financial Educators Council* found that 60 percent of Americans say their lack of financial knowledge cost them money, usually more than $500 a year. Another survey found that 43 percent don't know what a 401(k) is, and nearly half admit they've signed a lease or financial document without reading it. Add to that the millions of young men who've never changed their own oil, and it's clear: we've built a generation that's fluent in Wi-Fi but illiterate in real life. You're making six-figure decisions based on vibes and a quick Google search. Your grandfather could rebuild an engine, balance a checkbook, and negotiate a mortgage without blinking. You need a YouTube tutorial to hang a picture frame and you're still not sure if you're doing it right.

The average American young man today lives in his parents' house until he's twenty-eight. His grandfather owned a home, had a wife, and two kids by that age. His grandfather worked fifty hours a week building something real. He works part-time, if at all, staring at screens. His grandfather knew exactly what it meant to be a man. He has no idea.

That gap isn't evolution. It's devastation.

That's why every system that controls modern life, media, education, entertainment, attacks purpose at its root.

Media glorifies indulgence and mocks sacrifice. It rewards men for chasing status instead of building character. Every ad tells you that meaning can be bought: *the right car, the right watch, the right vacation.*

But purpose can't be purchased. It's earned through service, not spending.

Education stripped away the spiritual and practical lessons that once gave boys direction. Schools used to teach that a man's duty was to serve something bigger than himself, his family, his God, his country. Now they teach him to serve only himself. They've replaced vocation with ideology.

Entertainment finishes the job. Every movie, every series, every game tells men that life is about escape, not engagement. Heroes used to be builders and leaders. Now they're sarcastic loners, broken antiheroes who stumble through chaos. That's not storytelling, that's sabotage.

And social media turned all of it into a contest. Men no longer ask, *"What am I here for?"* They ask, "Who's watching me?" Purpose used to be measured in legacy. Now it's measured in likes.

When men lose purpose, they don't go neutral, they go numb. They retreat into distractions. They find identity in ideologies. They seek meaning in the extremes, politics, rage, self-destruction.

That's why we see so many young men radicalized, addicted, or withdrawn. They're not evil. They're empty. And the world keeps selling them more emptiness dressed as fulfillment.

Let me show you what this looks like in real life. There's a young man, call him *Jake*. He's twenty-four. He graduated college with decent grades and fifty thousand in debt. He's been applying for jobs for eight months. He lives in his childhood bedroom. He wakes up at noon, checks his phone for two hours, applies to three jobs he doesn't care about, plays video games until 3 AM, and repeats. His parents think he's depressed. His friends think he's lazy. The truth is simpler: he has no purpose. No one ever taught him what he was for. School taught him to pass tests. His degree taught him theories he'll never use. His father was too busy working to show him how to be a man. Social media taught him that his value is measured in likes. Every system told him what to avoid, toxic masculinity, aggression, dominance, but no one told him what to become. So he drifts. He's not suicidal, but he's not alive either. He's waiting for a reason to care. And every year, that reason feels further away. Jake isn't rare. He's the norm. There are millions of him.

This war on purpose didn't happen with violence. It happened with convenience.

The Convenient Truth

We built a society that rewards men for being comfortable. We told them the goal was pleasure, not progress. But pleasure without purpose destroys a man. Comfort without challenge kills his soul.

That's why depression and addiction are rising even as life gets easier. Men weren't built for easy. They were built for effort.

A man without struggle loses strength. A man without duty loses direction. A man without purpose loses peace.

Purpose isn't optional, it's oxygen. When you take it away, men start suffocating.

And here's what most people don't understand: *this isn't just tragic for individual men. It's civilization-level destruction.* A generation of purposeless men doesn't build, doesn't defend, doesn't create families, and doesn't pass on values. What we're watching isn't a temporary dip in male confidence. It's the slow-motion collapse of everything that requires masculine energy to survive. You can't run a country on men who don't believe their lives matter. You can't defend freedom with men who won't fight for anything.

You can't maintain a culture when the men who should be leading it are too numb to care. This is an emergency. Not in fifty years. Right now. Every day we lose more young men to purposelessness is a day we won't get back. The clock is running, and the consequences are irreversible.

That's why you can find despair in every corner of modern life, not just among the poor or powerless, but among the wealthy and powerful too. The pain doesn't come from lack of comfort. It comes from lack of meaning.

You can see it in the eyes of the man driving a luxury car he doesn't need, or in the posture of the man behind a desk scrolling through his phone during meetings. He has everything except clarity. He's winning the game, but he's forgotten what the game is for.

That's the trap of modern masculinity, success without satisfaction. We raised men to chase money, attention, and approval, and we wonder why they're anxious and bitter when they get it.

Purpose isn't found in applause. It's found in obedience, to duty, to principle, to something larger than yourself.

A man's purpose doesn't have to be heroic. It just has to be rooted in service. Protecting a home, building a business, mentoring a boy, leading a team, these are acts of purpose. They're small in scale but eternal in effect.

You can't mass-produce meaning. You can only create it through work that matters.

The modern man has to reclaim that truth. He has to stop asking what feels good and start asking what's worth doing.

The answer won't come from culture. It won't come from social media, politics, or a therapist's couch. It comes from action. From deciding that life isn't about what you get, but what you give.

Men rediscover purpose the moment they pick up weight again, literal or figurative. The moment they stop chasing ease and start building something hard, something lasting.

Because purpose doesn't come to men who sit. It comes to men who move.

Finding purpose isn't about motivation. It's about mission. Motivation fades the moment comfort returns. Mission survives everything, fear, fatigue, failure. A man with a mission can walk through fire and keep going because he knows why he's there.

If you're a young man reading this and you feel that emptiness, that sense that something's been stolen from you, you're right. It has. But here's the truth they don't want you to know: *you can take it back.*

The system is built to keep you weak, but it can't force you to stay that way. Every man who finds purpose becomes a threat to the machine. That's why they fight so hard to keep you distracted. They know that one man with clarity is worth a thousand men scrolling. You don't need anyone's permission to reclaim your life. You just need to decide that enough is enough. You weren't born to consume content and die. You were born to build something that lasts. The world is waiting for you to remember that.

Seven Steps To Reclaiming Purpose

The first step to finding purpose again is silence. The world today never shuts up. It fills every quiet moment with noise, news, entertainment, endless opinions.

But purpose can't be heard in chaos. You have to create space for it.

Purpose speaks in whispers, not shouts. It doesn't compete with the noise. It waits for you to be still. That's why ancient warriors, monks, and philosophers all shared one practice, *solitude.* They withdrew from the crowd long enough to hear themselves think.

Men today are terrified of silence because silence reveals truth. When the music stops, the notifications pause, and the distractions fade, you're left alone with the question every man avoids:

"What am I really doing with my life?"

You can't find purpose until you face that question honestly. And honesty hurts at first. It exposes the gap between what you're doing and what you're meant to do. But that discomfort is sacred. It's the starting line of every comeback.

The second step is service.

Purpose doesn't start with what you want. It starts with what you can give. You find meaning not by asking "What makes me happy?" but by asking "Who needs me?"

That one shift changes everything. When a man begins serving something beyond himself, his family, his community, his country, his God, he starts to come alive. The weight of responsibility doesn't crush him. It defines him.

Weak men run from obligation because they mistake freedom for escape. Strong men run toward it because they understand that freedom is found inside responsibility. The man who carries weight walks straighter. The man who avoids it crumbles under the illusion of ease.

The third step is structure.

A man without a plan drifts until the world gives him one. Purpose doesn't survive chaos. It needs order, routines, goals, accountability. That's why soldiers and craftsmen have always found peace in repetition. Discipline gives direction to desire.

Every man should have a code, written or unwritten. A set of rules that define how he acts when no one's watching. Not moral relativism, not situational ethics, but fixed principles.

Tell the truth. Keep your word. Protect the weak. Finish what you start. These aren't slogans. They're anchors. Without them, you'll be tossed by every emotional wave.

The fourth step is struggle.

You cannot have purpose without pain. The obstacle is the path. Every hardship you face is the training ground for what you're called to do. Modern culture treats struggle like a disease, something to avoid or medicate. But struggle is the forge of meaning.

The man who embraces struggle learns resilience. He discovers that his limits are lies. He stops fearing discomfort and starts using it. When you face pain willingly, it stops controlling you. That's when you become dangerous in the best way, untouchable by fear.

The fifth step is faith.

Not religion for show, but conviction that life is guided by something higher. Without faith, purpose collapses under pressure. You start believing that effort is pointless, that the universe is random. But faith gives every act weight. It turns work into worship, duty into devotion.

Even men who don't claim belief in God need something sacred to fight for, truth, family, country, honor. Something that can't be bought or faked. A man who believes in nothing will fall for everything.

The sixth step is brotherhood.

Purpose isn't sustained alone. Even the strongest man needs allies. Isolation kills mission. Brotherhood sharpens it. The right men will hold you accountable, correct you when you drift, and push you when you stall. The wrong ones will drain your will. *Choose carefully.*

No man finds purpose surrounded by people who want him comfortable. You need men who expect greatness from you. Who refuse to let you quit. Who tell you the truth even when it stings. That's not control, that's loyalty.

The seventh step is legacy.

Once a man finds purpose, he must pass it on. A mission that dies with you was never purpose, it was ego. Purpose multiplies through others. The father who teaches his son, the mentor who guides the next man, the leader who builds something that lasts, that's how purpose outlives mortality.

Legacy is built in ordinary moments. It's built when you keep your word after failing. When you show up on time. When you fix what you broke. When you build something that makes life better for people who may never know your name.

That's how men used to think. They weren't chasing fame. They were chasing contribution. They didn't care about *"personal brands."* They cared about family crests. They weren't influencers. They were builders.

Modern men have to return to that mindset, not nostalgic, but necessary. Because the world isn't starving for innovation. It's starving for direction. It doesn't need more noise. It needs meaning.

Finding purpose isn't a one-time revelation. It's a daily decision. You choose it every morning when you wake up and decide to live with intention instead of impulse. Purpose doesn't shout. It waits for your commitment.

If you're lost, start small. Clean your space. Call your family. Help someone quietly. Keep a promise. Read something true. Each act reconnects you with meaning. Each step rebuilds your sense of control.

Purpose doesn't appear. It's built brick by brick through work, sacrifice, and service. That's how you reclaim it, not in theory, but in action.

When you find it, everything changes. The noise fades. The temptations lose power. The opinions of others stop mattering. You wake up with a reason that no one can take away from you.

That's when you become unstoppable.

The Quiet Revolution

When a man finds purpose, his entire environment changes. His home steadies. His relationships deepen. His energy shifts from reaction to creation. The chaos that once controlled him begins to quiet. He no longer needs constant distraction because he finally has direction.

You can see it in his eyes. A man with purpose doesn't wander anymore. He walks differently. He doesn't flinch at criticism or envy. His mood isn't dictated by the headlines or the algorithm. He has his own compass now, and he follows it.

Purpose gives a man power that can't be bought. It gives him confidence that doesn't depend on success. Even when life hits hard, he knows why he's fighting. He doesn't crumble when he loses because he knows what the loss is for.

That kind of strength spreads.

When a man stands tall, others around him rise. His sons see it. His wife feels it. His friends start to match it. Purpose is contagious. It builds culture from the inside out.

That's how families are rebuilt, not by policies or programs, but by men who find purpose and live it consistently. Children don't need perfect fathers. They need purposeful ones. They need to see a man who works with intention, who corrects himself when he fails, and who gets back up every single time.

A father with purpose teaches his children that life has meaning even when it's hard. He doesn't protect them from struggle; he prepares them for it. That's how resilience is passed down.

Communities thrive the same way. When men live with purpose, they stop waiting for someone else to fix the problems. They fix them. They repair what's broken. They lead quietly but effectively. They don't need credit because the results are their reward.

Purposeful men don't complain about the state of the world. They build alternatives. They start businesses that serve others. They mentor boys who need guidance. They show up in civic life, not for power but for stewardship.

That's how nations are healed, not through speeches, but through purpose multiplied across millions of ordinary men who decide that strength and duty aren't outdated. *They're essential.*

Purpose restores order because it restores hierarchy, not one of domination, but of discipline. It teaches every man that his place matters. He's not a victim of circumstance. He's an agent of stability. He's responsible for the little corner of the world he occupies.

When every man takes that seriously, chaos loses ground.

A man with purpose also becomes immune to manipulation. You can't control a man who already knows what he's living for. He doesn't fall for false promises because he's already found fulfillment in service. That's why societies built on purpose are harder to corrupt.

Their men can't be bought.

Purpose gives men clarity about what matters and what doesn't. It teaches them to stop chasing status and start chasing excellence. It reminds them that meaning isn't found in what you get, but in what you build and protect.

That shift creates stability that no government can manufacture.

When men live with purpose, they stop being liabilities and start becoming anchors.

Families stop fracturing. Communities stop fracturing. The noise fades because leadership reappears where it's always belonged, in the home, in the workshop, in the quiet strength of men who know who they are.

That's why the war on purpose is so destructive, it robs men of that anchor. It convinces them that life is about pleasure, that values are flexible, that leadership is oppressive. But once men rediscover purpose, the lie collapses.

Men with purpose become protectors again. Not just of people, but of principles. They guard truth when it's unpopular. They defend order when it's mocked. They carry burdens that others drop. And because of that, civilization holds.

That's what every generation of strong men has done, carried weight so others could live free. *The war on purpose was meant to stop that.* It was meant to turn builders into consumers and leaders into followers. But it failed to understand something deeper: men are built for meaning. You can bury it, but you can't kill it.

Even now, under all the noise, the hunger for purpose is waking up. You can feel it in the conversations happening online, in gyms, in workplaces, and in churches. Men are quietly reclaiming their sense of direction. They're realizing that being useful feels better than being comfortable.

That's the start of a new movement, not a political one, but a moral one. A generation of men deciding that they won't be sedated anymore. That they'll trade numbness for responsibility. That they'll rebuild strength, family, and faith because the world still needs them.

The man who lives with purpose doesn't just change his own life. He changes his lineage. His children inherit confidence instead of confusion. His wife inherits partnership instead of chaos. His community inherits stability instead of decline.

That's legacy, and it always begins with purpose.

Purpose gives a man direction. But more than that, it gives him peace. Once you know why you're here, the chaos around you stops mattering. The fear fades. The confusion fades. The noise becomes background. You start living on mission instead of on impulse.

Men who live on mission don't drift. They decide. They move with certainty. They act with integrity. They're not searching for validation because they already know their value.

That's what modern culture doesn't understand, confidence doesn't come from affirmation. It comes from alignment. When what you do matches who you are, you stop doubting yourself.

That's why purpose is freedom. It breaks the chains of everything designed to control you, addiction, distraction, comparison. You can't manipulate a man who knows his mission. You can't shame him with lies about privilege or guilt. He's too busy building something real.

The world can't cancel purpose. It can mock it, fight it, distort it, but it can't kill it. Truth doesn't need popularity to survive. It just needs men willing to live it.

When men rediscover purpose, society stabilizes. Work regains meaning. Marriage regains trust. Children regain guidance. Every system that looked broken begins to repair itself because the foundation, men of conviction, is strong again.

That's the real revolution. Not anger. Not politics. Purpose.

We don't need more policies. We need men who wake up every day and live like their lives matter, because they do. We need fathers who guide, workers who build, soldiers who protect, teachers who inspire, pastors who lead, and friends who hold the line. Purpose turns those roles from jobs into callings.

The man with purpose no longer asks, "What do I get?" He asks, "What am I responsible for?"

That's how civilizations rise, when duty replaces desire as the highest goal.

And when men live that way, peace follows. Not comfort, peace. The kind that comes from doing what's right, even when it hurts. The kind that lets you sleep soundly at night because you carried your weight that day.

Peace isn't found in escape. It's found in endurance. In finishing the task when you're tired. In choosing character over convenience. That's the peace of a man who knows why he's alive.

Purpose doesn't erase pain, but it redeems it. Every struggle becomes part of the story. Every loss becomes instruction. Every scar becomes proof that you kept going. That's what gives meaning its power, it transforms suffering into strength.

Without purpose, men break. With it, they bend and recover. They can carry more than they ever thought possible. That's how heroes are made, not in comfort, but in calling.

Purpose makes a man dangerous again, not to others, but to weakness, to lies, to everything that feeds decay. A man who knows why he's here becomes a wall against chaos. He holds the line not because it's easy, but because he knows it's his.

The world needs more of those walls. The kind that don't crack under pressure. The kind that protect without hatred and lead without ego.

That's the kind of strength that built every free nation in history. And it's the only kind that will keep one alive.

Purpose is what separates surviving from living. It turns existence into legacy. It makes every small act matter. It makes every sacrifice worth it.

If you want to change the world, start by changing one man's purpose, your own.

Because every movement that ever shaped history started with one man deciding he would no longer live small.

Purpose isn't about saving the world. It's about doing your part in it with excellence. The world will follow men who live that way. It always has.

When this generation of men finally stops apologizing for being men, when they stop living for comfort and start living for calling, something remarkable will happen. Families will stabilize. Work will regain honor. Faith will return to daily life.

That's not a dream. That's a blueprint.

We were built for purpose. The proof is in our restlessness. The ache inside every man isn't a flaw, it's a reminder. A signal that you were made to build, protect, and lead. That longing you feel for more is the call of responsibility whispering, *"Get up. There's work to do."*

Answer it. Don't wait for permission. Don't wait for clarity. Just move. Purpose reveals itself through motion, not meditation.

Once you move, everything else begins to align, your energy, your focus, your peace. You stop being a passenger in your own life and become its author.

That's the power of purpose. It gives you ownership. It turns the ordinary into sacred ground. It reminds you that every action, no matter how small, ripples forward into eternity.

The war on purpose has done its damage. But it hasn't won.

The men who remember why they're here, who wake up, stand tall, and live with conviction, will rebuild what's been lost. They'll raise sons who aren't confused, daughters who aren't afraid, and a generation that believes in something again.

That's how you end the war. Not by shouting louder, but by living better.

Purpose is the quiet revolution that no one can stop.

7

THE INFORMATION WAR

There's a reason so many men feel stuck. It's not weakness. It's engineering.

The modern world is built to keep you addicted, not to drugs or alcohol, but to distraction. Every app, every screen, every ad has the same goal: *keep you scrolling, buying, and obeying.* The economy runs on your attention, and men have become its most profitable resource.

Here's what I see every day: grown men sitting in their cars in parking lots, scrolling through their phones before going into work because they can't face eight hours without a hit. Fathers checking their phones during dinner while their kids try to tell them about their day. Men who say they want to be successful but spend four hours every night watching other people live on screens. Twenty-five-year-olds who've never had a girlfriend but have premium subscriptions to three different porn sites.

This isn't living. This is slow-motion suicide. And you're paying for the privilege.

Every minute you give to these platforms is a minute you'll never get back, and they're making billions while you're getting nothing.

They Taught You Not to Think

Back in 2016, researchers at *Stanford University* decided to see how bad it really was. They tested 7,804 middle-school, high-school, and college students across twelve states. The question was simple: can young people, the most plugged-in generation in human history, tell the difference between real information and manipulation?

The answer was catastrophic.

"In every case and at every level, we were taken aback by students' lack of preparation," the *Stanford History Education Group* wrote in its official report (2016). Not concerned, but taken aback.

More than 80 percent of middle-schoolers believed that a paid advertisement labeled *"sponsored content"* was a legitimate news story. High-schoolers looking at two Facebook posts about Donald Trump's candidacy (one from verified Fox News, one from a fake account) chose the fake account as more trustworthy because it had better graphics. Only one-quarter even knew what the blue checkmark meant.

At the college level it didn't get better. Students assumed a polished design or a professional-looking *"About"* page meant credibility. *Stanford's* lead researcher *Sam Wineburg* put it bluntly: *"Fluency in social media does not equal discernment."*

That single sentence should have triggered a national panic. Because the boys who can't tell a verified account from a fake one are the same boys being told that masculinity is toxic, ambition is selfish, confidence is arrogance, and strength is dangerous. They're being programmed to doubt everything strong about themselves, and they don't even know it's happening.

They scroll through *TikTok* and get hit with endless posts claiming that *"real men cry," "real men apologize for existing," "real men defer."* The comments are full of bot approval and influencer sponsorships. No one teaches them to ask the most basic questions: Who's paying for this? Who benefits if I believe it?

Here's how it plays out. You're fifteen. You open Instagram. A post from an account with two million followers says, "Toxic masculinity is destroying mental health. Real men talk about their feelings." It has fifty thousand likes. The comments are full of applause emojis. You think, everyone believes this. It must be true.

What you don't see is that the account is sponsored by a therapy app selling monthly subscriptions. Half the comments are bots. The *"study"* cited doesn't exist. Dissenting opinions were deleted before you ever got there. But you weren't taught to check. You weren't taught to question anything that looks polished. So you internalize the message: my instincts are toxic; I need fixing.

Multiply that by ten thousand posts, and you've got the modern social-media boy: conditioned to distrust himself while worshiping algorithms.

> *Your grandfather questioned authority. You question your own existence because an influencer with good lighting told you to.*

The Algorithm Trap

The algorithms don't care about truth. They care about engagement. They feed whatever keeps you outraged or afraid. Click on one video about anxiety and you'll get a hundred more. Watch a clip mocking men and you'll get a flood of the same. The system rewards emotional chaos because it keeps your thumb moving.

> *The algorithm isn't your friend; it's your dealer.*

And you're hooked on outrage like it's digital fentanyl.

So if you're a young man who's struggling, who feels lost or purposeless, the algorithm notices. It starts showing you videos of other men talking about how lost they feel. Then it shows you videos blaming someone for why you feel that way: feminists, schools, society, your parents, the government, whoever. Then it shows you videos of someone selling a solution.

You didn't go looking for this content. The algorithm brought it to you. And because you watched one video, it assumes you want a hundred more just like it. Before you know it, your entire feed is curated to keep you feeling exactly the way you felt when you first clicked.

You think you're discovering truth. Really, you're being programmed.

The worst part? The algorithm doesn't care if the content is true. It doesn't care if it's helpful. It only cares if you keep watching. So it feeds you whatever keeps your eyes on the screen: outrage, fear, hopelessness, anger, whatever works.

And young men, who've never been taught to recognize manipulation, think they're "doing their own research" when really they're just watching the same propaganda loop on repeat.

It's like thinking you're well-traveled because you walked in circles inside an airport.

The information machine uses another trick: *manufactured consensus.* You see a post. It has fifty thousand likes. The comments are overwhelmingly positive. Everyone seems to agree. So you assume the idea must be valid. After all, fifty thousand people can't be wrong, right?

Except they can. Because half of those likes are bots. A quarter of the comments are from paid accounts. And the negative comments were deleted by moderators before you ever saw them.

What you're seeing isn't consensus. It's theater.

But you don't know that, because you were never taught how these systems work. So you adjust your own beliefs to match what you think everyone else believes. This is called preference falsification, and it's how you get entire populations to adopt ideas they don't actually agree with. Everyone thinks everyone else believes it, so they stay quiet and go along.

That's how you convince boys that masculinity is toxic even though most of them instinctively know it's not. They see the posts. They see the likes. They assume everyone agrees. So they suppress their own instincts and adopt the narrative, because fitting in feels safer than standing out.

It's cowardice masquerading as enlightenment.

But the algorithm doesn't just feed you lies about yourself. It also floods your feed with false idols: *men who look strong, sound confident, and promise they can teach you to be like them.* For a price, of course.

In *2018, University of Pennsylvania* researchers demonstrated the psychological damage this digital diet creates. Their experimental study linked higher Facebook, Instagram, and Snapchat use to increased depression and loneliness *(Hunt et al., Journal of Social and Clinical Psychology, 2018).* Translation: the more "connected" you are online, the worse you feel. Social media sold young people an illusion of community and delivered chronic isolation instead.

Congratulations. You've got five thousand followers and zero friends. That's not a network; that's a hostage situation with Wi-Fi.

So millions of young men scroll through curated images of success while their own lives quietly erode. They've been sold masculinity as a product, and they're going bankrupt buying it. They're told that masculinity itself is the problem, that ambition is oppression, and that the only safe emotion left is guilt. Then we act shocked when male suicide rates climb.

The *CDC (2023)* confirms that men still account for nearly 80 percent of suicides in the United States. You'd think that stat alone would stop the slogans and start a real conversation about meaning. But no, because guilt sells better than truth.

Performance Over Purpose

If the last generation of men was lost to silence, this one is being lost to noise.

The digital world is full of men shouting about strength, power, and dominance, yet very few of them have ever built, led, or protected anything in real life.

Let me tell you what I see every day: teenage boys who can quote every Andrew Tate line but can't change a tire.

Twenty-year-olds who post gym selfies with captions about *"grinding"* but live in their parents' basement. Men who talk about being "high value" but have never held a job for more than six months.

They know all the language of masculinity (alpha, sigma, dominance, frame), but they have zero substance behind it. They're performing strength for an audience that's equally fake. It's the blind leading the blind, except everyone's got a camera and a course to sell.

This isn't masculinity. This is cosplay. And an entire generation is confusing the costume for the character.

Social media has turned masculinity into performance art. The *"alpha male"* online looks like confidence, but it's mostly insecurity wearing sunglasses. Every post is a flex. Every video is a sales pitch. Every quote about discipline ends with a link to buy a course.

We've built a new digital masculinity, one that looks like leadership but is driven by ego. It promises men that if they say the right words, lift the right weights, and mock the right enemies, they'll be respected.

But real respect doesn't come from aesthetics. It comes from results.

The so-called digital alphas talk about conquering the world, but most of them can't conquer their own habits. They speak about freedom, yet they're slaves to attention. Their entire identity depends on validation: likes, followers, and money. Strip away the screens, and there's nothing left. *That's not strength. That's dependency.*

Here's the brutal truth: *most of those Lamborghinis are rented. Most of those mansions are Airbnbs.* Most of those women are paid to be there. The entire thing is a stage set designed to sell you the idea that you're not enough.

Because if you believed you were already enough, you'd stop watching, stop buying, and stop comparing yourself to fake success.

The digital alpha mirage runs on your insecurity. Every time you watch one of those videos and think "I wish I had that," they make money. They're not selling you success. They're selling you envy. And you're buying it by the gigabyte.

The problem isn't that young men want to improve. The problem is that improvement has become entertainment instead of transformation.

Look at the *"grind culture"* that's taken over the internet: endless videos about waking up at 4 a.m., drinking raw eggs, or talking about *"hustle"* and *"dominance."* It looks tough. It sounds inspiring. But ask most of these influencers what they've actually built, and the answer is nothing.

Their business is selling the illusion of progress to men who are desperate for direction.

Let me give you the real numbers: the average *"alpha male"* influencer makes his money selling courses to young men about how to make money selling courses. It's a pyramid scheme dressed up as self-improvement. They don't have businesses. They have audiences. They don't create value. They extract it.

They're digital parasites feeding on the desperation of fatherless boys who'll pay $997 for a twelve-week program that teaches them nothing they couldn't learn from a library card and some discipline.

And when the program doesn't work, when the kid is still broke and directionless three months later, the influencer blames him. "You didn't want it bad enough. You weren't willing to sacrifice."

It's a scam. They need your confusion more than you need their advice.

That's digital warfare: strength without sacrifice, confidence without competence, leadership without legacy. It's a fantasy that rewards image over integrity.

The worst part is that young men believe it because they have no one else to follow. When fathers and mentors disappear, boys will follow anyone who sounds sure of himself. Confidence becomes the only credential. The internet rewards certainty, not truth. So the loudest voice wins, even if it's lying.

Real masculinity isn't loud. It's steady. It's the man who gets up before dawn, not for a camera, but because his family depends on him. It's the man who keeps his word even when no one's watching. It's the man who doesn't need to broadcast strength because he lives it quietly every day.

Online, silence doesn't trend. But in real life, silence builds empires.

That's the difference between influence and impact. Influence makes people look at you. Impact makes them stand taller because of you.

The information war wants eyes. The real man wants results.

The Engineering of Dependency

This system wasn't an accident. It was designed.

Every major industry that thrives today depends on one thing: keeping men from mastering themselves. When you strip a man of focus, you strip him of freedom.

Porn keeps him isolated. Social media keeps him distracted. Gaming keeps him entertained. Processed food keeps him sluggish. Consumer debt keeps him obedient.

Every one of those industries turns male discipline into dollars.

Look at the numbers. The porn industry is a multi-billion dollar global business earning revenue from addiction *(Covenant Eyes, 2023)*. The average man under 30 spends more time watching porn than exercising or pursuing a hobby *(Fight the New Drug, 2023)*. Each click is data.

Each data point is profit. The more he watches, the weaker he becomes, and the richer someone else gets.

And here's what nobody talks about: porn isn't just stealing your time. It's stealing your ability to connect with real women. Young men in their twenties can't maintain an erection with an actual woman because their brains are so fried from years of hardcore porn that reality can't compete.

They're physically functional but psychologically destroyed. They can't look women in the eye. They can't handle normal intimacy. They're wired for fantasy and broken for reality.

That's not an accident. That's the business model.

Keep you hooked, keep you isolated, keep you consuming. And when you finally realize what's been stolen, when you hit thirty and you're alone with nothing but a porn addiction and crippling shame, they don't care. They already got your money and your youth.

Gaming is no different. In 2017, EA's Star Wars Battlefront II sparked international outrage when regulators in Belgium classified its loot box system as literal gambling. Major publishers spend millions engineering these reward systems because they work; they're identical to slot machines, and they're targeting your sons. Every level, every win, every kill gives the illusion of progress without producing anything real. Meanwhile, billions of hours of male energy vanish into virtual space.

And social media? It's the crown jewel of the addiction economy. It's where validation and envy meet. Every scroll gives you something to react to: outrage, desire, approval, fear. The emotional cycle never ends because it's meant to keep you hooked.

This is how empires are built now, not with soldiers, but with screens.
They don't need to control you if they can keep you busy.

The brain isn't built for this level of stimulation. Dopamine used to be a signal that meant you were moving toward something important: food, victory, survival. Now it fires for nothing. Your body releases the same chemical when you see a half-naked influencer or win a digital game as it does when you protect your family or close a business deal.

Over time, that confusion breaks the system. You start chasing the feeling instead of the purpose behind it. That's why you can scroll for hours and still feel exhausted. Your mind is overstimulated but under-satisfied.

It's like eating junk food for the soul: full of flavor, no nourishment.

You spent six hours on your phone and accomplished nothing. Congratulations. You just wasted a quarter of your waking life watching strangers live theirs.

This constant exposure rewires motivation. It makes long-term effort feel impossible. Why commit to a five-year plan when the phone offers a five-second hit? Why face the discomfort of rejection when fantasy is one click away? Why train for excellence when a filter can make you look like you've already achieved it?

That's the quiet war men are losing. Not because they're incapable, but because they've been sedated.

The system doesn't kill ambition directly. It just keeps it numb.

The Way Out

But here's the truth: your brain can heal. Focus can return. Drive can be rebuilt. It's not easy, but it's possible.

The first step is recognizing what's been stolen: time, attention, energy, clarity. Once you know that, you can start taking it back.

Start with a dopamine detox. It's not a gimmick. It's a reset. Go a week without porn, social media, or video games. The first few days will feel like withdrawal because that's exactly what it is. You've been trained to expect constant stimulation. Silence will feel unbearable.

That's how you know you're getting your mind back.

Then fill that silence with something that fights back: reading, training, prayer, building. The goal isn't to remove pleasure. It's to earn it again.

Every time you choose work over distraction, you rebuild your reward system. Every time you delay gratification, you strengthen your willpower. The same brain that was conditioned to seek comfort can be retrained to seek challenge.

That's what the system fears most: men who don't need it anymore.

Because when you no longer need distraction, you become dangerous in the right way. You see through manipulation. You stop reacting to bait. You focus your time and energy on what matters: your mission, your craft, your family, your body, your faith. *That's when real freedom starts.*

The addiction economy can't survive independent men. It can't monetize discipline. It can't profit from men who find purpose. That's why the system will always sell you the opposite: indulgence disguised as freedom, convenience disguised as progress.

It tells you *"do what feels good"* because it knows what feels good usually keeps you weak. It tells you "you deserve rest" because it knows rest becomes laziness. It tells you "you're fine the way you are" because improvement is bad for business.

The message sounds like self-love. It's really self-sabotage.

Every man has to choose who benefits from his time: *him or the system.* If the system profits more from your day than you do, you're not living; you're leasing your life. *Take it back.*

The ugly truth is this: the death of discernment didn't happen by accident. It was profitable.

Social media companies discovered that outrage keeps you on the platform longer than joy, so they fed us outrage. Universities discovered that moral panic sells tuition better than logic, so they sold that. Corporations realized guilt makes you buy more products, so they sold guilt.

And while everyone was busy chasing feelings, truth quietly left the building. Probably got tired of being called "problematic."

We now have a population that believes fact-checking websites are gospel but can't describe how a source is verified. A population that shares headlines they never read. A generation that thinks "research" means typing three words into TikTok's search bar and watching whatever the algorithm serves up.

Meanwhile, *Pew Research (2023)* found that trust in major institutions *(media, government, academia)* has collapsed to historic lows. Fewer than 35 percent of Americans say they trust traditional news. People sense they're being manipulated; they just don't know by whom.

That's the worst of both worlds: suspicious but still gullible.

It's like knowing there's poison in your drink but chugging it anyway because you can't figure out which glass is safe.

Your Move

So if you're a young man reading this and you know you're caught in the loop, if you wake up every day promising yourself you'll change and then spend the night exactly the same way, scrolling, gaming, watching, escaping, I need you to hear this:

You are not broken beyond repair. But you are running out of time.

Every day you give to the addiction economy is a day you don't get back. Your twenties aren't a practice round. This is your life. Right now. And it's slipping through your fingers while you watch other people live theirs.

Delete the apps. Block the sites. Go one week, just seven days, without the things you know are destroying you. It will hurt. That pain is proof you're still alive. Use it.

Because the alternative is spending the rest of your life as a consumer, a product, a statistic.

And you were made for more than that.

That's how civilizations are restored: one focused man at a time.

We live in a world that worships weakness. It rewards outrage, victimhood, and dependency. The system can't stand men who think, who build, who refuse to bow. That's why every distraction exists, to keep those men from rising.

But they will rise. You can feel it. The tide is turning.

There's a growing hunger among men who are done being entertained to death. They're tired of living small. They're ready to take back their minds, their bodies, and their purpose.

It starts with small acts of rebellion: silence over scrolling, discipline over desire, effort over ease. Each choice looks minor in the moment, but together they form a new kind of movement, one that doesn't need hashtags or politics. It just needs men who live differently.

The addiction economy can't survive that kind of man. He doesn't just resist it. He outgrows it. He stops being a consumer and becomes a creator again. He starts building the things the system destroyed: family, brotherhood, faith, strength, skill.

Those are the original antidotes to addiction. They give the male spirit something solid to hold on to. When men rebuild those foundations, the system loses its grip.

Because a man with a mission doesn't need escape. He's already at war, not with others, but with his own limits. That battle gives his life meaning, and meaning kills addiction.

A man with meaning doesn't waste time. He doesn't need approval. He doesn't chase the next high. He's too busy sharpening himself into someone who can be counted on when everything else falls apart.

That's what we've been missing: reliability. Men who show up. Men who endure. Men who carry weight without complaint.

The good news is that kind of man is still possible. He's in every man reading this who feels the quiet anger of knowing he's capable of more.

That anger isn't bad. It's the spark. Use it.

Every generation needs a few men who decide enough is enough, who step out of the fog, kill the distractions, and get to work. They don't wait for permission. They don't ask for motivation. They move.

That's how it starts. That's how the addiction economy ends, not with protests or slogans, but with men reclaiming their minds. The moment a man stops consuming, he starts creating. The moment he stops chasing comfort, he starts finding purpose. The moment he stops obeying distraction, he starts leading.

That's the cure. Not another program, not another product, but a return to the simplest truth: men are meant to build, to serve, and to lead.

The system can sell distraction, but it can't sell purpose. You have to forge that yourself.

So log off. Get quiet. Pick something hard and commit to it. Build calluses. Earn exhaustion. Create something that outlives you.

Because when you do, the noise fades. The temptations lose their power.

And what's left is freedom, the kind that no algorithm can ever take away. The kind your grandfather had. The kind your son deserves. The kind you're going to build, starting tomorrow morning at 5 a.m.

8

FEELINGS OVER FACTS

We've built a culture that treats emotion as truth and truth as optional.

Logic has taken a back seat to feelings, and the results are everywhere, weak minds, broken debate, and a generation that mistakes sensitivity for strength.

Here's what that looks like in practice: a grown man loses his job because he stated a biological fact. A teacher gets fired for refusing to pretend reality doesn't exist. A student is suspended or even expelled for questioning an ideology. A father loses custody for refusing to endorse his child's claimed gender identity. These aren't hypotheticals. These aren't just headlines. *This is America in today.*

We've created a society where hurt feelings have more legal weight than observable truth.

Where the most fragile person in the room gets to define reality for everyone else. That's not progress. That's tyranny with a therapy degree.

This isn't empathy. It's indulgence.

We've convinced people that their emotions are the ultimate authority, that if something hurts their feelings, it must be wrong. We've replaced objective reality with personal experience. You can't build a civilization on that.

For centuries, progress came from discipline, not comfort. It came from men and women who could act with reason when others panicked. They used facts to make decisions, not emotions. Today, the opposite is celebrated. We call it *"emotional intelligence,"* but what it's really become is emotional fragility.

We tell kids that their feelings are valid, and they are. But validity doesn't make them correct. You can feel offended and still be wrong. You can feel hurt and still need correction. That used to be common sense.

Now it's considered cruelty.

The danger isn't that people have emotions. The danger is that we've elevated emotions to the level of morality. The person who feels the most gets to claim the moral high ground. The louder the pain, the truer the argument. That's how you end up with mobs deciding truth instead of evidence.

In this new order, disagreement is hate. Correction is abuse. Debate is violence. The classroom teaches kids to *"share their truth"* instead of seeking truth. The media praises vulnerability but mocks discipline. The result is a society that confuses compassion with cowardice.

Real compassion isn't telling someone they're right when they're wrong. It's helping them see the truth even when it stings. That's what builds strong people. Shielding them from discomfort only makes them fragile.

Resilience used to be a virtue. Now it's a threat.

The same culture that glorifies *"safe spaces"* and *"trigger warnings"* has made fear a lifestyle. Instead of teaching people how to face hardship, we teach them how to avoid it. But avoidance doesn't eliminate pain. It just delays it until it becomes unbearable.

The numbers reflect it. Anxiety and depression rates have

skyrocketed, especially among young adults *(American Psychological Association, 2023)*. You'd think that with all our awareness campaigns, mental health apps, and self-care movements, we'd be happier. We're not.

Because comfort doesn't heal you. Challenge does.

When you tell people they never have to face discomfort, you rob them of the opportunity to grow. You trap them in emotional adolescence. They become adults who can't handle criticism, who melt under pressure, who believe every disagreement is an attack.

That's not compassion. That's cruelty disguised as kindness.

The shift from facts to feelings started small. It began in the schools when self-esteem became more important than performance. Instead of teaching kids how to earn confidence through mastery, we handed it out like a participation ribbon. We thought we were protecting them, but we were weakening them.

A boy who's never been challenged doesn't develop strength. A girl who's never been corrected doesn't develop judgment. You get 25-year-olds who need therapy because someone told them "no" at work.

When you remove friction from growth, you remove maturity with it.

By the time these kids become adults, they've been trained to believe that their emotions are shields against reality. If something offends them, the problem must be external. Someone else is to blame.

That's why victimhood has become the fastest-growing identity group in the world. It's the only one that guarantees power without responsibility.

And here's the sick genius of it: victimhood is addictive. It feels good to blame someone else. It's easier to stay broken than to fix yourself. It's safer to demand the world change than to change yourself.

We've created millions of emotional addicts who get their dopamine hit from being offended.

Every time they claim victim status, they get sympathy, attention, and power. They don't want to heal. Healing would cost them their identity. So they stay wounded on purpose, milking their pain for status while the people who actually suffered in silence get ignored. *That's not compassion. That's exploitation.* And your sons are being taught to join that game or be destroyed by it.

Victimhood feels good because it removes accountability. If everything that hurts you is someone else's fault, you never have to change. You never have to grow. You never have to face the fact that life isn't fair and never will be.

That's what separates strong men and women from everyone else. Strong people accept reality first, then act. Weak people deny reality until it destroys them.

You can't feel your way into strength. You earn it through resistance. Every time you face something painful and survive, you get tougher. Every time you avoid it, you get weaker.

We've trained a generation to believe that self-expression is the same as self-mastery. It's not. Expressing your feelings doesn't make you emotionally intelligent. Controlling them does. Real emotional intelligence is knowing when to speak and when to stay quiet, when to react and when to hold your ground.

But control isn't celebrated anymore. It's shamed. We call it repression. We tell men to "open up" but mock them when they do. We tell women to "speak their truth" even when it defies logic. We've turned honesty into therapy and therapy into identity.

The truth is simple.

Feelings are signals, not commands.

They tell you something is wrong, but they don't tell you what to do. Facts tell you what to do. That's the balance we've lost.

When facts become offensive, freedom dies. You can't have free speech and emotional censorship at the same time. You can't have justice if feelings replace evidence. And you can't have strong men if every act of discipline is labeled as trauma.

Emotions matter. But they're not supposed to lead. They're supposed to follow reason. A man who's ruled by feelings is a slave to them. He'll never stand firm, because his beliefs change with his moods. A nation full of those men won't stand either.

Strength isn't built in therapy circles. It's built in the moments you want to quit and don't. It's built in discipline, sacrifice, and truth. When we replaced those with comfort, validation, and emotion, we started the slow collapse of Western strength. And it all began when we decided that truth was secondary to how truth makes people feel.

The Infection Spreads Everywhere

The infection of emotionalism didn't stop at schools. It spread everywhere, into workplaces, media, politics, and even law. Companies no longer make decisions on results but on reactions. Public policy is written to prevent offense, not to produce outcomes. The news doesn't report truth; it curates feelings.

Workplaces are now social laboratories built around comfort. Performance reviews revolve around *"how people feel"* instead of what they achieved. Leadership has turned into management therapy. Instead of pushing teams to excel, managers are told to avoid confrontation. No one wants to upset anyone. But growth always upsets someone. Progress hurts before it helps.

Politics has become a performance of emotion. Anger and outrage are currency. Logic doesn't matter; volume does. Entire movements are built on hurt feelings, and the media rewards whichever side cries louder. Every issue turns into a morality play where the "most offended" win by default. That's not democracy. That's emotional blackmail.

You see it in the headlines. Facts are labeled *"problematic."* Data that contradicts a narrative is hidden or redefined. We don't debate truth anymore; we debate tone. If you speak calmly but say something unpopular, you're condemned.

If you scream something false but say it with emotion, you're celebrated. It's the triumph of noise over knowledge.

The cost is trust. When feelings replace facts, institutions collapse because people can no longer agree on reality. A society that can't share truth can't solve problems. You can't fix what no one is allowed to name.

The same logic has poisoned journalism. The press once saw itself as a watchdog, verifying facts, exposing lies, and keeping power in check. Now it sees itself as a therapist, soothing audiences, validating biases, and filtering stories through emotional safety. The result is propaganda wrapped in empathy.

We call it "advocacy journalism," but what it really means is selective truth.

Stories are judged by whether they make readers feel good, not whether they make them think. That's why the headlines change depending on who's involved. Facts are constant. Feelings are conditional.

Even science has bent the knee to emotion. Research is censored if it hurts feelings. Scholars are punished for studying inconvenient truths. The pursuit of knowledge used to demand courage. Now it demands conformity. We've turned laboratories into echo chambers.

At the individual level, the damage shows up in relationships. People end friendships over opinions. Couples break apart because one person *"doesn't feel seen."* Families fracture over emotional politics.

We've lost the ability to disagree without dehumanizing.

Maturity used to mean mastering your reactions. Now it means avoiding discomfort altogether. Adults behave like children who need constant reassurance. That's why so many relationships fail, because resilience, patience, and forgiveness have been replaced by instant outrage.

A culture that worships emotion eventually loses wisdom. Wisdom comes from reflection, not reaction. It's the pause between stimulus and response where judgment lives. When everything becomes urgent and emotional, there's no space for thought. That's exactly what social media exploits. The platforms are engineered to trigger emotion, anger, envy, fear, validation. The more people feel, the more they click. The more they click, the more profit the algorithm makes. It's not a digital town square. It's an emotional casino.

> *Let me spell out what this means for your sons: they're being raised by algorithms designed to keep them angry, insecure, and addicted.*

Every notification is a dopamine injection. Every argument is bait. Every post is designed to make them feel something, anything, so they stay scrolling. The tech companies have teams of psychologists whose entire job is to exploit human emotion for profit. They know exactly how to manipulate young men who feel purposeless. They feed them outrage, envy, and artificial validation in carefully measured doses to keep them hooked. Your son isn't weak for falling into it. He's a lab rat in the biggest psychological experiment in human history, and the experimenters are making billions while he rots in his room.

> *You don't leave a casino richer. You leave drained, confused, and addicted. That's how emotional culture works too. It keeps people reacting, so they never start thinking.*

Reclaiming reason doesn't mean rejecting emotion. It means putting it back in order. Feel first, think second, act last. Emotion should warn you, not rule you. Logic should decide what's true, not how you feel about it.

That's how strong people operate. A man who can master his emotions doesn't become cold. He becomes clear. He sees things as they are, not as he wishes them to be. That clarity is what separates leaders from followers.

We can't rebuild culture on validation. We can only rebuild it on truth. The truth doesn't care how you feel about it. That's why it's powerful. It cuts through confusion. It doesn't need approval to exist.

To restore balance, we have to re-teach the discipline of emotional control, in schools, in homes, and in public life. It's not repression; it's refinement. The ability to stay calm in chaos used to be the highest virtue. It made soldiers reliable, fathers dependable, and leaders trustworthy.

Imagine a generation raised to handle discomfort instead of avoiding it. Boys and girls who know how to debate ideas without personalizing them. Workers who can take criticism without collapsing.

Leaders who can make hard choices without apology. That's what civilization depends on.

The cure for fragility isn't cruelty. It's consequence. People grow when they face reality and adapt to it. If you never face resistance, you never develop backbone.

Truth and empathy can coexist. But truth has to lead. Empathy without truth is manipulation. Truth without empathy is cruelty. The balance is what defines maturity.

We need to rebuild that balance everywhere, in classrooms, in families, in media, in government. Facts have to come first again. Emotions have to serve reason, not replace it.

The goal isn't to create emotionless people. It's to create emotionally stable people. The kind who can feel deeply but still act wisely. That's the foundation of freedom. A population that can't control its emotions will always be controlled by those who can.

That's the real danger of feelings over facts. When people are ruled by emotion, they become easy to rule.

The War on Masculine Strength

No group has been damaged more by the feelings-first culture than men. Masculinity has been redefined not by science or ethics, but by emotion. We've been told that stoicism is cold, that discipline is oppression, that self-control is repression. But those were never flaws. They were virtues. They were what allowed men to build, protect, and endure.

For centuries, men were raised to lead with reason. They were taught to keep emotion in check so they could think clearly when it mattered most. The modern world calls that outdated. It calls emotional restraint *"toxic."* But the alternative hasn't created happier men, it's created broken ones.

We told men to open up. We told them to cry more, to express, to share. Some of that was healthy. Men need space for vulnerability. But we didn't stop there. We went from encouraging openness to shaming strength.

The man who stays calm under pressure is now *"emotionally unavailable."* The man who controls his anger is *"repressed."* The man who refuses to crumble is *"cold."*

So men tried to comply. They opened up. They cried. They shared their feelings. And you know what happened? They lost respect. Their wives left them. Their kids stopped listening. Their employers passed them over. Because nobody actually wants an emotionally uncontrolled man, they just said they did. Women don't want men who cry like them, they want men who stay strong when they cry. Children don't want emotional fathers, they want steady ones. Employers don't want reactive men, they want reliable ones. We told men to be vulnerable, and when they were, we punished them for it. That's not just mixed messages. That's a trap. And millions of men are stuck in it right now, trying to be what women say they want while watching those same women choose the men who ignore that advice. *That's backwards.*

Real strength isn't emotional blindness. It's emotional mastery. A man who can't feel is dangerous. But a man who can't control what he feels is just as dangerous, mostly to himself.

When you strip men of stoicism, you strip them of stability. Stoicism isn't about suppressing emotion; it's about giving it structure. It's the ability to feel deeply and still act rightly. It's the discipline of the soldier, the patience of the father, the calm of the leader.

We've mistaken calm for weakness. But calm is what keeps chaos from spreading.

When men lose it, families fall apart, tempers explode, and trust dies. The world depends on men who can keep their emotions in check when everything else is collapsing.

That's what fathers used to teach their sons. They taught them how to fight without hatred, how to love without dependency, and how to endure pain without self-pity. It wasn't about being unfeeling. It was about being reliable. A man who's ruled by emotion can't be relied on.

We're seeing that now. A generation of men who are emotionally reactive instead of emotionally grounded. They take everything personally, respond impulsively, and crumble when criticized. They confuse authenticity with volatility. They think that "being real" means broadcasting every feeling. But maturity means mastering your feelings, not displaying them.

Look at what this produces: thirty-year-old men who have breakdowns over job rejection. Twenty-five-year-olds who cut off their families over political disagreements. Men who ghost women after one uncomfortable conversation. Men who quit careers because their boss hurt their feelings. Men who spiral into depression because someone unfollowed them online. This isn't strength. This isn't even normal human weakness. This is emotional infancy in adult bodies. And we created it by telling men that emotional control was toxic and emotional expression was brave.

Now we have a generation of men who can't handle the most basic disappointments without collapsing. They're not equipped for marriage, fatherhood, leadership, or life. They're emotional children waiting for the world to validate them, and the world never will.

The irony is that this emotional overexposure hasn't made men more connected. It's made them more isolated. Because respect is built on restraint. No one trusts a man who can't control himself. No one follows a man who can't stay composed. Emotional excess doesn't create closeness. It creates chaos.

Men used to find emotional balance through purpose. When a man has a mission, his emotions serve that mission. They don't lead it. Duty gave him direction. That's why soldiers, builders, and leaders rarely fell apart emotionally, not because they didn't feel, but because they had something bigger than feelings to focus on.

Take away purpose, and emotion fills the vacuum. That's what's happened today. When men stopped leading families, building things, and defending values, they started internalizing emotion with nowhere to direct it.

Depression, addiction, and anxiety filled the gap.

You can see it everywhere, men overreacting online, seeking validation in likes and comments, exploding in anger or drowning in apathy. They're not weak by nature. They're weak because they've been told to trust their feelings more than their judgment.

The world doesn't need men who are emotionally reckless. It needs men who are emotionally strong, steady, calm, rational, compassionate but firm. That kind of man brings order. He brings peace.

You can measure a man's character by what it takes to break his composure. If it's criticism, he's fragile. If it's hardship, he's untested. But if he can stay grounded when everything around him shakes, that's a man with depth.

Stoicism is not the absence of empathy. It's empathy under control. It's knowing how to care without collapsing. It's strength in service of others, not in defiance of them. That's what the modern conversation about masculinity misses.

We've created emotional men without emotional discipline. That's why you see men crying on social media for attention instead of healing in private through purpose. That's why you see men blaming society for their pain instead of channeling it into productivity.

Feeling pain doesn't make you weak. Staying stuck in it does. Real emotional strength is quiet. It's a man who grieves in private and still shows up for work. It's a father who carries his stress without taking it out on his kids. It's a leader who absorbs pressure so others can stay calm.

That kind of emotional strength used to be respected. Now it's mocked as *"old-fashioned."* But the world will always need those men, because chaos will always need order.

The truth is, emotion and logic aren't enemies. They're partners. But one has to lead. Logic keeps emotion honest. Emotion keeps logic human. When emotion leads alone, it blinds. When logic leads alone, it hardens. The balance is what defines maturity.

The Path Back to Mastery

Men need to relearn that balance. It starts with restraint. Don't react instantly. Don't speak from anger. Don't confuse loudness with power. Real control looks quiet.

Next comes perspective. Ask:

"Is what I'm feeling true? Or is it just temporary?"

Most emotions fade when you stop feeding them. Facts don't. That's why grounding yourself in truth is so important.

Finally comes discipline, daily habits that reinforce strength over sensitivity. Wake up early. Move your body. Do hard things. Keep promises. Each act of discipline rewires the brain to follow logic instead of impulse.

A man who lives that way doesn't lose emotion. He leads it.

The path back to strength isn't complicated. It's not a secret formula or a hidden philosophy. It's a return to what every generation before us already knew, that emotion is a tool, not a master. It serves reason, not the other way around.

Men need to stop apologizing for being logical, direct, and composed. The world depends on those traits. Families depend on them. Civilization depends on them. We need men who can stay rational when everyone else is emotional. That's how bridges get built, how conflicts end, how nations survive.

When a plane loses an engine, you don't want a pilot who panics. You want the one who breathes, checks the instruments, and handles the problem. Life works the same way. The men who can stay calm in the storm are the ones who keep the rest of us alive.

That doesn't mean emotion has no place. It means emotion has to be led.

Courage is emotion led by reason.
Compassion is emotion led by principle.
Love is emotion led by commitment.

When emotion isn't led, it turns into chaos. That's what we're living in now, a culture where everyone feels everything, all the time, and no one can control it.

Silence Is Golden

Men once took pride in being steady. They didn't need to announce how they felt about every issue or every slight. They understood that their value came from what they could carry, not from how loudly they could complain. The more pressure they faced, the calmer they became. That's leadership. That's maturity.

The world used to reward that kind of composure. Now it rewards outrage. The loudest voice gets the attention, not the wisest one. But emotion doesn't build anything lasting. It burns hot, then dies fast. Discipline is what builds. Reason is what sustains.

The modern man has to relearn the art of self-control, not as a form of denial, but as a path to freedom. Because the man who can't control his emotions is controlled by whoever can trigger them. Every manipulative ad, every political movement, every social media trend thrives on emotional reaction. They sell outrage because outrage is easy. They fear discipline because discipline can't be sold.

Freedom starts with restraint. The man who can say no, to temptation, to distraction, to emotional impulse, is the man who's truly free. He's not a prisoner of mood or circumstance. He doesn't need constant validation. He's centered, grounded, and clear. That's real power.

Every boy should be taught that lesson early.

Strength isn't found in yelling, crying, or collapsing.

It's found in mastering yourself when everything in you wants to give up. It's found in holding your temper when someone insults you. It's found in showing up on time, every day, no matter how you feel.

That's what builds trust. That's what earns respect. People follow men who stay steady when others lose control. They know that kind of man won't be swayed by emotion or manipulation. He'll stay rooted in truth, even when it's unpopular.

You can see it in history. Every moment of progress was driven by reason. Every moment of collapse was driven by emotion. The reason-led build. The emotion-led destroy. A man who acts on emotion destroys faster than he can rebuild.

We need a generation of men who think before they react, who speak with purpose instead of impulse, who can be passionate without being reckless. That's not repression. That's refinement. That's how men become strong enough to lead families, businesses, and nations without turning them into chaos.

When men master their emotions, they don't become cold. They become warm in the right ways, protective, reliable, and steady. They can love harder because they're not ruled by fear or pride. They can forgive because they don't mistake emotion for ego. They can sacrifice because they don't confuse feelings with fulfillment.

That's the kind of man every society needs, and the kind of man every boy needs to see.

The solution starts simple: *stop worshiping emotion.* Stop teaching boys that every feeling is a crisis. Teach them that feelings are information. Listen to them, then decide what's true. Teach them to act based on principle, not mood. Teach them to stand firm when emotions tell them to run.

Resilience is a muscle. It grows every time you face discomfort and don't fold. Every small act of self-control is a rep that builds strength.

Skip the rep, and weakness becomes habit.

Our culture teaches the opposite. It glorifies reaction and mocks restraint. But look around. The loudest people are rarely the strongest. The most emotional are rarely the most fulfilled. The happiest men you'll ever meet aren't the ones who avoid pain. They're the ones who've mastered it.

The world doesn't need more emotional men. It needs emotionally disciplined men, the kind who can feel pain and still move forward, who can take insult without losing control, who can lead calmly through chaos. *That's not toxic. That's heroic.*

You can't feel your way into truth. You have to face it. And the truth is this: reality doesn't care about your feelings. It never has. That's what makes it reliable. You can build on it. *You can trust it.*

If you're a young man reading this and you've been taught that expressing every emotion makes you enlightened, I need you to understand something: you've been lied to. The people who told you to be vulnerable weren't trying to help you. They were trying to weaken you.

Every man who bought that lie is now stuck, emotionally unstable, relationally isolated, professionally stagnant, and wondering why life isn't working. Your emotions are tools, not masters. Feel them, understand them, then put them in their place. The world doesn't need more men who cry about their problems. It needs men who solve them.

The woman you want doesn't need you to understand her feelings better than she does. She needs you to stay calm when she can't. Your future kids don't need a father who's *"in touch with his emotions."* They need a father who's in control of them. Start there. Master yourself first. Everything else follows.

When men stop chasing comfort and start embracing clarity,

> *they stop being victims,*
> *they start being leaders,*
> *they stop reacting and start rebuilding.*

Facts don't change. Feelings do. That's why strength built on emotion collapses, and strength built on truth endures.

We don't need more men in touch with their emotions. We need more men in control of them.

Because a man who masters his emotions can lead a family, a team, a nation, and himself.

That's the foundation of freedom. That's the cure for chaos. That's how we rebuild men.

THE PRICE OF WEAKNESS

The decline of men isn't just a personal tragedy. It's a national liability. *Weak men make weak families, and weak families make weak nations.* For decades, we've been told that masculinity was optional, that society could function just as well without strong fathers, providers, or protectors. We were wrong. The evidence is everywhere, and it's written in the faces of our children.

Picture this: A twelve-year-old boy sitting in his bedroom at 2 a.m., screen-glow lighting his face, scrolling through social media, watching other people live while he slowly disappears. His father is either gone or present but checked out. His mother is exhausted trying to be both parents. His teachers think he's lazy. His peers think he's weird. He doesn't know what he's for, and no one has bothered to show him. In ten years, he'll either be in prison, on welfare, or medicated into functional numbness. Multiply him by ten million.

That's the cost. That's not a statistic. That's your neighbor's kid. That's your nephew. That might be your son.

Every major problem in modern America traces back to the same wound: *men stopped leading.* Not because they're incapable, but because they were told not to. And when leadership disappears, chaos fills the vacuum.

In Chapter 4, I showed you the fatherless nation, the boys growing up without male guidance, destined for prison, poverty, and despair. In Chapter 5, you saw the education trap, schools that medicate boys instead of mentoring them. Those chapters diagnosed the damage at the individual level.

But the price of weak men doesn't stop there. It scales.

When 25% of children grow up without fathers, you don't just get broken families, you get a broken economy. According to the Bureau of Labor Statistics (2023), prime-age male workforce participation has dropped from 98% in the 1950s to 89% today. Millions of working-age men aren't working, studying, or even looking for jobs. They've checked out. And when men check out, productivity collapses, tax revenue shrinks, and the economy runs on fumes.

When boys grow up medicated and directionless, you don't just get failing schools, you get a collapsing military. The U.S. Department of Defense (2023) reports the worst recruitment crisis in history. Only 23% of Americans aged 17-24 meet basic physical, mental, and moral standards for service. That's not a recruiting problem, that's a civilization problem. You can't defend a nation with men who can't do a pull-up or handle criticism.

When men stop leading churches, neighborhoods, and civic organizations, you don't just get lonely individuals, you get social collapse. Crime rises where fathers vanish. Communities fracture where men retreat. Every institution that depends on masculine leadership, from volunteer fire departments to Little League, is hemorrhaging participation because men don't believe they're needed anymore.

And here's the most terrifying part: this isn't a temporary dip. It's a generational cascade. Fatherless boys become fatherless fathers. Weak men raise weaker sons. The cycle doesn't break—it accelerates. We're not just losing this generation. We're losing the next three.

This is the price of weakness. Not measured in individual failures, but in civilizational collapse. Not counted in broken homes, but in broken nations. And if we don't act now, right now, there won't be anything left to rebuild.

The effects stretch beyond childhood.

Boys who grow up without male role models often become men who distrust authority or avoid responsibility. They drift. They seek validation in gangs, online echo chambers, or self-destructive habits. The surge in male crime, addiction, and suicide isn't random, it's what happens when a generation grows up without guidance and without purpose.

You can see it in relationships too. Weak men don't build strong partnerships. They either dominate or disappear. Many are terrified of women, unsure how to approach them without being accused of something wrong. Others chase approval instead of respect, creating shallow, unstable bonds. The hookup culture that dominates young adulthood isn't liberation, it's loneliness disguised as freedom. Swipe right, meet up, pretend you're not desperate for connection, leave before breakfast. Congratulations, you just participated in the emptiest transaction known to modern humanity. Two people using each other for validation isn't progress. It's a symptom of emotional poverty.

Marriage has suffered most. Half a century ago, marriage was a milestone of adulthood.

Today it's treated like a luxury or a risk. Men delay it or avoid it altogether, not because they hate commitment, but because they've been taught it offers no reward and endless liability. Divorce courts favor one side. Culture mocks husbands. The message is clear: men who marry are fools. The result is predictable. Fewer marriages mean fewer children. Fewer children mean a shrinking future.

A nation that stops reproducing has already surrendered. Recent research indicates that total testosterone levels in American men have fallen over recent decades. For example, one study found a significant age-independent decline in serum testosterone between 1987 and 2004 *(Travison et al., 2007)*. More recent data suggest the trend continues among younger men, though definitive national figures above 20% remain unconfirmed. Sperm counts are in steady decline *(Levine et al., Human Reproduction Update, 2017)*. These aren't just medical statistics, they're reflections of a deeper spiritual decay.

Men without purpose don't build, protect, or reproduce. They exist, but they don't continue.

The economic fallout follows. When men stop working, nations stagnate. Labor force participation among men of prime working age (25–54) has declined for decades, even after short-term rebounds. Though the rate reached about 89% in 2023, its highest since before the Great Recession, it remains well below the 97% levels seen in the 1950s and 1960s *(Bureau of Labor Statistics, 2023)*. Millions of able-bodied men are not working, not studying, and not looking for jobs. They've checked out. Some live off parents or government benefits; others retreat into digital escapism. They're 32 years old, living in their child-hood bedroom, explaining to their exhausted mother that they're "taking time to figure things out" while playing Call of Duty for 14 hours a day. An economy built on consumption can hide that for a while, but not forever. Eventually, someone has to build, repair, and defend. Without men doing that, the system collapses under its own weight.

The cultural cost is harder to measure but easier to feel. You see it in public spaces that no longer feel safe, in classrooms that no longer inspire respect, in cities where apathy has replaced pride. You hear it in the silence of communities that used to be led by fathers, coaches, and mentors who have vanished. A society that forgets how to produce strong men eventually forgets how to protect anything.

Even the military, once the last refuge of discipline, isn't immune.

Recruitment numbers are at record lows *(U.S. Department of Defense, 2023)*. Young men who once saw service as honor now see it as burden. They're physically weaker, mentally less resilient, and socially disconnected. When the guardians of a nation no longer believe in sacrifice, the nation is unguarded in every sense of the word.

This is what the price of weak men looks like: fragile homes, unsafe streets, empty churches, and aimless youth. It's not just emotional, it's structural. You can measure it in every broken promise and every lost potential.

A weak man doesn't just fail himself; he leaves everyone around him vulnerable.

And let's be brutally honest: *this isn't reversible overnight.* You can't undo a generation of damage with a motivational speech and a gym membership. The boys who grew up without fathers, who were medicated instead of mentored, who learned manhood from Instagram instead of real men, they're already here. Some of them are too far gone. That's the part no one wants to say out loud. We lost an entire cohort. The best we can do now is stop the bleeding and save the next generation. But that requires us to admit the scale of the catastrophe. It requires rage, not at the boys, but at the people who destroyed them. And it requires action, immediate, unapologetic, relentless action, before we lose another ten million sons to the same cultural slaughter.

The irony is that this weakness was sold as progress.

We told men they'd be happier once they let go of responsibility. We told them that comfort was the same as peace. But peace doesn't come from ease, it comes from earned confidence. A man who's never tested can't feel peace, only boredom. The more we sheltered men from struggle, the more they collapsed under the weight of it.

That's where we are today: *surrounded by comfort, starving for meaning.* We have more entertainment than any generation in history, yet less satisfaction. We have more information, yet less wisdom. We have more options, yet less courage to choose. That's not evolution; it's exhaustion.

The world still needs men who are strong, but strength today starts with clarity. Men need to understand that the cost of weakness isn't paid individually, it's paid collectively. Every man who quits leaves a hole that someone else has to fill. Every father who walks away leaves a son to wander. Every husband who retreats leaves a wife to carry the load alone. Weakness spreads faster than strength because it demands nothing and offers comfort. But comfort without purpose is decay.

Weak men don't just fail privately. They reshape the world around them.

They reshape the world around them. Every institution that depends on courage, restraint, and moral clarity begins to fracture when men no longer live by those values. The damage spreads slowly at first, then all at once.

When the Protectors Disappear

You can see it in the breakdown of public order. When men stop protecting their communities, predators step in. Crime doesn't rise in a vacuum; it rises where strong men have vanished. Look at any city plagued by violence and fatherlessness is always the common thread. The young men pulling triggers weren't born violent, they were born leaderless. They learned manhood from chaos. Without fathers, they seek power the only way they understand: through domination and fear. *That's not masculinity. That's desperation.*

Police departments across the country have watched the same story repeat. Officers respond to calls where there is no father, no authority, no stability, only exhaustion. Teachers see it too. They face classrooms filled with boys who can't focus, can't sit still, can't follow direction, and no longer respect authority. We keep asking schools to fix what only families can build.

The courts, prisons, and welfare systems are all monuments to the cost of weak men. They exist because strength failed upstream. A boy raised without boundaries grows into a man who tests them. A man who never learns self-control must learn it from the law. The billions we spend on incarceration and social programs are the invoice for abandoning fatherhood.

Weak men also make bad citizens. When responsibility disappears, entitlement grows. A generation raised without discipline will look to government for solutions to problems they created. That's why bureaucracies expand in proportion to cultural decay. The weaker the men, the stronger the state.

Free nations don't survive when their people trade self-reliance for dependency.

The ripple effect reaches culture. Weak men don't produce great art, great ideas, or great movements. Their output is imitation, not inspiration. They chase trends instead of truth. You can see it in the emptiness of modern entertainment, endless remakes, recycled ideas, and shallow virtue signaling. The creative spirit that built civilizations fades when men lose conviction. Art without courage becomes propaganda.

Even the spiritual cost is immense. Weak men can't lead in faith because faith requires strength, the strength to stand firm when the world mocks you. Churches that cater to comfort instead of conviction fill pews with indecision. Pastors afraid to offend stop preaching about sin and start preaching about feelings. But truth without discipline doesn't save anyone. It just keeps them numb.

Everywhere we look, softness is being mistaken for kindness. We've confused empathy with weakness, tolerance with apathy, humility with surrender. Those traits, when detached from principle, corrode the very things they pretend to protect. Weak men don't defend freedom; they apologize for it. They don't stand up for the innocent; they rationalize the guilty.

Their morality is whatever earns them approval in the moment.

You can trace every major cultural decline through the same pattern. First, men stop leading. Then families fracture. Then values fade. Then chaos fills the vacuum. Once chaos takes root, the same weak men who caused it demand that someone else fix it, through laws, through censorship, through control. That's how free societies die. Not with invasion, but with surrender.

The great irony is that the men most eager to avoid responsibility end up enslaved by their own comfort. The man who refuses to work becomes dependent on someone who does. The man who avoids conflict becomes ruled by those who don't. The man who won't discipline himself will eventually be disciplined by the world. Freedom and strength are inseparable. You can't have one without the other.

Weak men are dangerous in positions of power. They crave approval more than truth. They follow polls instead of principles. They use morality as a marketing strategy. They fear being disliked more than being wrong. And so they say whatever keeps them comfortable while their societies unravel.

History is filled with such men, soft rulers, timid generals, moral cowards, who let corruption grow because confronting it would cost them favor.

The same weakness infects leadership in modern institutions. Corporate boards, schools, media outlets, even churches are led by men who think risk is worse than failure. They avoid controversy at all costs, confusing silence with wisdom. But silence in the face of decay isn't wisdom; it's cowardice. The world doesn't need men who blend in. It needs men who will stand out and stand firm.

The cost of weak men is visible even in small things, the tone of conversation, the way people handle disagreement, the absence of accountability. We've created a generation that confuses emotion with evidence. A society run on feelings will always attack the people who tell the truth, because truth hurts before it heals. Only strong men can endure that discomfort long enough to fix what's broken.

You can't build safety on weakness.
You can't build trust on excuses.
You can't build peace on avoidance.

Every real improvement in human life, from invention to freedom to justice, was built by people who took risk and endured pain. Weak men avoid both. That's why they produce comfort instead of progress, compliance instead of character.

And yet, strength doesn't mean cruelty. The solution to weak men isn't aggressive men, it's good men. A good man is strong enough to act, humble enough to listen, and disciplined enough to control himself. He doesn't need to dominate others to prove his power. His restraint is his power. The problem with modern weakness is that it rejects both halves of that equation. It removes strength entirely and calls the leftover confusion *"kindness."*

Our culture is full of men who've been told they're virtuous because they never offend anyone. But virtue isn't avoiding offense; it's doing what's right regardless of reaction.

> *Weak men seek approval; strong men seek purpose.*
> *Weak men follow trends; strong men follow truth.*
> *Weak men build nothing; strong men leave legacies.*

The cost of weak men is written across every crumbling institution in this country. It's the reason our schools can't teach, our cities can't stay safe, and our politics can't stay honest. You don't fix those problems by hiring more bureaucrats or passing more laws. You fix them by producing men who can bear the weight of responsibility again.

Weak men don't just weaken families or neighborhoods. They weaken nations. A society is only as stable as the men willing to defend it, and when that instinct fades, the walls start to crack. History doesn't forgive softness. It replaces it.

You can see the pattern repeating itself on a global scale. Every empire that fell started by mocking its own defenders. Rome didn't collapse because its enemies were stronger; *it collapsed because its citizens grew comfortable.* Bread and entertainment replaced duty and sacrifice. The same signs are showing now. The United States still has unmatched resources and technology, but those mean nothing if the spirit that built them dies.

Our military struggles to meet recruitment goals. Fewer young men are fit to serve. Many fail physical exams or background checks. Some just aren't interested. They've been raised to see patriotism as outdated and masculinity as a liability. Instead of calling that a national emergency, our leaders celebrate inclusivity campaigns that have nothing to do with readiness. The armed forces don't need more slogans. They need strong men who believe in something bigger than themselves.

Strength has become controversial. Discipline is framed as aggression. Duty is mocked as blind obedience.

The very traits that used to define leadership are now treated like defects. That's why our institutions look paralyzed in the face of crisis. Weak men can't make hard choices. They wait for someone else to act, someone else to take the risk, someone else to be blamed. But no nation survives on hesitation.

We're already paying the price abroad. Enemies respect strength and exploit weakness. They study our confusion and use it as a weapon. They see a country obsessed with pronouns and celebrity gossip, too distracted to defend its own values. You can't intimidate your rivals with hashtags. You can't deter adversaries with apologies. Power respects power, it always has.

The cost of weak men also shows up in diplomacy. Negotiations built on guilt instead of confidence end in concession. Nations led by weak men trade principle for approval. They mistake compromise for peace. They talk endlessly about unity while handing their sovereignty away piece by piece. History remembers those moments not as progress but as decline.

Economically, the pattern is identical. Weak men don't innovate; they maintain. They don't build industries; they manage decline. The spirit that created the airplane, the microchip, and the space race came from risk-takers who weren't afraid to fail. Weak men avoid risk entirely, which means they also avoid greatness. That's why so many young men now dream not of invention or exploration but of attention, the hollow currency of the digital age.

You can see how this has reshaped the global playing field. Nations that once looked to America for leadership now look elsewhere. Strength commands respect. Weakness invites challenge. Every time our leaders apologize for success or hesitate to act decisively, the world takes note. The vacuum doesn't stay empty for long. Other powers step in, and they're led by men who have no confusion about what strength means.

Civilization Itself Is Crumbling

The decline of men doesn't just affect nations; it affects civilization itself. Every major advancement in human history, agriculture, architecture, exploration, science, governance, came from men who accepted risk and responsibility. They built the world we live in. To dismantle masculinity is to dismantle progress. Civilization depends on men who build and protect, not men who wait for someone else to handle the burden.

When men lose their sense of purpose, societies become reactive instead of proactive. They stop thinking about the next generation and focus only on the next comfort. They trade legacy for leisure. That's what we see now, a world that can't plan beyond the next election cycle, can't sustain families beyond one generation, and can't inspire young men beyond the next dopamine hit. That's not just a moral failure; it's an existential one.

Weak men also weaken faith in leadership itself. When people see their leaders cowering before mobs, apologizing for truth, or prioritizing self-preservation over service, they lose respect for authority entirely. That erosion of trust is the beginning of anarchy. The world doesn't fall apart when people stop believing in God or country. It falls apart when they stop believing in each other.

We're already seeing that erosion at every level, in politics, policing, education, and even family life. A generation that doesn't trust leadership will not follow rules. And without rules, civilization becomes chaos wrapped in comfort. The police can't fix it. The courts can't legislate it. Only strong, principled men can restore it.

But there's another layer to this cost, the psychological one. Weak men live in quiet misery. They know something is wrong, but they've been trained not to name it. They feel anxiety without understanding its source. It's not always depression in the medical sense; it's despair in the moral sense. Deep down, every man knows he was made for something more than consumption and comfort. When that purpose goes unfulfilled, it turns inward as shame.

The Quiet Despair

That shame is what fuels so many of today's addictions. Pornography, gaming, gambling, and drugs are symptoms of the same disease: men trying to feel something real in a world that no longer gives them purpose. Weak men escape into fantasy because the real world no longer respects what they are built to do. But escapism never cures emptiness; it deepens it. Every hour spent avoiding responsibility makes it harder to return to it.

That's why this crisis can't be solved with slogans or self-help books.

It's not about confidence coaching or mental hacks. It's about rebuilding the core of manhood, purpose, discipline, and duty. That foundation has been stripped from boys for decades. If we want to reverse decline, we have to rebuild that foundation from the ground up.

The nations that endure are those that still value duty over comfort. Look at history again: after every collapse, the societies that rose from the ashes were built by men who refused to stay weak. They rebuilt through faith, work, and sacrifice. That's the pattern. The question now is whether we have enough strong men left to repeat it.

The cost of weak men is the quiet collapse we live in every day.

It's not a single moment of destruction but a slow erosion of standards, duty, and pride. You see it in the man who stops showing up for his family. You see it in the teenager who won't look anyone in the eye. You see it in the leader who says nothing when everything he built starts to rot. The problem isn't that we ran out of strength overnight. It's that we stopped believing strength mattered.

The culture tells men they can be anything except what they were meant to be. They can chase money, attention, and comfort, but not meaning. The result is predictable. A generation of men who don't know what they stand for can't hold a line against anything. They bend to pressure, apologize for success, and call their compliance empathy. But real empathy isn't surrender. It's sacrifice. It's doing what's right even when it hurts. Weak men have forgotten that distinction.

The truth is, strength and goodness were never opposites. They were designed to coexist. The man who protects his family isn't oppressive. The father who sets rules isn't cruel. The soldier who defends his country isn't violent, he's disciplined. But when strength disappears from virtue, virtue becomes fragile. You can't defend truth with weakness. You can't raise children on excuses. You can't keep peace by refusing to fight for it.

We're now living with the full harvest of that weakness. Boys are raised to doubt themselves. Women are exhausted from doing everything alone. Families are falling apart. Communities are leaderless. And at the highest levels of power, people mistake appeasement for diplomacy. None of it works. Because none of it was built on strength.

The remedy won't come from government programs or social campaigns. It won't come from hashtags or awareness months. It will come from individual men deciding that they've had enough. It will come from fathers choosing to raise their sons, husbands choosing to honor their wives, and young men choosing responsibility over comfort. The turnaround begins when men remember that they're needed, not as accessories, not as equals in the vague modern sense, but as protectors, builders, and anchors.

How the Reversal Begins

A weak man waits for rescue. A strong man rescues himself and then reaches back for others. That mindset shift is the hinge between collapse and recovery. History never changes direction through committees or slogans. It changes when individuals rediscover duty.

When enough men do that, cultures heal.

It starts in the smallest places, in homes, in gyms, in churches, on job sites. Every man who sets a standard raises the ground for everyone around him. Every man who lives with discipline gives the next generation permission to do the same. You don't rebuild a nation by yelling at the darkness; you rebuild it by lighting fires of purpose in every man who's still willing to fight for what's right.

The cost of weak men can only be paid back through the work of strong ones. That's the simple truth no ideology can erase. And it's not just physical strength that matters. It's moral strength, the willingness to speak truth when it's unpopular, to stand firm when it's risky, to say no when the world demands yes. Courage is contagious, and cowardice is too. The choice each man makes spreads further than he thinks.

If every man in America woke up tomorrow and decided to take responsibility for one thing, his health, his work, his family, his community, the cultural decay would stop within a generation. That's not theory; it's math. Responsibility scales. Every strong man creates stability. Every stable home creates stronger children. Every strong community creates a stronger nation.

It's a chain reaction waiting to happen.

The cost of weak men is high, but it's not final. Collapse is not destiny. Weakness can be reversed. Strength can be rebuilt. Every era that lost its way eventually found it again when men stopped apologizing for being men. The world doesn't need perfection. It needs courage. It needs men who aren't afraid to be what they were designed to be, decisive, protective, selfless, and strong.

If there's a message to take from this chapter, it's this: strength is not the problem. It's the solution. The world doesn't fall apart because men are too strong. It falls apart because too many refuse to be strong at all. When men are grounded in purpose, guided by morality, and unafraid of responsibility, everything else follows.

Women thrive.
Children thrive.
Nations thrive.

We can debate policies and systems all day, but it always comes back to the same point: a country rises or falls on the character of its men. Weak men create hard times. Hard times create strong men. Strong men create good times. We are somewhere in the middle of that cycle now, and which direction we go next depends on whether men decide to rise again.

It's not too late. But it will be if we keep pretending weakness is virtue. The cost of weak men has already been counted in lost families, broken communities, and dying nations. If we don't stop the bleeding now, there won't be anything left to rebuild.

Strength is not about domination. It's about stewardship. It's about being the man your children can count on when life turns hard, the husband your wife can respect when everything feels uncertain, the citizen your country can rely on when danger comes. That's not toxic. That's noble. That's manhood.

If men want to save their world, they must first save themselves. No policy can do that for them. No law can legislate it. It begins when one man decides to stand up and lead again. Then another. Then another. Until once again, we look around and see a country that stands tall because its men do.

That's the closing truth of this chapter, the cost of weak men is destruction, but the reward of strong men is renewal. Everything else in this book, and everything that comes next, depends on whether we choose one or the other.

PART TWO

THE FIGHT BACK

10

THE BOYS WHO FIGHT BACK

When you silence a generation long enough, they eventually start to shout. That's what's happening with young men today. After years of being told that their instincts are wrong, their masculinity is toxic, and their presence is a threat, they've started pushing back.

You can see it in classrooms, online, in politics, and even on the streets. It's not hate that drives them. It's hunger, hunger for truth, for belonging, for permission to exist without apology.

And before we go any further, let me be absolutely clear: I'm proud of them. I'm proud of every young man who refused to apologize for being male. I'm proud of every teenager who stood up in class and said "no" when asked to pretend reality doesn't exist. I'm proud of every boy who walked away from a system designed to break him and found his own path. They're not radicalized. They're awake. And the people who spent decades demonizing masculinity are terrified because their experiment failed.

The boys didn't break. They fought back.

That's not a problem. That's exactly what men are supposed to do when threatened.

The media calls it radicalization. Teachers call it rebellion. But it's really restoration. Young men are trying to reclaim something that was taken from them, the right to be proud of who they are.

For years, we've told boys to sit down and shut up while the world lectured them about privilege. They watched as their fathers were mocked in sitcoms, their heroes erased from history, and their values rewritten as oppression. They were told they were born guilty for crimes they didn't commit. Eventually, they stopped listening.

When people feel unheard, they shouldn't disappear... they should organize.

That's what we're seeing now. A growing number of young men are rejecting the culture that raised them. They're turning off the propaganda and turning toward communities that speak to their frustration, sometimes healthy ones, sometimes dangerous ones.

And here's what makes the establishment panic: they can't control it. They tried censorship. They tried de-platforming. They tried calling everyone who disagreed with them Nazis. None of it worked. Because you can't shame someone who's already been told they're worthless for existing. You can't scare someone who has nothing left to lose. These young men watched the system destroy their fathers, medicate their brothers, and mock their nature. They have zero loyalty to it. And when the system realizes it lost an entire generation's trust, it doesn't apologize. It doubles down. It calls them extremists. That just proves they were right to walk away.

This backlash didn't come from nowhere. It was built, brick by brick, by the same institutions that now condemn it.

Schools taught boys to be ashamed of strength. Universities mocked tradition. The media celebrated every form of rebellion except masculine pride. So these boys built their own spaces.

Online communities became their new locker rooms and town halls. They found other men who felt the same, angry, isolated, searching. They started talking openly about what they saw: the double standards, the hypocrisy, the constant messaging that men are expendable. For the first time, someone was saying what they'd been thinking.

That's the power vacuum created by a culture that demonized manhood.

When fathers, teachers, and leaders stop speaking truth, someone else fills the silence. And not everyone who fills it is good.

Enter the influencers. Some preach discipline and purpose. Others preach resentment and chaos. But they all have one thing in common, they tell young men that it's okay to be men again. That message alone is enough to make them listen.

People love to attack figures like Andrew Tate, Jordan Peterson, and others who speak directly to male frustration. But what they miss is why these figures resonate in the first place. They didn't create the crisis, they answered it. They stepped into the space where institutions failed.

Peterson told men to clean their rooms and take responsibility. Tate told them to fight, build, and stop apologizing. One spoke to order, the other to defiance. Together they filled the vacuum of fatherhood and leadership that modern culture left behind.

And here's the part that should terrify every institution: these aren't fringe figures anymore. Peterson has tens of millions of followers. Tate reached hundreds of millions before they tried to silence him. These numbers represent boys and young men who the system completely failed. Every subscriber is a son who didn't have a father to teach him. Every view is a student who got nothing from school except shame. Every like is a young man saying "finally, someone who doesn't hate me for being male."

You can ban the messengers, but you can't ban the hunger.

When young men are starving for masculine guidance, they'll find it somewhere. The only question is whether it comes from wise men or angry ones.

You can disagree with their delivery. You can even criticize their flaws. But you can't deny their reach. Millions of young men are listening because no one else is talking to them. The world lectures men. These figures speak to them.

When you spend a decade telling boys they're the problem, you shouldn't be surprised when they start looking for people who call them the solution.

This backlash isn't just political, it's spiritual. Young men are starving for purpose, for clarity, for truth that isn't filtered through ideology. They're tired of being told that masculinity needs to be fixed instead of refined. They want rules, not feelings. Order, not chaos. Challenge, not comfort. *And they're right to want those things.*

The establishment calls their rebellion dangerous, but the real danger came first, the collapse of meaning. When men lose meaning, they don't stay neutral. They either give up or fight back. The ones who give up disappear into addiction, depression, and isolation. The ones who fight back are the reason there's still hope.

These boys aren't extremists. They're displaced traditionalists.

They believe in discipline, honor, and identity, but they've been raised in a world that mocks all three. Their rebellion isn't against progress. It's against the emptiness that replaced it.

You see it even in places like Beverly Hills, boys raised in comfort, surrounded by luxury, yet starving for purpose. When they put on a red hat or speak out of line, it's not always political. It's personal. It's the only way left to assert that they exist.

I've sat across from teenagers in Beverly Hills, kids with every material advantage, who are angrier and more lost than kids from broken homes. *You know why?* Because money doesn't fix purposelessness. Comfort doesn't cure emptiness. These boys have everything except a reason to exist. Their fathers are gone, working 80-hour weeks to maintain a lifestyle. Their mothers are medicated and distracted. Their schools teach them they're oppressors. Their therapists tell them to find themselves. So they rebel, not with violence, but with refusal.

They refuse to play the game. They refuse to pretend. They refuse to apologize. And every adult in their life calls that the problem. It's not. It's the symptom. The problem is that we gave them wealth but not worth.

When the system rewards conformity, rebellion becomes the only path to authenticity. And when rebellion is mislabeled as hate, the divide grows.

These young men are not lost causes. They're canaries in the coal mine, warning us that something is deeply wrong with how we're raising boys.

They're the product of fatherless homes, feminized schools, and a culture that replaced respect with shame. Their frustration isn't baseless, it's earned.

They're tired of being told that every problem is their fault.

They're tired of being told to be softer while the world gets harsher.

They're tired of watching men who built everything be replaced by men who apologize for it.

They want something real to believe in again. And right now, no one in authority is offering it.

That's why the voices they follow, even the controversial ones, sound like truth. Not because those voices are perfect, but because they're the only ones telling young men to stand up.

The backlash isn't the problem. It's the symptom. The problem is that the institutions responsible for raising and guiding young men abandoned their role. Schools, churches, media, and families stopped speaking to masculine identity. Now we're shocked that the vacuum got filled by louder, rougher voices.

We can criticize the messengers, or we can ask why they're the only ones left speaking.

Political Course Correction

The political shift among young men isn't accidental. It's a reaction to rejection. When every major institution, schools, universities, Hollywood, and corporate America, tells you that you're the villain, you start looking for a side that doesn't treat you like one.

The left used to be about rebellion. Now it's about conformity. The right, once the side of tradition and restraint, has become the side of resistance. So when young men look around for somewhere to belong, they don't see the left offering them purpose. They see it offering shame.

They see the right offering identity, even if it's rough around the edges.

Let me be specific about what that looks like. A young man graduates college with student debt, no job prospects, and a degree that taught him he's inherently evil for being white and male. The left tells him he's privileged and should be grateful. The right tells him he's been lied to and should be angry. Which message do you think resonates? He's not choosing an ideology. He's choosing survival. One side tells him to apologize for existing. The other side tells him to exist unapologetically. It's not even a contest. And then the left wonders why young men are leaving in droves. They're not leaving. They were pushed out. And they're never coming back.

That's why the modern conservative movement looks different than it used to. It's younger, angrier, and more outspoken. It's not just about taxes or policy anymore. It's about belonging. It's about young men saying,

"You don't get to call me toxic for existing."

The left can't understand it because they still believe they're fighting their parents' generation, old men in suits, holding power. But this new movement isn't coming from the powerful. It's coming from the ignored. These are 20-year-olds who feel cheated, not privileged. They're living with their parents, drowning in debt, watching TikTok feminists explain why they're the problem, and you expect them to vote for more of that? Good luck. They grew up being told they had every advantage, only to realize that the system has no place for them.

So they turned to the one place that still allows bluntness and strength. That's why you'll find these boys in online conservative spaces, or showing up at rallies, or making memes that mock the same institutions that once lectured them. To them, this isn't just politics, it's survival.

The media paints these young men as hateful or extremist because that's easier than admitting they failed them. It's easier to label them dangerous than to ask what made them angry. But behind the rage is pain, the pain of disconnection, of being raised in a culture that preaches tolerance but practices contempt toward traditional masculinity.

For many, this isn't even about Trump or politics. It's about rebellion against hypocrisy. When they see adults who celebrate tolerance but scream at anyone who disagrees, they recognize the lie. When they're told that "diversity" means excluding their opinions, they realize diversity doesn't include them. When they see women told they can be anything but men told they're the problem, they stop listening.

You can't lecture a generation into compliance. You can only inspire them into loyalty.

And right now, no one in power is inspiring them.

The irony is that this rebellion could have been prevented. If schools had kept mentoring boys instead of medicating them, if fathers had stayed home instead of leaving, if our institutions had honored masculine strength instead of dismantling it, these boys wouldn't be looking to social media influencers for direction. They'd already have it.

But instead, we created the perfect storm... an ideology that treats masculinity as a threat. We broke the natural transmission of manhood from fathers to sons, and now we're shocked when boys go looking for new fathers online.

This is why the cultural elites can't stop the movement. They don't understand it.

They think it's about politics when it's really about identity. These young men don't see themselves as Republicans or Democrats. They see themselves as survivors, survivors of a culture that told them they were broken for being born male.

Every time a late-night host mocks them, every time a journalist calls them "fragile," every time a professor calls masculinity "toxic," the movement grows stronger. Because mockery doesn't shame them anymore. It confirms what they already believe, that the system is rigged against them.

This is the danger of labeling everyone who disagrees as hateful. When you silence men who just want to talk, they'll eventually find someone who will talk to them, even if that someone is radical. When you shame men for wanting order, they'll find it in chaos.

But there's a better way. The rebellion doesn't have to stay angry. Anger is fuel, not a destination. It can power something better if it's guided, by truth, purpose, and discipline.

That's what the next generation of leaders must do. We don't need to tame young men. We need to train them. We don't need to shame them for their aggression. We need to teach them how to aim it.

Aggression is not evil. Unfocused aggression is. When it's disciplined, it builds armies, companies, and families. When it's untrained, it destroys them.

That's the task now, to turn rebellion into responsibility. To take that spark of defiance and shape it into self-control. The same fire that makes a boy stand up against hypocrisy can make him stand up for honor. It's the same energy, just refined.

We can't meet this rebellion with censorship or lectures. We have to meet it with truth and respect. Young men don't need to be scolded. They need to be challenged. They need to hear, "You're strong enough to build something better, now prove it."

That's what the best mentors and coaches used to do. They didn't shame boys for being competitive or intense. They channeled it. They said, *"You want to fight? Good. Fight for something that matters."*

When men have nothing worth fighting for, they fight against everything. But when they find purpose, they become unstoppable. That's the transformation this generation needs, from outrage to order.

The boys who fight back aren't the problem. They're the sign that we still have a chance.

Because apathy is death. Anger means there's still life in them. It means they still care enough to want something different.

The question is whether we'll lead that energy somewhere constructive or let it spiral into chaos.

History shows us that movements born from frustration either reform the system or burn it down. The direction depends entirely on whether wise men step up to guide it. If they don't, the vacuum will once again be filled by loud, reckless voices instead of principled ones.

We have a choice, to lead these boys back to strength, or to keep mocking them until their anger turns to despair. And despair is what leads to destruction.

From Rage to Purpose

Rebellion alone doesn't build anything. It's raw energy, a natural reaction to pressure. But if it's not directed, it becomes noise. The boys who fight back are full of that raw energy, the same energy that once built nations, carved mountains, and defended freedom. The problem isn't their fire. It's that no one has taught them where to aim it.

Every generation of men has faced rebellion. It's how boys test their strength. But past generations had mentors to guide it. A father, a coach, a sergeant, someone who could say, *"Alright, you're angry. Now do something useful with it."* Today's generation rarely hears that. Their rebellion has no outlet. So it goes online. It becomes sarcasm, mockery, meme warfare, and endless debate.

They fight because they still want to feel powerful. They want to feel like men again in a culture that tells them they aren't allowed to be. But that power can be reclaimed without hate. It can be channeled into creation instead of destruction.

The first step is leadership. These young men need examples of what strength looks like when it's calm and steady. They need to see men who aren't afraid to be masculine, but who also don't need to prove it every second. That's what separates real strength from performative masculinity, quiet confidence.

A strong man doesn't need to shout about it. He doesn't need to dominate to feel powerful.

His strength is visible in how he carries himself, how he treats others, and how he handles pressure. That's what these boys are craving to see.

Right now, the loudest men online are entertainers, not leaders. They make noise, not impact. They sell rebellion because it's profitable. But rebellion without direction doesn't free you. It traps you in a loop. The more you fight without purpose, the more lost you become.

That's why this movement of young men needs fathers, mentors, and teachers who can turn that frustration into fuel. Instead of telling them to *"calm down"* or *"grow up,"* we should be telling them, *"Stand up, here's what to fight for."*

Because deep down, every young man wants to fight for something. It's in their nature. Men were built to protect, to build, to compete, to win. You can suppress that instinct for a while, but you can't erase it. The goal isn't to make men less aggressive. It's to give that aggression a purpose.

That's where society has failed them most. We've taken away purpose and replaced it with distraction. We told them to focus on feelings, not outcomes. We told them to chase comfort, not challenge. And then we're shocked when they grow restless and angry.

Look at history. Every great generation of men was forged through hardship and guided by vision.

The young men of World War II didn't storm beaches because they hated the enemy. They did it because they loved what they were defending. That's what we've lost, love of purpose.

The boys who fight back today are fighting against something. They need something to fight for.

That's why this backlash doesn't have to be destructive. It can be the start of a revival, if guided with truth and honor. These young men already have courage. They're already willing to take heat for what they believe. What they need now is wisdom.

Wisdom is what tempers courage. It turns chaos into discipline.

Without it, energy burns out fast. With it, energy becomes legacy.

We can't tell these boys to stop fighting. We should teach them what's worth fighting for, faith, family, community, craftsmanship, loyalty, and freedom. Those aren't outdated values. They're the backbone of every civilization that survived.

There's a lesson in every young man's rebellion: when society stops giving boys meaningful rites of passage, they'll create their own. That's why they're drawn to intense influencers, physical challenges, political movements, or online tribes. They're looking for initiation, a test that proves they're capable and worthy.

We used to give that to them through real-world trials, military service, apprenticeship, athletics, or hard work. Now we call everyone a winner and wonder why they're frustrated.

That's what's driving this movement beneath the surface. It's not politics. It's pain. These boys don't want to destroy society. They want to be part of something real again. They want to build. They just don't know how.

They're not the enemy. They're the unfinished product of a culture that stopped forging men.

That's why our response can't be condemnation. It has to be reconstruction. If we shame them, they'll double down. If we guide them, they'll rise up.

We have to teach them that true rebellion isn't yelling into the void, it's living differently from the system that failed you. It's refusing to be weak in a world that rewards weakness. It's standing for principle when it costs you something.

That's the kind of rebellion that builds leaders.

The boys who fight back are the same boys who can rebuild America. They just need the right blueprint, discipline instead of outrage, purpose instead of pride, respect instead of resentment.

Once that energy is refined, it becomes unstoppable. The same fire that built revolutions and rebuilt nations still burns in them. It's just buried under confusion and shame. The job now is to uncover it and aim it toward something noble.

The next decade will decide which way this rebellion goes. Either it gets hijacked by grifters who turn it into chaos, or it gets reclaimed by leaders who turn it into virtue. The choice is ours, as fathers, teachers, mentors, and men.

These young men don't need more enemies. They need examples. They need men who've walked through fire and come out disciplined, not bitter. Men who can say, *"You don't have to destroy everything to prove you're strong. Build something instead."* That's how we turn rebellion into rebirth.

The boys who fight back aren't lost. They're searching. Every insult they throw online, every political rally they join, every defiant post they make, it's all an expression of the same thing: a need to be seen, respected, and led. When society refuses to provide that leadership, they build it themselves. Sometimes it looks messy. Sometimes it goes too far. But the instinct behind it is ancient and good, the instinct to stand up when something feels wrong.

That's why the worst thing we can do is dismiss them. The more they're ignored, the louder they'll get. The more they're mocked, the more extreme their anger becomes. The solution isn't more censorship or condemnation. It's re-engagement. These young men need to be reminded that strength and civility aren't opposites, they're partners.

The truth is that this rebellion, if handled correctly, could save an entire generation. It's a sign that the masculine spirit isn't dead. It's been buried under apathy, confusion, and shame, but it's still alive. These boys are digging it back up with their own hands. What they need now is guidance, not guidance that weakens them, but guidance that tempers them like steel.

That's where men come in. Real men. Not influencers, not academics, not politicians, men of integrity who lead by example. Men who work hard, keep their word, and protect their families. Men who understand that leadership isn't about control; it's about service. When young men see that kind of leadership up close, it changes everything.

A father doesn't have to lecture his son about masculinity. He just has to live it. A teacher doesn't have to debate politics to shape a young man. He just has to hold him to a standard and expect him to meet it. A coach doesn't need a degree in psychology to raise confidence. He just needs to demand effort, teach discipline, and model respect. *We've made mentorship too complicated.*

Boys don't need theory. They need truth, structure, and someone who believes they can be better.

That's how rebellion becomes growth, when someone shows them what strength looks like when it's guided by purpose.

The boys who fight back are responding to a vacuum of leadership. They're saying, "We want something real." It's up to the rest of us to give it to them before the wrong people do.

And to the young men reading this who've been labeled radicalized, toxic, or dangerous for refusing to bend: I see you. I know what you've been through. I know you were told to sit down and shut up while adults who never built anything lectured you about privilege. I know you watched your fathers destroyed by divorce courts and your brothers medicated into zombies. I know you're angry, and you have every right to be. But here's what I need you to understand: *your anger is fuel, not a destination.* You can burn the world down with it, or you can use it to forge yourself into something unbreakable. The system that failed you wants you to stay angry and directionless, because that makes you manageable. The second you channel that anger into purpose, discipline, and competence, you become a threat they can't control. Don't give them the satisfaction of watching you self-destruct. Build yourself into the man they're afraid you'll become.

That's how you win. Because the truth is, they're going to follow someone. The only question is who?

If we want this movement to mature, we have to reconnect these young men with responsibility. That's the antidote to aimless rebellion. Responsibility gives them ownership of their lives. It replaces outrage with action. It teaches them that the way to prove their worth isn't through noise but through contribution.

> **You don't fix a generation of angry boys by telling them to calm down.**
> **You fix it by giving them something worth getting fired up about.**

Faith, family, country, craftsmanship, excellence. Tell a young man he's strong, and he'll flex. Tell him he's responsible for something bigger than himself, and he'll rise.

That's how men are wired. The more weight they carry, the stronger they get. We've spent too long telling them to drop the weight, to relax, to emote. It's time to tell them to pick it back up. That's how they'll find meaning again, under pressure.

We also have to remind them that masculinity isn't about dominance. It's about direction. It's not about being in control of others. It's about being in control of yourself. The man who can master himself can lead anyone. The man who can't master himself shouldn't lead anyone.

That's what separates rebellion from leadership. Rebellion breaks rules because it feels powerful. Leadership writes new rules because it understands power. A rebel wants attention. A leader wants progress.

The goal is to help these boys evolve from one to the other, from defiance to direction.

That transition starts with truth. Boys need to be told what's real, even if it stings. They need to hear that no one's coming to save them, that strength comes from struggle, and that victimhood is a dead end. They need to be challenged, not coddled. Because deep down, they want that.

Every man remembers the moment he was tested and passed. Every boy is waiting for that test. We've removed those moments from modern life, and now we're seeing what happens when boys never get the chance to prove themselves. *They stay boys.*

That's the silent tragedy behind this entire movement; it's a generation of men trying to grow up without guidance. They're desperate for initiation into something real. The world mocked them for wanting it. Now they're forcing their own initiation through rebellion.

We can end that cycle by giving them real rites of passage again, physical challenges, apprenticeships, service, faith, responsibility. Tasks that teach discipline and purpose. Moments that say,

> *"You are capable.*
> *You matter.*
> *You belong."*

When a young man feels those three things, he doesn't need to rebel anymore. He doesn't need to prove anything. He starts building instead of fighting.

That's the point we have to reach, turning rebellion into reconstruction. Because the boys who fight back today can become the men who rebuild tomorrow. The same defiance that rejects weakness can protect freedom. The same courage that says "no" to lies can say "yes" to truth. The same energy that burns in anger can blaze in purpose.

It's all the same fire. The question is how it's used.

We don't have to fear this generation. We just have to lead it. These boys aren't the end of masculinity. They're the start of its revival.

They've already taken the first step; they stopped apologizing for being men. Now they need to learn what being a man truly means.

And that's where we come in.

Because if we can help them aim that fire toward building, protecting, and serving again, we won't just save them, we'll save the country they're supposed to inherit.

11

REBUILDING MEN

Every generation eventually faces the same question: what kind of men will we become?

For too long, we've been answering it with silence. We've pointed fingers, blamed culture, blamed politics, blamed parents, but blaming never rebuilds. The truth is that men broke, and only men can fix it.

Let me be brutally clear about what's at stake: we are watching the first generation of American men who will be weaker, poorer, lonelier, and more desperate than their fathers. According to a 2023 study by the Brookings Institution, millennial men are earning approximately 20 percent less than their fathers did at the same age, even with higher levels of education.

The life expectancy gap between men and women has widened to 5.8 years, the largest in decades *(CDC National Center for Health Statistics, 2021)*. Male suicide rates have increased 35 percent since 2000 *(American Foundation for Suicide Prevention, 2023)*.

We are not "struggling." We are dying.

And if we don't rebuild now, there won't be anything left to save.
This isn't theory. I'm watching it happen in real time. As a school

board member in Beverly Hills, I've sat in meetings where administrators celebrate "progress" because suspension rates are down, while completely ignoring that boys are failing at record rates. I've seen seventeen-year-old boys who can't look adults in the eye, can't shake hands, can't speak in complete sentences. These aren't kids from broken homes in forgotten neighborhoods. These are sons of millionaires, and they're just as lost. Money can't save your son if he has no purpose. Wealth without worth creates the emptiest kind of man.

Rebuilding men doesn't mean returning to some outdated version of masculinity. It means returning to the timeless principles that make men stable, useful, and honorable.

The world doesn't need more tough talk or empty bravado. It needs men who are competent, disciplined, and trustworthy. Men who know how to protect what matters. Men who carry weight without complaint.

The Five Pillars of Rebuilding

The first step in rebuilding men is rejecting the lie that *masculinity is toxic.* Masculinity isn't the problem, it's the foundation. Every civilization that has endured was built on the back of male courage, self-control, and responsibility. Those qualities aren't cultural; they're biological and moral. When we suppress them, men wither. When we cultivate them, men thrive.

And let's talk about what "withering" actually means in 2025. It means that according to the National Marriage Project at the University of Virginia (2023), only 20 percent of men aged 18-29 are married, compared to 59 percent in 1978. It means that nearly one-third of men under 30 haven't had sex in the past year (General Social Survey, 2021), a number that has tripled since 2008. It means that prime-age male employment, men aged 25-54, has dropped from 98 percent in the 1950s to 88 percent in 2023 (Bureau of Labor Statistics, 2023), meaning millions of men in their prime years are sitting at home doing nothing. This isn't a trend. This is collapse in real time. And every man who checks out, who gives up, who retreats into video games and porn and self-pity, makes it easier for the next one to do the same. Weakness is contagious. So is strength. Choose which virus you want to spread.

A man who has no purpose is a danger to himself. He becomes restless, bitter, and reckless. That's why the first task of rebuilding is purpose. Every man needs a mission, something larger than comfort, something worth suffering for. It doesn't have to be a war or a business empire. It can be as simple as raising a family, building a trade, or serving a community. But it must be real. A man without a mission is a machine without power. *Purpose alone isn't enough.*

The second step is discipline. Weak men chase motivation. Strong men build systems. The difference is simple: motivation fades, discipline endures. A disciplined man doesn't wait to feel ready, he acts because it's time to act. He trains his body and his mind to obey principle instead of impulse. He understands that freedom comes through structure, not the absence of it.

Every great man, in any era, lived by structure. The soldiers of Sparta, the builders of Rome, the founders of America, all were bound by discipline. They understood that comfort is a drug and struggle is medicine. Modern men have been overdosed on ease. The cure is discomfort. Wake up early. Train. Read. Work. Serve. The path back to manhood isn't glamorous, but it's honest.

The third step is responsibility. This word has been twisted into something negative, as if carrying weight is punishment. It isn't. It's privilege. Responsibility gives life direction. When a man says, "This is my problem," he takes ownership of his fate. That's where respect begins, not in power, but in accountability. You can't respect a man who runs from his own mess. You respect the one who faces it and fixes it.

Responsibility also means leadership. And leadership doesn't require a title. A father leads his family. A worker leads by example. A coach leads by discipline. Leadership is about action, not position. When men lead well, everyone benefits. When they don't, everyone pays.

We've raised a generation that's terrified of leadership because it comes with blame. But that's the point, leadership always comes with risk. You can't lead without being criticized. You can't stand for truth without being attacked. The measure of a man isn't how comfortable he feels but how much he can endure without quitting. The world doesn't need flawless men. It needs unbreakable ones.

And here's the brutal truth about why so few men lead anymore: we've taught them that taking responsibility makes you a target. A man steps up to coach Little League, and suddenly he's running background checks and signing liability waivers like he's applying for the FBI. A man tries to mentor a young employee, and HR monitors every conversation for potential lawsuits. A father disciplines his son in public, and strangers pull out their phones ready to destroy his life on social media. According to AmeriCorps and the U.S. Census Bureau (2022), overall volunteer rates have fallen to their lowest levels on record, barely 23% of Americans now give their time, down from nearly 30% in the early 2000s. Men are showing up less, especially in youth programs, and honestly, who can blame them? We've turned leadership into a minefield. But let me be clear: the men who walk away because it's hard aren't leaders. They're cowards. Real leaders step into the fire knowing they'll get burned, because the alternative is letting boys grow up without any men to guide them. If you're not willing to risk your reputation to save a generation, you never had character worth protecting in the first place.

The fourth step is community. Men weren't designed to live in isolation. That's why brotherhood has always been essential to male strength. The ancient warriors trained together. The early settlers built towns together. The soldiers who fought wars trusted the men beside them with their lives. Modern men sit alone behind screens, confusing connection with communication. You can't rebuild manhood without rebuilding community.

The data on male isolation is staggering. According to the Survey Center on American Life (2021), 15 percent of men report having zero close friends, up from just 3 percent in 1990. Men aged 18-34 are now twice as likely as women to report feeling lonely "most or all of the time" (Cigna Loneliness Index, 2023). This isn't just sad, it's deadly. Studies from Harvard's Adult Development Study show that men without strong social connections have a 50 percent higher mortality rate than those with robust relationships (Waldinger & Schulz, 2023). You read that right:

being alone kills you faster than obesity or smoking. Your grandfather had a bowling league, a church group, a union hall, and neighbors he actually knew. You have a Discord server and 847 Instagram followers who wouldn't piss on you if you were on fire. That's not connection. That's the illusion of it. And it's killing you slowly, one lonely night at a time.

Every man needs other men who will challenge him, correct him, and stand beside him when things get hard. That's what brotherhood is, not drinking buddies or shallow validation, but men who sharpen each other like iron on iron. A lone man can survive. A band of men can change history.

Finally, the fifth step is faith, not necessarily religious faith, but belief in something above yourself. A man without reverence for something higher will eventually worship himself, and self-worship always ends in decay. Faith grounds a man. It reminds him that he didn't create truth and can't bend it. Whether you believe in God or the moral order of the universe, the lesson is the same: humility anchors strength.

These five pillars, purpose, discipline, responsibility, community, and faith, are the blueprint for rebuilding men.

They aren't new ideas. They're old truths that never stopped working. The reason our society is crumbling isn't because these principles failed, but because we abandoned them. Reclaiming them is how we begin again.

Rebuilding won't be quick. Weakness is easy to grow and slow to fix. It took decades to dismantle manhood; it will take years to restore it. But every small act of strength matters. Every father who teaches his son respect. Every man who refuses to lie. Every worker who takes pride in his craft. These moments don't make headlines, but they build civilizations

The world changes when men change. Not through protests or hashtags, but through consistent, quiet excellence. A strong man doesn't need to announce himself. His results do it for him. He walks with integrity, and others rise to meet his example. The modern world loves loud men with no depth. What it truly needs are silent men with conviction.

That's what rebuilding looks like, not a movement, but a mindset.

Not a campaign, but a commitment. It's a return to the simple, timeless truth that strength is service. The man who carries more than his share keeps the world from collapsing. The man who does his duty when no one's watching is the reason his community holds together.

Rebuilding men isn't complicated. It's just hard. But hard things have always been the forge where real men are made.

Raising Boys to Be Men

Rebuilding starts with boys. If we want strong men, we have to raise them. You cannot expect boys raised in chaos to grow into disciplined adults. Strength is learned by example. That means fathers have to show up. Not just in the house, but in the lives of their sons.

A boy who watches his father lead learns that leadership is normal. A boy who sees his father work learns that work is part of life. A boy who hears his father say no learns that boundaries matter. You can tell a boy a thousand lessons, but he will remember what you did, not what you said.

Fathers are the first teachers of honor. They teach a boy that discipline comes before reward, that patience comes before success, and that failure is not the end. Boys who grow up with strong fathers don't just learn rules. They learn identity. They learn who they are and where they belong.

When fathers are absent, mentors must step in. Every boy needs an older man to guide him. A coach, a teacher, a pastor, a neighbor. Someone who sets standards and expects him to meet them. It does not take a bloodline to build a man. It takes presence. When men start mentoring again, we stop losing boys to confusion.

Mentorship is not about speeches. It's about consistency. It's about showing up on time, keeping promises, and setting the example of steadiness. A boy who sees that pattern learns to trust himself. He learns that steadiness is power.

We also have to rebuild the spaces where boys learn to compete. Schools have replaced competition with comfort. That was a mistake. Boys grow through testing themselves. Sports, trades, and physical challenges teach lessons that no classroom can. When a boy trains, fails, adjusts, and tries again, he learns resilience. He learns that life is not about avoiding pain but mastering it.

We need a culture that rewards healthy aggression instead of punishing it. Controlled aggression is not violence. It is drive. It is the energy that pushes men to finish a job, defend a friend, or protect a stranger. When we suppress that, we turn strength into frustration. That frustration becomes the depression and apathy we see everywhere now.

> *Discipline must return to education.*
> *Respect must return to homes.*
> *Accountability must return to communities.*

You cannot build strong men in an environment that rewards weakness. Boys should be allowed to fail. They should be allowed to lose. They should be corrected when they lie and praised when they take responsibility. Real love is not indulgence. It is guidance.

We also need to fix how we talk to young men. Too often, boys only hear what they are not supposed to do. Don't fight. Don't speak. Don't interrupt. Don't disagree. That constant stream of restriction turns into shame. Instead of teaching boys what not to be, we should teach them what to be. Teach them that confidence is good. Teach them that strength is noble. Teach them that service is the highest form of masculinity.

It's time to make respect cool again. The modern world has convinced young people that rebellion is maturity. It is not. True maturity is knowing when to stand tall and when to stand down. A real man can do both. The world doesn't need more rebels without cause. It needs builders who know when to fight and when to work.

Fathers can start this shift today.

Set expectations.
Enforce rules.
Love with strength, not softness.

Mothers can help by letting fathers lead without resentment. Society works best when men and women support each other's roles, not when they compete for control.

Communities can help too. Support trades. Support apprenticeships. Bring back programs that teach boys real skills. Every young man should know how to fix, lift, or build something. Work creates confidence, and confidence builds responsibility. You cannot learn purpose sitting still.

Churches, schools, and civic groups can become training grounds for manhood again. We should be proud to say the word masculine without apology. We should celebrate the man who shows up, works hard, raises his kids, and never quits. Those are not outdated values. They are survival skills.

Rebuilding men also means redefining success.

We've spent too long worshiping wealth and fame. A man's worth is not measured by his car, his watch, or his follower count. It's measured by his consistency. By how many people rely on him. By whether he leaves his world better than he found it. A man who earns little but builds strong children has achieved more than a millionaire who abandons his family.

We have to make that truth loud again. Boys should grow up seeing real men respected. Not the loudest, not the richest, but the most dependable. The man who works two jobs to keep his family afloat should be a hero. The soldier, the firefighter, the mechanic, the coach, the farmer, those men hold the country together, quietly, every day. They deserve more honor than any celebrity ever will.

Rebuilding men is not about changing laws. It's about changing examples.

Boys copy what they see. If they see cowardice, they'll learn fear. If they see strength, they'll learn courage. Every man alive today is teaching, whether he means to or not. The only question is what lesson he's giving.

If we want to save a generation, we must remind men that they are not victims. They are stewards. They are protectors. Their lives have weight. Their choices matter. The world may not thank them, but history will.

Rebuilding Yourself

Not every man had a father to teach him discipline or a mentor to guide him. Many grew up in chaos and learned to survive, not to lead. But survival is not living. The good news is that it's never too late to start. A man can rebuild himself at any age if he's willing to face the truth about where he is and who he wants to become.

But let's be honest about what rebuilding actually requires. It means looking at yourself and admitting that you're weak. That you've wasted years. That you're thirty-five and still living like you're twenty-two. That your wife doesn't respect you. That your kids don't listen to you. That your friends make jokes about you behind your back. That you can't do ten push-ups. That you're in debt. That you're addicted to porn or video games or social media or alcohol or whatever drug you're using to avoid facing the fact that you've become the man you swore you'd never be. And here's the hardest part: most men won't do it. According to the American Psychological Association (2023), less than 30 percent of men who recognize they need help actually seek it. The rest just keep decaying, year after year, until they die full of regret and unspoken potential. Don't be that man. Be the one who had the guts to admit he was lost and the discipline to find his way back.

Rebuilding yourself begins with honesty.

No excuses, no distractions, no blame. You have to look in the mirror and say, *"I did this."* Whatever pain, weakness, or failure you carry, own it. That's the first act of strength. You can't change what you refuse to claim.

Once you accept responsibility, you need order. Chaos feeds weakness. Structure feeds strength. That means setting a schedule, keeping it, and repeating it every day until it becomes second nature. Wake up early. Make your bed. Train your body. Read something that builds your mind. Keep a written record of progress. These are small acts, but they create momentum.

> **Most men don't fail because they're lazy. They fail because they have no structure.**

They drift from one emotion to the next, waiting for motivation to strike. But motivation is a liar. It shows up when it wants to and disappears when you need it most. Discipline is what keeps you moving when motivation is gone.

Physical training is the cornerstone. Not for vanity, but for control. A strong body teaches a man that pain has value. It teaches that limits can be pushed, that endurance is earned. When a man trains, he's not just building muscle. He's building the habit of showing up for himself. That habit will carry into every part of his life.

And let's talk about the state of the modern male body, because it's a disgrace. According to the CDC (2023), 74.4 percent of American men aged 20 and over are overweight or obese. That's nearly three out of every four men. Testosterone levels continue to plummet, muscle mass is at historic lows, and the average American man today is weaker than his grandfather was at the same age (Stanford University, 2016). You can't protect anyone if you can't walk up a flight of stairs without wheezing. You can't lead anyone if you're a slave to sugar and processed food. Your body is the first thing you're supposed to master, and most men can't even do that. If you can't control what you eat or whether you exercise, what makes you think you can control anything else in your life? Physical weakness is moral weakness made visible. Fix your body first. Everything else gets easier after that.

Then comes mental strength. Read real books. Study history. Learn from men who built things before you. Stop consuming empty entertainment designed to pacify you. Fill your mind with truth and skill. Learn something useful, how to fix something, how to negotiate, how to defend yourself, how to teach. Knowledge is power only when it's applied.

The next step is cutting out weakness. That means substances, distractions, and habits that rob you of energy or clarity. A man who spends six hours a day scrolling on his phone isn't resting, he's decaying. Replace consumption with creation. Replace fantasy with purpose. Every minute you give to something meaningless is a minute stolen from something that could build you.

You also have to rebuild integrity. In a world that lies constantly, truth becomes a weapon. Be honest even when it costs you. Keep promises even when it hurts. Admit when you're wrong. Those habits separate men from boys. Weak men hide behind excuses. Strong men stand behind results.

Rebuilding also means making peace with failure. Too many men fear mistakes more than mediocrity. They'd rather stay comfortable than risk falling short. That's why they never grow. Failure is the tuition of mastery. You pay with discomfort, but you graduate with wisdom. Every great man you admire has failed more times than the average man has tried.

Forgiveness is part of rebuilding too. Not the kind that excuses wrongdoing, but the kind that frees you to move forward. If you stay angry at your father, your ex, or your boss, you give them power over you. Let it go. You can't rebuild while living in resentment. Strength and bitterness can't live in the same heart.

After forgiveness comes focus. The modern world wants men distracted. It sells addiction as entertainment and confusion as compassion. Rebuilding means turning your focus inward, to your body, your craft, your circle, and your purpose.

Every time you say no to distraction, you say yes to growth.

Once a man begins to rebuild, his world changes. *People notice.* Some will resent it because your progress reminds them of their stagnation. Others will be inspired and follow your lead. That's how culture shifts, not through lectures, but through example. One man decides to rise, and others remember that they can too.

The process is not glamorous. It's not meant to be. You will wake up tired. You will be tempted to quit. You will question whether it matters. That's where most men fail, not because they can't do it, but because they expect it to feel good. Growth rarely feels good. It feels heavy. That's why it builds strength.

Rebuilding yourself is not about ego. It's about duty.

A strong man benefits everyone around him. His presence calms chaos. His discipline inspires others. His word builds trust. When men rebuild, society rebuilds quietly behind them.

And here's the most important truth: you don't need permission to start. You don't need a program, a coach, or an audience. You just need to begin. The hardest part of rebuilding isn't the work itself, it's deciding that weakness is no longer acceptable. Once you make that choice, everything else follows.

Once a man rebuilds himself, his influence multiplies. The same discipline that changes one life starts changing everything around it. A man who becomes strong again reminds others what stability looks like. He sets a tone. His children walk taller. His wife feels safe. His friends respect him. People begin to trust that someone still knows how to hold the line.

Strong men are contagious. Their presence changes a room. They don't need to dominate or boast. They lead quietly, by example. You can feel it in how they carry themselves, how they treat others, how they stay calm when the world panics. They don't need attention because they already have purpose.

When enough men live that way, families heal.

Fathers who show up and stay steady teach their children how to face life. Sons learn discipline. Daughters learn respect. Women relax because they know they are protected, not controlled. Strong men don't compete with women. They complete the balance that keeps families whole.

Communities start to change next. When men take pride in their neighborhoods, things get fixed instead of ignored. Schools improve because fathers get involved. Businesses thrive because men show up to work with integrity. Crime drops because discipline returns. It's not politics that saves communities. It's men deciding to take ownership again.

The next ripple is cultural. Entertainment begins to reflect strength instead of mock it. Heroes stop being ironic and start being honorable again. Masculinity becomes something admired, not mocked. That doesn't happen because of marketing campaigns. It happens when men stop apologizing for being men.

We also need to rebuild brotherhood on a larger scale. Men have been isolated long enough. They need places to gather, train, talk, and build. Not online forums full of anger, but real circles of accountability. The gym, the workshop, the church, the range, the business group, anywhere men can push each other to be better. Brotherhood is the fence that keeps men from slipping back into weakness.

When men rebuild together, they rediscover meaning. They find pride in teamwork and respect in effort. They remember that iron sharpens iron. The man who refuses to isolate himself will never fall as far as the one who stands alone.

As this spirit spreads, nations rise. History always turns when strong men return. After every collapse, the rebuilding begins the same way: men take responsibility again. They rebuild the farm, the workshop, the home, the faith. They don't wait for orders. They act. They protect what is theirs and restore what was lost.

And we need this now more than ever, because America's enemies are watching. China is training millions of young men for war while we're teaching ours about microaggressions. *Russia is rebuilding traditional masculine culture while we're celebrating men in dresses. Iran is indoctrinating boys with purpose and discipline while ours are getting participation trophies for showing up.* According to the Department of Defense (2023), the U.S. military is facing its worst recruitment crisis in history, with only 23 percent of Americans aged 17-24 meeting the basic physical, mental, and moral standards for service. That's not a recruiting problem. That's a civilization problem.

You can't defend a nation with men who can't do a pull-up and cry when someone hurts their feelings. Our grandfathers stormed Normandy at 19. Today's 19-year-olds need a trigger warning before reading a book. If you don't see the danger in that, you're not paying attention.

That's the path forward now. Not political revolution, but personal restoration. The revolution begins inside the individual man.

It happens when he stops blaming the world and starts mastering himself. When he stops chasing comfort and starts chasing purpose. When he stops apologizing for his strength and starts using it for good.

Rebuilding men is not just about men. It's about the survival of civilization. Without strong men, there are no safe streets, no secure borders, no lasting families, and no freedom. Every generation forgets this until it's too late. We are living in that forgetful generation now. But it can still be reversed if enough men wake up.

It starts with a simple truth: being a man is not a problem that needs solving. It's a responsibility that needs honoring. A man's worth isn't defined by what he owns or what others think of him. It's defined by what he builds, protects, and endures. Weak men crumble under pressure. Strong men carry it until the weight becomes their strength.

We cannot wait for institutions to fix this. Schools are too confused, media too compromised, and politics too divided. The solution will come from the ground up, from fathers, coaches, tradesmen, soldiers, pastors, and workers who decide that they will stand firm again.

Foundations of Principle

Every man must ask himself one question: will I add to the decay, or will I become the foundation? The answer isn't written in slogans or speeches. It's written in daily choices. Will you keep your word? Will you stay when it's hard? Will you defend what's right when it's unpopular? That's what separates strong men from weak ones.

A man who lives with principle leaves a legacy that outlives him. His sons inherit his habits, his community inherits his stability, and his country inherits his example. That's how nations are reborn, not through politics, but through character. The future is always built by the men willing to carry it.

Rebuilding men isn't about looking backward. It's about restoring forward. It's about taking what worked, discipline, courage, purpose, honor, and bringing it into the modern world with clarity and pride. The tools have changed, but the mission hasn't. The world still needs protectors, providers, inventors, and leaders. It always will.

This generation has a choice. We can continue down the path of weakness and watch the world collapse, or we can rebuild ourselves and lift it back up. History will remember whichever we choose.

So let me say this directly to every man reading these words:

You're running out of time.

Not in some abstract, philosophical way. In a real, concrete, your-life-is-passing-you-by kind of way. You're thirty-five and you've spent fifteen years "figuring things out." You're forty and your kids barely know you. You're fifty and you've built nothing that will last. Every day you wait is another day you'll never get back. Every year you waste is another year your son grows up without a model. Every moment you spend scrolling, gaming, watching porn, getting drunk, making excuses, is a moment you're choosing weakness over strength.

The world will not wait for you to be ready. Your wife won't wait forever to see if you'll become the man she hoped you'd be. Your kids won't stay young long enough for you to "figure it out later." Your body won't repair itself. Your career won't build itself. Your character won't develop itself. And one day, sooner than you think, you'll be old and weak and full of regret, sitting in a chair wondering where your life went. *Don't let that be you.*

Rebuilding starts *TODAY.*

Not Monday.
Not January 1st.
Not after you "get through this rough patch."
Today!

Wake up earlier tomorrow. Go to the gym. Read something real. Turn off the video games. Delete the porn. Call your dad. Hug your kids. Fix something in your house. Do ten push-ups. Pray. Write down one thing you're going to improve this week and then DO it. Small steps compound into transformation, but only if you *START*.

This isn't a self-help book. This is a warning. We are losing an entire generation of men, and if we don't rebuild NOW, there won't be anything left to save. But if enough men wake up, if enough men decide that weakness is no longer acceptable, if enough men commit to becoming the protectors, builders, and leaders this world desperately needs, we can turn this around. *It won't be easy. It won't be fast. But it's possible.*

The question is: are you going to be one of the men who rebuilds, or one of the men who just watched it all fall apart?

The work starts now.

Get up earlier.
Get stronger.
Speak truth.
Raise your sons.
Defend your values.

Live like someone who knows he was born for responsibility, not comfort. The road back to manhood is not easy, but it's open to anyone willing to walk it.

Because in the end, it's simple: strong men build, and the world needs builders again.

12

THE NEW CODE OF MANHOOD

Every generation of men has lived by a code. Sometimes it was written in law, sometimes in faith, sometimes in silence passed from fathers to sons. For centuries, it was understood that being a man meant more than existing. It meant serving, protecting, producing, and providing. But somewhere along the way, we stopped teaching that code. We replaced it with slogans and theories. We told men to be nice, not to be good.

Now we live in a world without standards. Men are praised for weakness and punished for strength. We celebrate victimhood and mock virtue. The result is chaos. Men don't know what they're supposed to be anymore. They drift between guilt and confusion, chasing comfort and calling it peace.

And the data proves it. A 2022 *National Research Group* study found that 43 percent of young men said they *'don't know what it means to be a man today.'*

Let that sink in.

Nearly half of America's young men are growing up unsure of what masculinity even is and nobody's rushing to tell them.

In 2019, the *American Psychological Association* released its first-ever guidelines for treating boys and men, warning that traits like stoicism, competitiveness, and aggression, what it called *'traditional masculinity ideology'*, could be psychologically harmful.

Translation?

The establishment started labeling the same strengths that built civilization as symptoms of a problem. *Gallup's 2023 research* found that nearly half of Gen Z, men included, say they don't feel a sense of purpose in their daily lives. Half. They're showing up, scrolling through life, but not living it. And nobody seems to care that an entire generation of young men feels like nothing they do actually matters. *This isn't confusion. This is civilizational sabotage.*

> **We've raised an entire generation of men who've been taught that everything masculine is toxic, and now we wonder why they're lost, angry, and checking out of life entirely.**

It's time to write a new code. Not a new ideology or religion, but a clear set of principles that remind men who they are. This code doesn't belong to any political side or generation. *It belongs to truth.*

It's the code that built every great civilization and will build the next one.

The New Code

The first rule of the new code is *Responsibility Before Rights.*

Freedom means nothing without discipline. A man who demands rights but refuses responsibility isn't free, he's spoiled. Every liberty you enjoy was earned by men who bore burdens. You honor their sacrifice by carrying your own. If something breaks, fix it. If someone needs help, offer it. If the world goes wrong, stand up instead of complaining. Responsibility is the weight that keeps men grounded.

The second rule is *Strength in Restraint.*

Power without control is chaos. A real man can fight but chooses peace. He can speak but knows when to stay silent. He can dominate but prefers to serve. The strongest man is the one who masters himself. That doesn't mean he hides emotion, it means he owns it. Anger, lust, pride, and fear all serve him; they don't rule him. Self-mastery is the difference between a protector and a predator.

The third rule is *Truth Over Comfort.*

A man who lives by lies dies by them. The world will pressure you to stay quiet, to play along, to pretend. Don't. Tell the truth, even when it costs you. Especially when it costs you. A man who lies to protect his comfort is weak, but a man who tells the truth to protect others is courageous. Truth is the foundation of strength, because only the honest can be trusted.

The fourth rule is *Work Builds Worth.*

Every man needs to produce something. It doesn't matter if you build houses, run a company, or teach children, work gives meaning. Laziness rots the soul. You don't work just to make money; you work to create value. A man who refuses to work isn't free. He's dependent. And dependence is the quiet death of manhood.

The fifth rule is *Honor Your Word.*

Character is not built on what you say. It's built on whether you mean it. Keep your promises, even when it's inconvenient. Be the man people can count on when everything else fails. A man who keeps his word earns respect that no title can buy. In a world of empty talk, integrity is rebellion.

The sixth rule is *Protect What Matters.*

A man's strength isn't for show. It's for defense, of his family, his community, his country, and his values. That doesn't mean living in constant aggression. It means living with constant awareness. Evil wins when good men stop guarding the gates. You don't need to save the world, but you must protect your corner of it.

The seventh rule is *Lead Quietly, Serve Loudly.*

Modern culture teaches men to chase followers instead of respect. But leadership isn't about being noticed. It's about being useful. The best leaders don't seek attention; they seek improvement. They don't demand loyalty; they earn it. Real leadership begins with service.

The eighth rule is *Master Pain.*

Weak men run from pain. Strong men learn from it. Pain is a teacher that never lies. It shows you what matters and what doesn't. It strips away excuses. Every scar a man carries is a reminder that he endured and kept moving. Pain doesn't make you broken. It makes you honest.

The ninth rule is *Respect Women, Reject Weakness.*

Men and women were designed to complement each other, not compete. A strong man protects, provides, and partners. He doesn't manipulate or exploit. But respect for women doesn't mean surrendering manhood. You can be kind without being passive, firm without being cruel. The man who respects women by first respecting himself sets the tone for generations to come.

The tenth rule is *Leave the World Better.*

Every man dies, but not every man contributes. Legacy is not about fame. It's about impact. Leave something behind, children, wisdom, art, work, protection, peace. The question every man must ask is simple: if I disappear tomorrow, will anyone's life be better because I was here?

These ten rules form the backbone of the new code of manhood.

They're not a theory. They're a call to live differently in a time when everything is pulling men downward. This isn't about perfection. It's about direction. It's about having a compass when the world tells you to drift.

And let me be brutally clear about what happens when men don't live by a code. I see it every week as a school board member. I see teenaged boys who've never been held accountable for anything, who've never been told "no," who've been given everything and taught nothing.

They can't look you in the eye. They can't take criticism. They fold the first time life punches them in the mouth. And these aren't kids from broken homes. These are sons of doctors, lawyers, and executives who had every advantage except one: a father who gave them stuff instead of standards.

I've watched boys destroy themselves because nobody taught them discipline. I've seen seventeen-year-olds with $80,000 cars wrapped around trees because nobody taught them restraint. I've sat across from parents weeping because their son OD'd on fentanyl, and the first thing they say is "we gave him everything." Yeah. Everything except a reason to be strong.

> *Money without meaning creates the most dangerous kind of man: one with resources and no purpose. That's not wealth. That's a loaded gun with no safety.*

Men who live by this code will not be popular with everyone. They'll be mocked by the weak and respected by the strong. That's fine. Strength has never needed approval. What matters is impact. The man who follows this code becomes the anchor in a storm, the builder when others tear down, the calm voice when others panic.

Rebuilding civilization begins here. Every strong nation started with men who lived by codes like this. They didn't wait for permission. They acted because it was right. They stood tall because the world needed examples of how to stand at all.

The code means nothing unless it's lived. Words are cheap. Action is what separates belief from posturing. Every man who chooses to follow this code has to translate it into daily life, where the tests are quiet but constant.

The Code Is Your Family

At home, the code starts with presence. A man's family should never wonder where he stands. He shows up, not just physically but mentally. He listens when his children talk. He pays attention to his wife. He makes decisions instead of avoiding them. A home led by a strong man feels safe, not ruled. His steadiness sets the rhythm of the household.

Leadership at home isn't about control. It's about responsibility. The man of the house takes ownership of its direction. If the finances are bad, he fixes them. If the marriage is weak, he invests in it. If the kids are struggling, he steps in. The weak man blames others. The strong man finds solutions.

Strength at home is quiet. It's in the tone of voice you use with your family. It's in how you handle frustration. It's in whether you keep your word when no one's watching. Children don't remember lectures; they remember patterns. The man who lives his code creates the blueprint his sons will follow and the standard his daughters will expect.

At work, the code means integrity before opportunity. The modern workplace rewards conformity more than competence. Men who live by the code refuse to play that game.

> *They don't lie to get ahead.*
> *They don't hide their values for a paycheck.*
> *They take pride in being reliable, focused, and honest.*
> *They don't cut corners.*
> *They produce excellence, not excuses.*

Every trade, every profession, every business still depends on the same thing it always has, men who take pride in their work. The best worker is not the one with the loudest opinions but the one who does his job so well that others want to match his standard. Excellence is its own rebellion in a lazy world.

The code also applies to relationships beyond family. A man living by the code treats friendship as loyalty, not convenience. He keeps confidences. He speaks truth, even when it risks comfort. He refuses to flatter weakness or feed delusion. His word carries weight because it's not for sale.

> *Brotherhood is the backbone of this new generation of men. Strong men recognize each other instantly.*

They don't need to agree on everything. They recognize integrity, courage, and discipline when they see it. They challenge each other without resentment. They compete to rise, not to destroy. In a world full of shallow connections, this kind of brotherhood becomes sacred.

We The People

Community matters too. The code demands engagement. The man who follows it doesn't hide from the world's problems, he confronts them. He votes. He volunteers. He mentors. He takes interest in the safety and direction of his community.

> *A neighborhood full of responsible men is safer than one patrolled by fear.*

Modern life tries to convince men that isolation is independence. That's false. Isolation weakens. Connection strengthens. The man who lives by the code doesn't isolate; he connects with purpose. He builds networks of trust, among family, friends, and neighbors. He becomes part of something greater than himself.

The code also calls men to guard their digital lives with the same discipline as their physical ones. The internet is full of noise designed to steal a man's focus and corrupt his character. A man living by the code treats his online habits like his home, clean, disciplined, and under control. He avoids garbage because he knows it poisons his thoughts. He uses technology as a tool, not a master.

In health, the code demands respect for the body. You only get one, and it's your responsibility to keep it strong. You don't need to look like an athlete, but you do need to be capable. A man who can't lift his child or defend himself is unprepared for life. Physical strength builds mental resilience. Training the body trains the mind.

Spiritually, the code reminds men to stay humble. No matter how strong you are, life will test you. Faith, in God, in moral order, in purpose, keeps pride from becoming arrogance. The man who prays, reflects, or gives thanks stays grounded. He understands that strength without humility becomes tyranny.

The code also means mastering emotion without denying it. Men aren't robots. They feel fear, sadness, frustration, and love. But emotion is a signal, not a steering wheel. A man who lives by the code listens to emotion, learns from it, and then acts by principle. He's calm when others panic because his decisions are rooted in order, not impulse.

This doesn't mean living without joy. The strong man still laughs, plays, and enjoys life. He simply does it without losing himself in it. Pleasure is a gift, not a goal.

When men start chasing constant comfort, they stop growing. The code calls men to embrace challenge and earn rest.

Following the code doesn't make life easier. It makes it meaningful. You will still face hardship. You will still fail. But your response to those moments defines you. When you live by principle, even pain has purpose.

A man who follows the code becomes a lighthouse. Others look to him not because he shouts louder, but because he stands taller. His steadiness in chaos draws others to stability. The people who mock him today will depend on him tomorrow when everything else starts to shake.

That's why the new code matters so much. It's not about history. It's about survival. Civilizations don't collapse because of bad ideas alone. They collapse because men stop defending what's good. The code restores that defense, one man at a time.

Living this way isn't an act of rebellion. It's an act of restoration. The world doesn't need new ideas about manhood. It needs men willing to live by the old truths that built everything worth protecting.

A code only matters when it's shared. One disciplined man can change his family. Ten can change a neighborhood. A thousand can change a city. When enough men live by principle, the culture begins to shift. Strength stops being the exception and becomes the expectation again.

Building Brotherhood

Men who live by the code recognize each other without saying a word. They shake hands firmly. They show up when they say they will. They don't gossip or play victim. They hold each other accountable. The bond between such men is not about convenience; it's about commitment. It's built on trust earned through action, not talk.

That's the brotherhood the modern world has forgotten. We used to have it in trades, in teams, in churches, and in the military. Men worked, sweated, and fought beside each other. They learned that loyalty matters more than status and that respect can only be earned. That kind of brotherhood gave meaning to manhood. It gave men a tribe. *Today, most men are alone.*

They live surrounded by people but feel invisible. They hide behind screens, drowning in comparison and noise. The result is quiet desperation. But the cure is not found in sympathy; it's found in brotherhood. Men need each other again. *The code calls for rebuilding those bonds.*

Create circles of accountability.

> *Train together.*
> *Learn together.*
> *Serve your communities together.*

Don't just talk about strength, demonstrate it.
When one man stumbles, the others pull him up. When one succeeds, the others celebrate without envy. Brotherhood replaces competition with collective rise.

A group of strong men bound by principle is a force few can stand against. You don't need massive numbers. You need consistency and character.

Ten disciplined men can outlast a hundred soft ones. They'll build businesses, families, and legacies that outlive any trend. The world doesn't need more influencers. It needs anchors.

Leadership born from this code looks different. It isn't loud or self-promoting. It's steady. It leads by example, not declaration. These men don't demand loyalty through fear; they earn it through integrity. People follow them because they trust them, not because they have to.

Real leadership is not about control; it's about responsibility multiplied.

The code also redefines strength for the modern age. Strength today isn't about dominance; it's about dependability. It's not about how much you can lift but how much weight you can carry for others. It's about being the man who doesn't fold under pressure. The one people call when things fall apart. That's the kind of strength that restores faith in masculinity.

When men live by this code, women win too. Families stabilize. Children grow up safer. Communities get cleaner and calmer. The modern world keeps pretending that strength and kindness are opposites. They aren't. A good man is both firm and fair. He protects what's right because he loves what's good.

Living by this code also demands humility.

Strength without humility becomes arrogance, and arrogance always collapses.

The man who lives by the code knows he isn't perfect. He admits mistakes quickly and corrects them. He doesn't pretend to have every answer. He just refuses to stop searching for truth.

Men of humility lead differently. They don't seek followers; they raise leaders. They invest in others instead of hoarding power. They build trust instead of fear. The best measure of a man isn't how many people obey him, it's how many grow because of him.

Passing The Torch

The code reminds men that legacy isn't about fame. It's about what lasts. A man's name might fade, but his influence echoes through the people he shaped. A father's strength lives on in his children. A mentor's wisdom lives on in his students. A builder's work lives on in the lives improved by his effort. That's immortality in its truest form.

Every generation of men must decide whether they will pass down excuses or standards.

Weak men hand off excuses. They blame circumstances. They tell their sons life is unfair. Strong men hand off standards. They say,

"This is how we live.
This is how we fight.
This is how we carry weight."

Standards build nations; excuses bury them.

If enough men start living by this code, the ripple will be unstoppable. Schools will change because fathers get involved again. Workplaces will improve because integrity becomes contagious. Politics will clean up because voters start demanding strength instead of charm. The shift won't come from speeches. It will come from example, millions of men quietly living like men again.

That's how every cultural revival starts. Not through movements or marketing, but through men deciding that weakness is no longer acceptable. The world has mocked strength for long enough. It's time to make honor fashionable again.

To live by this code is to live with clarity.

You know who you are, what you stand for, and what you refuse to tolerate. You stop asking permission to lead. You stop apologizing for being masculine. You stop confusing humility with hesitation. A man who knows his values doesn't need validation.

Following the code doesn't make life easier. It makes it worth living. The storms still come, but now you have an anchor. The losses still hurt, but now they have purpose. The noise still surrounds you, but now it can't reach you. That's what strength feels like, not comfort, but calm.

The world is starving for that calm. It's starving for men who live by principle, not impulse. It's starving for fathers, mentors, builders, and

RECLAIMING MEN

protectors. And it will follow the first group of men who show what that looks like again.

The new code of manhood is not a suggestion. It's a necessity. Without it, chaos wins. With it, order returns.

Men who live this way won't just survive the times, they'll define what comes next.

The code is not theory. It's not something you post about or debate online. It's something you live. The real proof of manhood is not in what you say but in how you act when nobody is watching. The code is tested in quiet moments, when temptation knocks, when fear whispers, when quitting feels easier than continuing. Every decision you make either strengthens or weakens the man you are becoming.

A strong man is built through choices.

The small ones, repeated daily, forge the steel that big moments demand. The code gives direction to those choices. It keeps you grounded when emotion rises. It reminds you that your strength is not for ego but for duty.

The man who lives by this code understands that every day is training. Every conversation, every failure, every victory is shaping who he will be when life truly tests him. That test always comes, in the loss of a job, the betrayal of a friend, the death of a loved one, the temptation to give up. Weak men fall apart. Strong men bend but do not break. They face the pain, process it, and move forward with more purpose than before.

The code will isolate you at times. The world doesn't reward conviction. It rewards conformity. You'll lose friends who prefer comfort. You'll be mocked by people who can't match your consistency. That's fine. Great men have always walked alone for stretches of their lives. Loneliness is not a punishment. It's a filter that separates those who talk from those who act.

And let's be honest about what living by this code will cost you.

184

You'll lose job opportunities because you won't lie in the interview.
You'll lose relationships because you won't pretend to agree with things you know are wrong.
You'll be passed over for promotions because you refused to throw someone under the bus.
You'll watch weaker men get ahead by playing politics while you're stuck doing the actual work.

A 2023 study published in the *Journal of Experimental Social Psychology* found that men who show traditionally masculine traits like assertiveness and dominance are rated significantly less promotable than those who appear more 'communal.' In other words, the modern workplace doesn't reward strength, it punishes it. Translation: the corporate world punishes strength and rewards compliance. But here's what they won't tell you: the men who get promoted by being weak still go home and hate themselves. The man who gets passed over for standing on principle? He sleeps like a rock.

Choose your suffering wisely.

The reward for living by the code isn't applause. It's peace. You sleep better knowing you lived honestly. You walk taller knowing you didn't compromise. You look in the mirror and see someone you respect. That's real success. The kind that can't be bought or faked.

Every man alive today is standing at a crossroads.

The path of weakness leads to comfort, decay, and regret. The path of strength leads to purpose, growth, and legacy. One road feels easier today. The other will still feel right fifty years from now. The choice is simple, but not easy.

Men who live by this code must also pass it on. You can't let the next generation grow up without it. Teach your sons early. Show them that respect is earned, that work matters, that truth stands taller than popularity. Don't lecture them about being good men. Be one in front of them.

If you have no sons, teach someone else's. Volunteer. Coach. Mentor. The next generation is starving for guidance. They've seen too many examples of what not to be. Show them what to be. Give them standards that no one can cancel.

The man who teaches others multiplies his strength. He becomes part of a chain that can't be broken by time or culture.

Every young man who learns honor carries it forward. Every generation that holds that standard keeps the flame of civilization alive. That's what this code really is, a torch. It's meant to be carried and passed, not hidden or hoarded

The modern world mocks words like duty, honor, courage, and faith. That's how you know they still matter. The values society laughs at are always the ones it needs most. Weak cultures make fun of strength until they need it again. When the storms come, and they always do, people will look for men who are anchored in something unshakable. Be that man.

This code will not make you perfect. It will make you real. You will still fail, still stumble, still fall short. But every time you get back up, you become the proof that strength is possible. That's how you inspire others, not by pretending to have it all together, but by refusing to stay down.

The new code of manhood isn't just a way to live. It's a way to rebuild the world.

It's the antidote to the confusion, cowardice, and chaos that have poisoned this generation. It's how we reclaim the foundation of family, community, and freedom.

If men return to this code, everything else will follow. Children will grow up safer. Women will be respected. Homes will be stable. Work will have meaning. Truth will matter again. You can't legislate that. You have to live it.

And it starts with you. Not tomorrow, not someday, today. Stand up. Take responsibility for your life. Fix what you can fix. Forgive who you need to forgive. Build what you can build. Protect what you can protect. Speak truth even when it shakes the room. That's how the world changes.

The new code of manhood is not a slogan. It's a standard. It's the set of rules that every man knows deep down but has been too distracted or afraid to follow.

This book isn't asking you to reinvent yourself. It's asking you to remember who you already are.

And here's the final truth: if you don't adopt this code, someone else will adopt one for you. The culture will tell you what to be. Your employer will tell you what to think. The algorithm will tell you what to want. You'll wake up at fifty realizing you never made a single real decision in your life. You just did what you were told, liked what you were supposed to like, and became exactly the kind of weak, dependent, replaceable man the system wanted you to be.

That's the real danger. Not that you'll fail. But that you'll succeed at becoming everything you were never meant to be. You'll climb the ladder, get the title, make the money, and still feel empty because none of it was YOURS. None of it came from principle. All of it came from compliance.

The code breaks that cycle. It gives you back control. Not over the world. Over yourself. And a man who controls himself can't be controlled by anyone else.

You were born to carry weight. To lead. To build. To protect. To serve. To love with strength and fight with purpose. That's not outdated. *That's human. That's eternal.*

The code is your compass. Follow it, and you'll never be lost again. Live it, and others will find their way through you. Teach it, and generations will thank you long after you're gone.

Because when men rise again, everything rises with them.

And if you don't rise? Your sons won't either. Your daughters will marry weak men. Your grandchildren will grow up in a world where strength is illegal and cowardice is celebrated. The decay will continue. The collapse will accelerate. And one day, your great-grandchildren will look back and wonder why your generation let it all fall apart without a fight.

Don't let that be your legacy. Adopt the code. Live the code. Pass it on. That's how civilizations survive. That's how men reclaim what's been stolen from them. *The time to start is NOW.*

Not when you feel ready. Not when it's convenient. *Now. Today. This moment.* Pick one rule and live it. Tomorrow, pick another. Build the code into your bones until it's not something you think about, it's something you *ARE.*

Because the world doesn't need more men who talk about principles. It needs men who embody them. And if you're reading these words, that's you. That's your calling. That's your mission.

Don't run from it. *RUN TOWARD IT.*

13

THE RECONSTRUCTION

The decline of men broke more than individuals. It broke systems. It weakened schools, families, businesses, and even governments. It stripped away the order that used to hold communities together. Now we live among the ruins. Polite, digital, distracted ruins, where everything still looks functional, but nothing feels solid.

And by "functional," I mean we've replaced actual function with the illusion of it. We've got apps for everything except responsibility. Your phone can order you dinner, find you a date, and track your sleep, but it can't teach you how to change your own oil or have a difficult conversation without crying. According to the *Bureau of Labor Statistics (2023)*, the average American now spends 2.8 hours per day on "leisure and sports" (mostly screens) but only 19 minutes on "caring for household members." Let me translate: We spend nine times longer scrolling TikTok than talking to our own kids. That's not a society. That's a daycare center for adults with a smart phone.

Rebuilding men was the first step. Reconstructing society is the next.

Because a strong man doesn't just fix himself; he rebuilds what's around him.

Strength is contagious when it's put to use.

It Starts at Home

The first place reconstruction has to begin is the home.

We need to make fatherhood sacred again. A man's legacy isn't the car he drives or the money he earns, it's the character he plants in his children. That truth has to return to the center of male identity. A man who builds a strong home is not less ambitious. He's doing the most important work a man can do.

But here's where we are: According to national time-use data analyzed by the University of Michigan and the Institute for Family Studies, today's fathers spend less than an hour a day in genuine interaction with their kids and most of that time isn't truly engaged. Break it down to real connection, and it's closer to 30 minutes. That's the modern definition of fatherhood in America. Thirty minutes. Most men spend longer deciding what to watch on Netflix. You've got time to binge-watch eight episodes of some bullshit about dragons or serial killers, but you can't sit down and ask your kid how school was? That's not bad time management. *That's bad fathering.*

Fathers must stop outsourcing parenting to screens and schools. The world will not teach their values. If a father doesn't shape his children's worldview, someone else will, and it will rarely be someone who wants them strong. Right now, that "someone else" is an algorithm designed by a 28-year-old in Silicon Valley who's never changed a diaper but somehow knows exactly what your twelve-year-old should think about gender, politics, and morality. Dinner tables need to replace devices. Conversations need to replace scrolling. Fathers have to speak truth, not just assume their children will find it.

Education Reimagined

The next phase of reconstruction is education. For decades, schools have taught young men how to conform, not how to think. They've replaced competition with comfort, discipline with indulgence, and truth with ideology. That has to end. We need schools that teach skill, strength, and reason.

Trade programs *must return*. Not every boy belongs in a lecture hall. Some belong in a workshop, a garage, or a field. There's no shame in building with your hands. There's honor in producing something real. America needs carpenters, electricians, mechanics, and builders again. Men who can fix, lift, and create. We've spent too long pretending those jobs are second class. They aren't. They're the foundation of everything else.

Here's the reality: According to the *National Center for Education Statistics (2023)*, only 11 percent of high schools now offer comprehensive vocational training, down from 42 percent in 1982. Meanwhile, we've pushed 70 percent of high school graduates into college *(NCES, 2023)*, where half of them will drop out or graduate with a useless degree and $50,000 in debt.

> *We convinced an entire generation that sitting in a cubicle with a college degree is "success" while the guy who can actually fix your toilet, wire your house, or build your deck is somehow "lesser."*

Spoiler alert: when your Wi-Fi goes down and your toilet backs up, your *Gender Studies* degree isn't going to help you. But the plumber you looked down on? He's making $90,000 a year, owns his own business, and isn't drowning in student loans. *Who's winning?*

Teachers must also stop treating boys like defective girls. Boys learn differently. They need movement, challenge, and structure. They need to compete, fail, and try again. When schools remove risk, they remove growth. The classroom must once again become a place where boys can test themselves without being punished for energy or curiosity.

Calling All Victims

The third arena for reconstruction is culture. For too long, entertainment has ridiculed fathers, mocked marriage, and glamorized dysfunction. The heroes of film and television are no longer builders or protectors; they're narcissists and victims. That's not culture, that's corrosion.

Let's be honest about what modern entertainment has done to the image of men. Media watchdogs like the *Geena Davis Institute on Gender in Media* have found that fathers, when featured at all, are shown as more likely to be incompetent or buffoonish rather than strong or present. One 2022 report found male caregivers were nearly twice as likely as female caregivers to be portrayed that way. The "bumbling dad" who can't pack a lunch, change a diaper, or handle basic household tasks without his wife saving him has become the default. Meanwhile, every commercial, every sitcom, every movie shows women as hyper-competent while men are one step away from accidentally setting the house on fire trying to make toast. And then we wonder why boys grow up thinking masculinity is a joke. You spent 20 years watching Homer Simpson and Peter Griffin as your male role models. *Congratulations, you're fucked.*

We need new stories. Stories that celebrate courage, sacrifice, and perseverance. Stories where men do hard things and are proud of it. Art shapes values. It always has. If we want to restore strength, we must demand media that honors it instead of mocking it.

This doesn't mean every story must be about violence or dominance. It means the heroes must stand for something again. We need modern stories of quiet men who work hard, love deeply, and protect what's good. When boys see that, they imitate it. When they see cowardice glorified, they imitate that too.

Music, movies, and social media have become the loudest teachers in our culture. It's time for men who create to step up. Musicians, writers, filmmakers, and influencers who still believe in honor must flood the space with better content. If you don't like what the culture produces, replace it. Build your own platforms. Speak truth where silence has become normal.

In God We Trust

The next field of reconstruction is faith. The collapse of male leadership in churches has left many men spiritually lost. Faith institutions often chase trends instead of truth. They talk about comfort instead of character. Men stop showing up because they aren't challenged. They hear sermons about feelings when what they need are calls to courage

Churches need to speak to men again. Not by watering down the message, but by strengthening it. Faith was never meant to be comfortable. It was meant to shape warriors of conscience. Every great movement of moral clarity began with men who feared God more than man. That fear, that humility before something greater, is the root of strength.

Reconstruction also means reclaiming the public square. Men must return to leadership, not for ego, but for service. Politics has become theater because strong men left it to actors. We need men who lead with conviction, who can't be bought, and who stand firm when the mob screams. Leadership should once again mean duty, not fame.

That means local leadership too.

School boards.
City councils.
Community watch groups.

Leadership isn't always about running for office. It's about taking responsibility for the place you live. Weak communities are those where good men stay quiet. Strong communities are those where men stand guard.

Reconstruction will not be quick. The systems that failed took decades to corrode. But rebuilding starts the moment men start showing up again, at home, in schools, in churches, and in government. Society changes when strong men return to their posts.

And every man has a post. A father at home. A coach on a field. A worker on a site. A soldier on duty. A pastor in a pulpit. A business owner who treats his people right. Those are the cornerstones of civilization. When they stand firm, the nation stands firm.

When Men Stop Teaching

The next step in reconstruction is mentorship. You cannot rebuild a culture of strong men without men teaching boys. No society has ever survived that broke that chain. In the past, apprenticeship and mentorship were built into life. Boys grew up working beside their fathers or under men who taught them trades, discipline, and ethics. They learned not just how to make a living but how to live.

Today, most boys are raised by algorithms. Their mentors are strangers on a screen who sell distraction instead of direction. We have to reverse that. Every man who has built something of value owes it to the next generation to teach. Mentorship doesn't have to be formal. It starts with one man saying, "Come with me." Watch. Learn. Try. Fail. Try again.

But here's the problem: we've made it terrifying for men to mentor boys. One awkward comment, one misunderstood interaction, and you're done. *Canceled. Fired.* According to *CDC and Census data*, about 40 percent of first marriages fail, with worse odds for second and third marriages. Still, the message hasn't changed: commitment is collapsing, and fewer people even bother to try. So men just... don't. *They stay away.*

According to *Big Brothers Big Sisters of America (2022)*, male volunteer applications have dropped 38 percent since 2015, while demand for male mentors has increased by 55 percent.

Translation: boys are desperate for guidance, and men are too scared of being accused of something to help them. So instead, fourteen-year-olds get their life advice from *Andrew Tate* and *Jordan Peterson* YouTube clips. Not because those are the best mentors available, but because they're the only ones willing to talk to them without running everything past HR first.

When men stop teaching, boys grow up thinking manhood is instinctive. It isn't. It's learned. A boy becomes a man when older men demand more of him and help him reach it.

Without that demand, he stays lost.

Apprenticeship needs to return, not just in trades but in life. Every profession should have a path where young men can learn directly from older ones. Nothing replaces proximity. Wisdom can't be downloaded; it's transferred. You can't text someone discipline. You have to live beside it.

Communities that rebuild mentorship rebuild stability. When older men invest in the young, the young grow into protectors instead of problems. The cycle reverses. Boys who are taught by good men rarely grow up to harm others. They grow up to help them.

Presence Is Leadership

The next piece of reconstruction is civic responsibility. For too long, good men have stayed silent because politics became corrupt or distasteful. That silence created a vacuum, and the wrong kind of people filled it. Weak men crave control because it's the only form of strength they understand. Strong men don't crave power, they shoulder responsibility.

Civic duty starts small. Attend school board meetings. Support local law enforcement. Help organize community projects. Serve in local government. You don't need to fix everything, but you do need to show up. Presence is leadership. When men stop showing up, disorder wins.

Good governance depends on men of integrity.

That doesn't mean perfect men; it means honest ones. Men who keep their word, even when no one's watching. Men who put principle before popularity. Every great leader starts that way, grounded, humble, and willing to take hits for what's right.

Reconstruction also depends on respect for institutions, but only when those institutions are worthy of respect. A man's loyalty should never be blind. The new generation of men must rebuild trust by reforming the systems that lost it. That means honesty in business, transparency in government, and accountability in education.

Strong men hold systems accountable instead of abandoning them. They don't burn it all down; they clean it up. They walk into broken places and restore order through truth and persistence. That's what reconstruction looks like in real life, not slogans, but steady repair.

The Dignity of Work

The next foundation of reconstruction is work. Economic decline always follows moral decline. When men lose pride in their labor, nations lose strength in their economy. Work is more than survival; it's purpose in motion.

We have to restore respect for every form of honest labor. The man who builds with his hands, the one who drives a truck, the one who farms, the one who repairs, they're all holding civilization together. Their work deserves honor. The young need to see that success isn't only wearing a suit. It's doing a job well.

That means rebuilding apprenticeship networks, trade schools, and small business mentorships. It means older men teaching younger ones how to manage money, save, invest, and build. Financial literacy is part of strength. Debt and dependence are the tools of control. A man who can provide for himself and his family can't be easily broken.

Reconstruction must also include moral education. Schools can't fix what families won't teach. The moral code that once guided men has to return, honesty, courage, discipline, and faith. These are not religious slogans; they are civic necessities. A society full of men without morality becomes a playground for corruption.

We need communities where truth is not negotiable. Where children learn right from wrong without apology. Where families teach gratitude instead of entitlement. Where men model humility without weakness. That moral clarity used to be America's greatest export. It can be again.

Reconstruction also means confronting modern addiction, to screens, to substances, to comfort. These addictions have robbed men of focus and energy. The strongest nation on earth is now full of distracted men. We need a cultural detox. Time off devices.

Real conversations.
Real sweat.
Real skill.

Physical training should once again be viewed as moral training. A weak body weakens the mind. A man who disciplines himself in one area learns to discipline himself in others. Gyms, sports, martial arts, and trades all teach this. Every time a man pushes through pain, he strengthens his will. Every time he quits, he weakens it.

The same applies to emotional discipline. The world tells men to vent, not to master. That's a trap. Feelings aren't meant to rule a man. They're meant to inform him. Reconstruction requires men who can think clearly in chaos, who can feel deeply without being ruled by emotion. That kind of control is leadership.

As communities rebuild, accountability must return. Weak societies fear judgment. Strong ones depend on it. Men should hold each other to standards again. Correct each other in truth, not in cruelty. A friend who tells you the hard truth is more valuable than a thousand followers who flatter you. Accountability keeps pride from becoming arrogance and weakness from becoming habit.

None of this reconstruction will happen through policy alone. It will happen through people.

Systems follow culture, and culture follows men. When men rise, order follows. When men fall, chaos fills the space. The equation has never changed.

This chapter is about responsibility. The reconstruction of a nation begins with the reconstruction of its men. When fathers, mentors, workers, and leaders stand tall again, everything else begins to align.

Reconstruction will not come from government programs or think tanks. It will come from the quiet, consistent acts of millions of men deciding that enough is enough. It will come from men who choose honor over comfort and action over apathy.

Reconstructing the Union

Reconstruction cannot happen if men and women stay at war. The culture made enemies out of allies. It convinced men that women were obstacles to their freedom and convinced women that men were threats to their safety. Both sides lost.

For generations, the relationship between the sexes was built on partnership. Men and women were different but complementary. That balance created stability. When we erased those distinctions, we didn't create equality, we created confusion.

The modern narrative tells women they don't need men. It tells men that women are untrustworthy or burdensome. Neither message is true, and both are destroying the foundation of family. A society that cannot unite its men and women cannot raise its children.

And the data shows exactly how this is playing out. According to the *Pew Research Center (2023)*, 63 percent of men under 30 are single, compared to 34 percent of women. Why? Because women are dating older or not at all, and men are... playing video games and watching porn. Surveys from Pew and Match's own *Singles in America* report show a dating market that's collapsing for men. Women are increasingly saying they'd rather be single than 'settle,' and men, especially those under 40, say they feel invisible. You can see it in the numbers: fewer relationships, fewer marriages, and more disconnection on both sides.

So we've got women refusing to "settle" for average men, and average men giving up entirely because they can't compete with the top 10 percent of guys getting all the attention on dating apps. The result? Nobody's happy, nobody's pairing up, and birth rates are cratering.

In 2023, the U.S. fertility rate hit 1.62 children per woman *(CDC, 2023)*, well below the 2.1 replacement rate. Congratulations, we've turned dating into an economy where nobody can afford to participate. At this rate, the last American will die alone, swiping left on Tinder.

Rebuilding trust begins with truth.

Men and women are not competitors. They are co-builders. One provides strength; the other provides stability. One protects; the other nurtures. These are not outdated roles. They are natural design. Trying to erase that has only left everyone lonelier.

Men must learn to lead with respect, not resentment. Strength without respect becomes control. Respect without strength becomes weakness. A healthy relationship requires both. A man who leads with arrogance loses trust. A man who refuses to lead leaves chaos.

Women need strong men, not perfect ones. They need men who protect, provide, and commit. Men need women who believe in them, challenge them, and hold them accountable. Each brings balance to the other. A healthy family is not a hierarchy or a democracy; it's a mission. Everyone has a role, and everyone matters.

We have to make marriage sacred again. Not as a prison, but as a promise. It's not just a personal choice; it's a civilizational foundation. When families are strong, nations thrive. When families collapse, governments expand to fill the void, and freedom dies a little more each time.

But we've spent the last 50 years treating marriage like a Netflix subscription: try it for a month, cancel if you're not 100% satisfied.

We've all heard the line that half of all marriages end in divorce, but that's a myth that refuses to die. The real numbers are lower. According to *CDC and Census data*, about 40 percent of first marriages fail, with higher failure rates for second and third marriages. Still, the message hasn't changed: commitment is collapsing, and fewer people even bother to try. Let me translate those third-marriage numbers: *if you've been divorced twice and you're getting married again, there's a 73 percent chance you're an idiot.*

At some point, it's not *"bad luck"* or *"we grew apart."* You're the problem. The median duration of a first marriage that ends in divorce is now just 8 years *(U.S. Census Bureau, 2022)*. Eight years. People keep their cars longer than that. We've turned "till death do us part" into "till I get bored or find someone hotter on Instagram."

Reconstruction means raising the cultural value of marriage back to what it deserves.

We should stop glorifying endless "self-discovery" and start glorifying commitment. We should honor long marriages the same way we honor military service. It takes discipline, sacrifice, and courage.

We should celebrate fatherhood publicly again. A man walking with his children should be seen as heroic, not routine. Fatherhood is not an optional accessory to adulthood. It is the test of it. A man who raises his children well contributes more to society than any celebrity, politician, or influencer ever could.

Rebuilding fatherhood means teaching men how to be emotionally present without losing their strength. Children don't need perfect fathers; they need dependable ones. A father's calm during chaos becomes a child's confidence for life. A father's example of discipline becomes the template for his son's success and his daughter's standards.

Reconstruction also requires forgiveness between men and women. The past few decades have created resentment on both sides. Women feel unheard. Men feel unappreciated. Neither can move forward until both stop seeing the other as the enemy. Forgiveness doesn't mean ignoring real pain. It means refusing to live in it forever.

We must build a new respect for the masculine and the feminine. Not the extremes that divide us, but the harmony that unites us. Masculinity should protect femininity, not suppress it. Femininity should refine masculinity, not resent it. That balance is what makes humanity whole.

The war on gender roles didn't liberate anyone; it destabilized everyone.

We replaced cooperation with competition. We traded families for followers. We taught women to distrust men and men to fear women. And now we wonder why loneliness is an epidemic.

The reconstruction must reverse that by restoring honor to relationships. Men must earn women's respect by acting like protectors, not predators. Women must reward strength, not cynicism. Modern dating culture treats loyalty as weakness, and selfishness as empowerment. *That's why no one is happy.*

Restoring Love

We have to redefine love as responsibility. Not feeling, but action. Love is showing up, sacrificing, staying when it's hard, and protecting what you build. That's the kind of love that built nations. It's the kind that rebuilds them too.

Marriage, family, and community are not old-fashioned ideas. They are the infrastructure of civilization. A man who commits to his wife, raises his children, and serves his community is doing more for progress than any activist ever could.

The next step in reconstruction is creating environments that support that vision. Workplaces should respect fatherhood instead of punishing it. Media should portray marriage as strength instead of suffocation.

We also need to restore ritual and rite of passage. For most of human history, cultures had clear moments when a boy became a man. Today, that line is gone. Boys drift into adulthood without ever being challenged, tested, or initiated. They never learn what responsibility feels like because no one makes them face it.

Rebuilding that means creating new traditions, community challenges, mentorship programs, and symbolic milestones that teach boys accountability, discipline, and self-control. It doesn't have to be military or religious. It just needs to mean something. Boys crave meaning. Without it, they invent their own in dangerous ways.

The same is true for men. We need spaces for men to gather, train, and talk without shame. Brotherhood is not toxic; it's necessary. A man who isolates becomes weaker. A man who connects with others who hold him accountable becomes stronger.

When men and women both reclaim their natural roles and respect each other's strengths, the culture starts to heal.

Families stabilize. Children grow up confident. Neighborhoods feel safe again.
None of that requires permission from government or approval from

media. It requires men and women deciding that rebuilding is more important than resentment.

That's reconstruction in its truest form, rebuilding trust, purpose, and unity from the ground up. It starts in one home, one marriage, one family, and then spreads like wildfire. Every time a man leads with integrity and a woman supports with strength, the world becomes a little saner.

Reconstruction doesn't begin with institutions. It begins with individuals. Systems are just reflections of the people who run them. The only way to rebuild a nation is to rebuild the men who lead, teach, protect, and provide for it. Once that foundation is restored, everything else follows.

When a man lives with integrity, he stabilizes his family.

When a hundred men live with integrity, they strengthen a community. When millions do, they rebuild a nation. That's not poetic; that's structural. History shows that societies rise or fall on the character of their men.

Look back through history. Every empire that collapsed followed the same pattern, discipline eroded, duty faded, men stopped defending what mattered. Once comfort became the highest goal, decline was guaranteed. The world doesn't end with an explosion. It ends with apathy.

Reconstruction means refusing apathy. It means rejecting the lie that the world can't be fixed. It means standing tall even when everything around you leans. The culture will tell you that one man can't make a difference. History says otherwise. Every movement of renewal began with one man who wouldn't back down. *That's where you come in.*

You may not control the world, but you control your house. You control your choices. You control how you treat others. That's your kingdom. Rule it well. That's where reconstruction starts.

Turn off the noise. Stop waiting for permission. Fix what's broken in front of you. Be the man your children can look at and say, *"That's what strength looks like."* You don't need a title for that. You just need courage and consistency.

The culture around you may not change overnight, but your influence will ripple outward. When a man leads with honor, other men notice. They might not say it, but they feel it. They start raising their standards too. Change begins quietly, one household, one decision, one example at a time.

The reconstruction is not just about men surviving modern life. It's about men rebuilding a civilization worth living in. It's about bringing back the standards that make peace possible: truth, order, respect, and courage. The world is starving for it, even if it doesn't know how to ask.

When men live by principle again, women will feel safer, children will feel protected, and society will feel stable. The chaos we see today isn't permanent; it's just the consequence of absence. When men return, order returns.

That's the deeper truth behind reconstruction: it isn't political; it's moral. It's not about left or right; it's about right and wrong. It's not about nostalgia; it's about necessity. You don't need to be perfect to join it. You just need to be willing to fight for what's real.

The Three Pillars of Strength

Men must rebuild the three pillars of strength... *discipline, duty, and direction.*

Discipline means doing what's right even when you don't feel like it.

It's waking up early, staying steady, controlling impulses, and finishing what you start. Discipline makes a man trustworthy.

Duty means living for something bigger than yourself.

It's taking responsibility for your family, your community, and your country. It's standing guard where others run. Duty makes a man dependable.

Direction means knowing where you're going and why.

A man without direction is a man waiting to be controlled. Know your values, know your purpose, and live by them. Direction makes a man dangerous, in the right way.

Together, these three pillars form the structure of reconstruction. Without them, every effort collapses into chaos or comfort. With them, a man becomes unshakable.

Reconstruction isn't theory anymore. It's action. It's choosing order over chaos, purpose over pleasure, truth over convenience. It's leading quietly, working hard, and protecting what's right. It's building when everyone else is talking.

The modern world laughs at those values because it fears them. It knows that disciplined men can't be manipulated. Men with duty can't be distracted. Men with direction can't be controlled. That's why the attack on masculinity happened in the first place, to make men weak enough to manage.

That attack ends when men stop participating in their own defeat. When they stop apologizing for strength. When they stop believing they're the problem. Men are not the problem. Weakness is. Cowardice is. Apathy is.

Every man who wakes up tomorrow and decides to live by principle instead of impulse becomes part of the reconstruction. Every father who shows up, every worker who gives his best, every leader who tells the truth, they're the real revolutionaries.

The reconstruction is not a call to nostalgia. It's a call to rebuilding the future with the best parts of the past, courage, family, faith, discipline, respect, and sacrifice. Those are not outdated values. They are eternal ones.

Civilizations don't fall because enemies attack them. They fall because men stop defending them. But the opposite is also true. Civilizations rise when men rise. Every great recovery in history began the same way, when men remembered who they were.

That's what this book is about.

Not politics.
Not outrage.
Not trends.

It's about remembering what manhood means and proving that it still matters. It's about rejecting the narrative that strength is toxic and reclaiming it as the virtue it's always been.

Reconstruction doesn't need permission or consensus. It only needs commitment. When you stand for what's right, you become a living example. And examples change more minds than arguments ever will.

One man of conviction is worth a thousand who conform. Be that man. Be the one who rebuilds instead of complains. Be the one who leads when others hide. Be the one your son wants to become and your daughter can trust.

That's how nations rise again. One man, one family, one standard at a time.

The reconstruction starts with you, *and it starts right now.*

14

THE COST OF STRENGTH

Every generation talks about wanting strong men, but few are willing to pay the price it takes to make them. Strength doesn't come from comfort. It comes from resistance, pressure, and pain. It's built in the long nights, the lost battles, and the moments when quitting feels easier than continuing.

The truth is simple: strength costs everything that weakness protects.

Men who try to better themselves, to stay disciplined, fit, or focused often get mocked for it. Research on social conformity and male peer dynamics shows that when a man steps outside the pack to improve his life, friends and even family tend to cut him down rather than cheer him on (American Institute of Stress, 2023; Psychology Today, 2022).

When you stop drinking with the boys, they call you boring. When you start eating clean, they say you're "obsessed." When you get up at 5 AM to train, they tell you you're "overdoing it."

Your weakness made them comfortable. Your strength makes them feel guilty.

So they'll do everything they can to drag you back down to their level, because watching you improve is a daily reminder that they're not.

The Toll Nobody Talks About

You can't be strong and stay popular. You can't be strong and stay comfortable. You can't be strong and still live to please everyone. Every man who chooses strength will be misunderstood, criticized, and sometimes hated. That's the toll.

But that's also what makes it rare.

The culture sells the image of strength, muscles, status, power, but it hides the price. It hides the discipline it takes to train when no one's watching, the hours spent in silence, the sacrifices made that no one ever thanks you for. Strength looks glamorous from a distance. Up close, it's blood and blisters.

Real strength is built in private. It's the father who works two jobs to keep food on the table. The veteran who keeps fighting nightmares so his family can sleep. The man who admits his mistakes and rebuilds himself from scratch. Strength isn't loud. It's steady. It's choosing to do the hard thing, quietly, over and over, until it becomes normal.

Every man who chooses that path will pay a price. You'll lose people who loved your weakness because it made them comfortable. You'll outgrow environments that once felt safe.

You'll walk alone sometimes. That's part of the cost.

The world rewards compromise. It punishes conviction. When you stand for something real, people will project their own weakness onto you. They'll call it pride, arrogance, or toxicity. Don't flinch. The criticism is proof that you've stopped playing by their rules.

The cost of strength is loneliness. Not forever, but for a while. Most men never learn to walk alone, so they settle for belonging over growth. But isolation can be a forge. If you use it right, it burns off everything false. It leaves only what's real.

And here's the brutal math on that loneliness: Start bettering yourself and you'll find out how fast people disappear. The data backs it up. According to the *Survey Center on American Life* (2021), the share of men reporting they have no close friends has increased fivefold since 1990, from just 3 percent to 15 percent. Pew Research (2023) found that 28 percent of men under 30 say they have no close social connections at all. The *Atlantic* reported that men are forming fewer deep bonds because adulthood now demands more emotional labor than most male friendships are built to handle.

So when a man starts improving, getting disciplined, focused, and intentional, he often exposes how shallow many of his old friendships were.

He doesn't lose people because he became worse; he loses them because they were only comfortable with the version of him who wasn't growing.

Why? Because weak men can't stand being around strength. It's like sunlight to a vampire. Your gym routine makes them feel bad about their beer gut. Your discipline makes them feel guilty about sleeping till noon. Your ambition reminds them they gave up on theirs. So they ghost you, talk shit about you, or just slowly fade away. Good. Let them go. They weren't friends. They were accomplices in your mediocrity.

The Price Every Man Pays

The cost of strength is discipline. You'll wake up earlier than others. You'll work when others rest. You'll sacrifice pleasures most people think are normal. You'll eat differently, train differently, live differently. You'll be called obsessive or extreme. That's fine. Ordinary never built anything worth remembering.

The cost of strength is rejection. The moment you stop living for approval, the world will test you. You'll be criticized for leading, questioned for standing firm, mocked for your values. You'll be told you're outdated. You'll be told you're harsh. You'll be told you're wrong. That's the tax on truth.

The cost of strength is responsibility. Weak men look for someone to blame. Strong men look for something to fix. The stronger you get, the more weight you carry. At first it feels unfair. Then it feels natural. You stop asking why the world is broken and start working to repair your part of it.

Strength also costs comfort. Comfort feels good, but it rots courage. The man who chooses easy today will face hard tomorrow. The man who chooses hard today will face peace tomorrow. That's the exchange. You can't escape the pain, you only get to choose when to face it.

And let's talk about what "choosing easy" actually costs you. Men who choose discipline over comfort win over time. Decades of research link self-control and conscientious habits to higher earnings, better health, and greater life satisfaction, while low self-control tracks with obesity, debt, and regret. That isn't a slogan. It's the record.

Translation: every time you hit snooze, skip the gym, eat the garbage, or take the easy path, you're not *"treating yourself."* You're mortgaging your future.

Your comfort today is your regret tomorrow.

That couch feels nice now, but it's going to feel like a prison when you're 55, overweight, broke, and wondering where your life went. Spoiler: *it went to Netflix and DoorDash.*

The cost of strength is sacrifice. You'll have to give up things that make you weak, certain habits, certain people, sometimes even certain dreams. You'll lose temporary happiness for permanent peace. Weak men chase pleasure. Strong men chase purpose.

Strength demands suffering, but suffering with meaning. You'll be tired, misunderstood, and doubted. But that pain refines you. It exposes who you really are. No man discovers his character until it's tested. Pain is the mirror that shows what's real.

You'll pay a price in time, too. Years spent training, building, working, studying, growing. Progress feels slow. Others seem ahead. That's fine. The race for strength isn't won in speed, it's won in endurance. The man who refuses to stop always passes the one who quits halfway.

The cost of strength is emotional control. You can't react to everything.

You can't let anger rule you. You can't let fear drive your choices. You have to be steady even when everything inside you is shaking. Leadership demands that kind of restraint.

The cost of strength is humility. The more powerful you become, the more temptation you'll face to use it selfishly. Power without humility turns men into tyrants. Strength is not domination. It's service under control. Every strong man has to remind himself daily: this power is for protection, not pride.

The cost of strength is constant pressure. The higher you rise, the more you'll be tested. Every victory will bring new challenges. Every step forward will attract resistance. That's how it's supposed to work. Strength without opposition is fantasy.

And the greatest cost of all, the one few ever talk about, *is peace with misunderstanding.*

> **You'll be lied about, misquoted, and judged unfairly. You'll watch people twist your motives. You'll be told you're the problem simply because you refuse to kneel.**

The strong man learns to stand still through that storm. His conscience is louder than the crowd.

But with every cost comes clarity. The more you sacrifice, the clearer you see. You stop craving applause. You stop needing comfort. You stop fearing failure. That's freedom. The freedom that only comes after paying in full.

Strength will isolate you, but it will also define you. Weakness wins friends. Strength builds respect. And respect is worth more than popularity ever was.

The world doesn't need more agreeable men. It needs men willing to pay the price for truth, honor, and courage. Men who carry the scars of the fight and still choose to show up again. That's the cost of strength. *And it's worth every drop of it.*

The Rewards of Paying the Price

The man who pays the price for strength gains something no one else can give him, peace that doesn't depend on circumstance. The storms still come, but they don't shake him anymore. He doesn't chase the highs or collapse in the lows. He moves forward with calm certainty. That calm is earned, not gifted.

Strength is expensive, but the return is permanent.

When a man learns to carry weight, the weight no longer breaks him. When he's been through the fire, he stops fearing it. The pain that once controlled him becomes proof that he can survive worse. That's the quiet confidence of a man who's been tested.

The world calls that arrogance. It isn't. It's stability. The man who knows he's been through hell and came out standing walks differently. He speaks less, listens more, and wastes no time explaining himself to people who haven't done the work.

When you live with strength, you no longer need permission to lead. You don't wait for validation. You stop negotiating with weakness. The strong man doesn't need to shout because his results do the talking. He doesn't need to prove anything because his life already proves it.

The reward for strength is clarity. You see the world for what it is, not what you wish it was. You stop expecting fairness, and you start creating justice through your actions. You stop arguing about right and wrong, and you start embodying it.

Strength brings peace because it removes confusion. You know who you are, what you stand for, and what you won't tolerate. You stop trying to live fifty different lives at once. You simplify. You focus. You live by code, not impulse.

That simplicity is rare today because everyone is chasing everything. Men are pulled in every direction, career, status, pleasure, attention, and end up exhausted, empty, and numb. The strong man says no. He chooses fewer things and gives them everything he has.

When a man pays the price of strength, he also gains time.

Not extra hours in the day, but control of them. He stops wasting time on meaningless talk, aimless scrolling, and temporary escapes. He uses his time with precision, to train, to build, to connect, to rest with purpose. Weak men kill time. Strong men invest it.

The cost of strength also buys credibility. In a world full of talkers, people trust the man who delivers. They know he'll show up. They know he'll keep his word. They know he won't fold when things get hard. That kind of reputation can't be faked or bought. *It's earned through years of consistency.*

Strength refines relationships. You'll lose shallow ones, but you'll attract real ones. Strong men don't bond over convenience. They bond over loyalty and shared struggle. The people who remain in your life once you've paid the price for strength are the ones who were meant to be there all along.

Strength also changes how you view failure. Weak men see failure as proof they aren't good enough. Strong men see it as feedback, as training. Every failure becomes a lesson, not a verdict. You stop being afraid to try because you stop being afraid to fall.

That fear of failure keeps most men average. They'd rather stay comfortable than risk humiliation. But humiliation is temporary. Regret lasts forever.

Once you've failed enough times and learned from it, you realize that failure doesn't define you, quitting does.

The man who has paid the price for strength doesn't crave shortcuts anymore. He's seen what easy gets you, dependence, mediocrity, and self-doubt. He'd rather take the long road because he knows the climb is where character grows.

That kind of man becomes dangerous, not in violence, but in discipline. You can't threaten a man who has already learned to suffer. You can't bribe him with comfort, and you can't control him with fear. He's already faced worse within himself. That's real freedom.

Strength also gives you perspective. You stop resenting struggle because you see what it produces.

You start to understand that the hardest moments of your life were also the ones that shaped your soul. The pain that broke you also built you. The betrayal that hurt you also taught you boundaries. The loss that crushed you also revealed your resilience.

The man who has walked through enough pain stops blaming others. He starts thanking God for the training. Every scar becomes a story of survival, every loss a lesson in endurance. The strong man doesn't look for escape anymore, he looks for purpose inside the pain.

That purpose turns suffering into fuel. It transforms hardship into strength and discipline into identity. Once you understand that, pain loses its sting. It becomes the gym where your character lifts its weight.

Paying the price for strength also gives you control over your emotions. You stop reacting to everything. You learn to pause. You respond with reason instead of impulse. That pause is power. Weak men react. Strong men respond.

When you can stay calm in the middle of chaos, people start looking to you. Not because you asked for authority, but because peace is magnetic. The world follows men who can keep their head while everyone else loses theirs.

The final reward of strength is *purpose.*

You stop asking "What's in it for me?" and start asking "What can I build?"

You stop thinking about what you deserve and start thinking about what you owe. The strong man doesn't live for himself anymore, he lives for what he can protect, create, and pass on.

That's the trade. Comfort for clarity. Ease for peace. Pleasure for purpose. Weakness offers the illusion of freedom but demands your soul.

Strength costs everything up front, but it gives you everything worth having in return.

Strength without morality is just force.

History is full of strong men who used power to dominate instead of protect, to enslave instead of serve. Real strength doesn't corrupt, ego does. Strength is neutral. What you build or destroy with it defines your character.

That's why the foundation of true strength must be humility. Humility doesn't mean weakness. It means knowing you're capable of power but disciplined enough to use it for good. The humble man is dangerous to evil because he isn't ruled by pride or greed. He acts from principle, not impulse.

Faith anchors humility. It reminds a man that his strength comes from somewhere higher. Without that anchor, power always turns inward. It becomes self-worship. That's how corruption begins, when men start believing they're gods instead of servants.

The man who fears nothing except losing his integrity is the freest man alive. Faith gives that freedom. It teaches restraint. It teaches gratitude. It keeps strength honest.

Every strong man will face moments where he could take the easy win, cut corners, lie, or dominate others to get ahead. Those moments define him more than victory ever could. The world may never know the temptation he resisted, but he will. That's where self-respect is forged.

The strong man who stays humble understands that leadership isn't a privilege, it's a burden. The higher you climb, the more people you serve. Weak men chase titles. Strong men chase responsibility.

To Protect and To Serve

That's the paradox of strength: the more you gain, the more you owe. The more capable you become, the more you're called to protect those who can't protect themselves. Strength always comes with duty attached. Without duty, it turns poisonous.

The true test of strength is what you do with power over others.

Do you protect or exploit?
Do you build them up or break them down?
Do you lead them toward virtue or toward your own
vanity?

Those answers decide whether your strength blesses or curses the world around you.

A strong man should make people feel safe, not scared. He should inspire others to rise, not to submit. His presence should bring calm, not tension. People should know that his discipline is their shield, not their threat. *That's leadership. That's honor.*

Faith also keeps strength patient. The man who believes in something eternal doesn't panic in temporary storms. He knows his role is to plant seeds, not control outcomes. That kind of patience is power, the ability to act with purpose without demanding instant reward.

In the absence of faith, men turn to pleasure or rage to fill the void. That's why modern culture feels so unstable. It's full of men with energy but no direction. Men with ambition but no virtue. Power without purpose always ends in destruction.

A society that mocks faith will always end up worshipping something else, money, fame, politics, or self. And all of those false gods eventually devour their followers. Only truth can anchor strength long enough to sustain it.

When a man's strength is rooted in faith, it serves others naturally. It becomes protective, not performative. It creates order instead of chaos. His home becomes peaceful. His work becomes meaningful. *His legacy becomes stable.*

That kind of man doesn't just survive, he multiplies. His influence spreads through his family, his community, and his nation. He raises sons who understand that power must be disciplined and daughters who trust that strength can coexist with goodness.

The strong man who stays humble and faithful becomes a cornerstone. He's not perfect. He doesn't pretend to be. But people around him know that he's consistent. That's why they follow him. Not because he's loud, but because he's reliable.

Strength combined with humility creates wisdom. Strength combined with faith creates peace. Strength combined with duty creates civilization.

Those three combinations are what the modern world is missing most.

The strong man must also be willing to kneel, not to man, but to principle. That's what keeps him upright when everyone else bows to pressure. Humility before truth keeps arrogance from destroying everything he's built.

Every empire that fell began with pride. Every leader who collapsed started believing his own legend. Every generation that lost its freedom stopped fearing God and started worshipping itself. The pattern never changes.

Strength without restraint becomes tyranny. Restraint without strength becomes fragility. The balance of both is what built every great civilization in history. The moment that balance disappears, decline begins.

The cost of strength, then, isn't just sweat or struggle, it's surrender. Not surrender to weakness, but surrender to principle. The willingness to say, "I'll do what's right, even if it costs me everything." That's the highest form of courage.

That courage isn't loud. It's quiet, steady, and unshakable. You see it in the firefighter who runs toward flames, in the soldier who stays behind to cover his team, in the father who sacrifices comfort for his family. None of them need applause. They already have peace.

Peace isn't given. It's earned through a life lived in truth.

A strong man can lay his head down at night and rest, not because life is easy, but because his conscience is clean. That's the reward for all the sacrifice, knowing you carried your weight well.

And when his time comes, that man won't fear death. He's already died a thousand small deaths, of ego, of fear, of temptation. What's left is pure conviction. A man like that doesn't leave behind wealth or fame; he leaves behind stability. He leaves behind people who are stronger because he was there.

That's the legacy of true strength. Not dominance. Not perfection. Stewardship. Protection. Integrity.

That's the kind of strength that rebuilds nations and holds families together long after the man himself is gone.

It's Always Collection Day

Strength is not a trophy you win once. It's rent you pay every day. The moment you stop training, stop guarding your mind, stop choosing discipline, it fades. That's why strong men stay humble, because they know they can fall at any time.

Every day is another test. You wake up to temptation, distraction, and doubt. The world wants you to soften, to let your edge dull just a little. One skipped workout. One compromise. One excuse. *That's how weakness sneaks back in.*

Strength is maintenance. It's not glamorous. It's not always exciting. It's repetition, doing the hard thing again and again until it's instinct. The men who stay strong the longest aren't the most gifted; they're the most consistent.

Discipline is the glue that holds strength together. Without it, motivation burns out. Motivation depends on feeling; discipline depends on choice. You'll have days when nothing feels right, when no one believes in you, when everything you built feels pointless. That's when strength proves itself. You keep going anyway.

Endurance separates the strong from the loud.

Anyone can start a challenge. Few can finish it. The man who endures pain without losing faith, who stays kind when he's angry, who keeps his standards when no one's watching, that's the man the world can trust.

Strength isn't about winning. It's about holding the line. It's about standing firm when everything around you shakes. Sometimes that means carrying the weight for others. Sometimes it means taking the hit that would have crushed someone else.

There's a reason real leaders have scars. They're proof that they stood in the fire and didn't run.

They're reminders of battles survived, lessons learned, and pain transformed into purpose. The scarred man isn't broken; he's seasoned.

Strength also means forgiveness, the hardest kind, the one that comes without apology. Letting go of bitterness takes more power than holding on to hate. Weak men blame. Strong men release. They don't forget, but they refuse to let pain own them.

The strong man also forgives himself. He accepts that failure is part of the process. He doesn't stay stuck in guilt. He learns, adjusts, and moves forward. That's how you grow without growing cold.

Legacy comes from that mindset. You can't control how long you live, but you can control what your life stands for. Every day you choose strength, you're writing part of your legacy. Every hard thing you endure becomes a lesson for someone else.

The goal isn't perfection, it's progress. It's being a little stronger, a little wiser, a little more useful than you were yesterday. Strength compounds. The man who improves one percent every day becomes unstoppable over time.

The next generation isn't watching what you post. They're watching how you live.

They'll remember the tone of your voice more than your words. They'll copy your actions more than your advice. Strength is contagious when it's consistent.

If you want your sons to grow up strong, show them what it looks like to stay calm under pressure, to tell the truth when it's costly, to protect what's right even when it's unpopular. If you want your daughters to believe good men still exist, be one.

Every man leaves behind evidence of what he believed. The weak leave chaos; the strong leave order. The weak leave excuses; the strong leave example. The weak talk about what should be done; the strong do it.

That's why strength matters. It's not vanity. It's not dominance. It's survival of everything that makes life stable and free.

We don't rebuild civilization with slogans. We rebuild it with men who refuse to break.

When your body gives out someday, when the noise of the world fades, your name won't matter as much as your influence.

Did you make people stronger or softer?
Did you protect truth or profit from lies?
Did you stand your ground or hide behind the crowd?

Those are the real measures.

Strength doesn't promise comfort, but it promises peace. It doesn't guarantee success, but it guarantees respect. It doesn't make life easier, but it makes it worth living.

Every day you wake up and choose to do what's right instead of what's easy.

Rebuild your world in small ways. Every honest act, every hard choice, every moment of restraint is a stone in the foundation of something greater.

That's the quiet revolution of strong men. No hashtags. No headlines. Just the daily discipline of showing up, building, protecting, and leading.

It's the man who fixes the broken fence before it becomes a problem. The man who checks on a friend who's slipping. The man who holds his temper instead of lashing out. These small choices create order in a world that feeds on chaos.

> **Strength at scale is what saves nations. But it always starts with one man making a decision: "Not today. Not on my watch."**

So, if you've paid the price, if you've carried the weight, if you've walked through pain and kept your soul clean, stand tall. You're what this world still depends on.

The cost of strength is high, but the cost of weakness is higher. Weakness destroys families, nations, and futures. Strength holds them together.

And when your story is told long after you're gone, the people who come after you won't talk about your comfort. They'll talk about your courage. They'll say, *"He didn't quit."* That's how you know you lived right.

The cost of strength is everything you have. The reward is becoming the kind of man who can handle anything that comes.

That's the trade. That's the truth. And that's what this generation of men must remember before it's too late.

15

REBUILDING THE TRIBE

The greatest lie told to modern men is that they can do it alone. Independence has its place, but isolation kills. Men aren't meant to be solitary. They're meant to stand shoulder to shoulder with other men who hold them accountable and fight beside them.

For thousands of years, every society built its men inside tribes, not digital ones, real ones. Hunters, soldiers, workers, builders, fathers. Men who trained together, prayed together, ate together, and protected what was theirs. They didn't need to talk about brotherhood; they lived it.

Then came modern life, suburbs, screens, and silence. We built bigger houses and smaller communities. Men lost their tribes. They lost the circles where toughness was tested and loyalty was earned. The cost has been enormous. And by *"enormous,"* I mean catastrophic. Loneliness is now one of the leading causes of depression and suicide among men.

The Lonely Island

Loneliness is now one of the leading causes of depression and suicide among men. Your body is literally eating itself because you don't have any real friends. But hey, at least you've got 847 followers on Instagram and three guys you play Call of Duty with who don't even know your real name.

A man without a tribe becomes vulnerable. He drifts. He doubts himself. He hides his pain because no one is there to challenge him.

That's how weakness spreads, one isolated man at a time.

Rebuilding the tribe begins with connection. Real connection. Not likes or messages, but proximity. You have to be around other men who demand your best. You can't sharpen steel without friction. The right kind of brotherhood will push you further than you can go alone.

Every man needs a group that calls him out when he drifts and lifts him up when he falls. That's not judgment; that's accountability. Weak men fear correction because they confuse it with criticism. Strong men welcome it because they know it keeps them sharp.

The tribe doesn't need to be large. In fact, the smaller it is, the stronger it becomes.

Five good men who share values and live by standards can do more than fifty who just talk about them.

Quality beats quantity every time.

The true numbers tell a story most people refuse to face. According to the American Perspectives Survey (2021), 15% of men have zero close friends, and another 28% have only one or two. The Survey Center on American Life found that 28% of men under 30 report no close social connections at all. In 2023, nearly one in five young men aged 18–24 were classified as NEET, Not in Education, Employment, or Training, which means they're doing nothing at all.

Your grandfather had a poker night, a church group, a bowling league, and friends he could call any hour of the night. Most men today can't even name five real friends. They've got a group chat that hasn't been active since 2019 and a guy from high school who likes their posts sometimes. *That's not a tribe. That's isolation with Wi-Fi.*

Find men who refuse to let you settle. Men who tell you when you're wrong. Men who celebrate your wins without envy and correct your failures without cruelty. Brotherhood isn't about comfort. It's about growth.

Where Brotherhood Begins

You can build a tribe anywhere, in a gym, a workshop, a church, a unit, or a neighborhood. It doesn't need uniforms or slogans. It needs standards. A shared code. A reason to show up.

> **The moment men agree on a mission, they stop being strangers and start being brothers.**

A tribe built on purpose can change everything. You train together, and strength multiplies. You plan together, and vision expands. You protect each other's families, and community forms. That's how civilizations rise again, not through politics, but through men who choose to stand together.

Rebuilding the tribe also means restoring mentorship between generations. Modern culture cut that bridge. Young men no longer sit with old men. They don't hear stories of mistakes, victories, and lessons learned the hard way. That silence has left them unprepared for real life. And I mean *UNPREPARED*.

Older men have a duty to teach. Their experience is a weapon that can protect the young from destruction. Wisdom that isn't shared dies with the man who holds it. The tribe is how it stays alive, through conversation, correction, and example.

> *Younger men must also learn to listen again.*

Pride is the first enemy of wisdom. You don't have to agree with every word an elder says, but you should respect the ground he's already walked. The path to strength is shorter when you learn from those who've fallen before you.

The tribe teaches what institutions can't. It teaches courage through challenge, loyalty through struggle, and humility through accountability. No government or app can replace that. It has to be lived.

Rebuilding the tribe will feel uncomfortable at first. Most men today have forgotten how to connect without distraction. You'll sit with silence. You'll face truth. You'll hear things you don't want to hear. That's the point. Brotherhood isn't therapy, it's sharpening.

Forward Together

In a tribe, weakness is treated, not excused. Men tell each other the truth because lies destroy trust. If a man is failing his wife, his children, or his duty, the tribe steps in. Not to shame him, but to save him. That's real love, discipline in disguise.

But modern men are terrified of this kind of accountability. We've replaced brotherhood with "safe spaces" where nobody's allowed to tell you you're screwing up. Studies on male friendships show that most men avoid confronting each other even when they see self-destruction up close. In one national survey on male friendship, over half of men said they've stayed silent when a friend was drinking too much, neglecting his family, or spiraling, not because they didn't care, but because they were afraid of 'ruining the friendship.' It's cowardice disguised as respect, and it's killing accountability.

Translation: we'd rather watch our boys drive off a cliff than risk an uncomfortable conversation.

Your grandfather's friends would have grabbed him by the collar and told him he was being an idiot. Your friends? They'll just unfollow you on social media and talk shit behind your back. That's not friendship. *That's cowardice.*

The tribe isn't just about talk. It's about action. Shared goals, shared work, shared struggle. Train together. Build something. Serve your community.

Men bond through effort, not conversation. Respect grows from sweat, not slogans.

Tribes should also honor hierarchy, not in arrogance, but in order. Every group needs leadership. Someone has to make the call when it's time to act. The best leaders in a tribe are servants first. They lead by example, not command. Their authority comes from consistency, not position.

Rebuilding brotherhood doesn't mean idolizing the past. It means reclaiming what worked. The future will belong to the men who build strong tribes, disciplined, loyal, faith-driven, and purpose-bound. Those men will shape schools, businesses, and governments from the ground up.

When men reconnect, society reconnects. Strong tribes build strong families. Strong families build strong communities. Strong communities build strong nations. It's not theory. It's architecture.

The tribe is how we rebuild everything we've lost. It's how we make manhood honorable again.

The Blueprint

Rebuilding the tribe starts with intention. Brotherhood doesn't appear by accident. It has to be built deliberately, the same way you build strength or skill. You start small, with consistency and trust. You meet, you train, you talk, you hold each other accountable. Then, slowly, it becomes something unbreakable.

Start with three things: a mission, a standard, and a rhythm.

The *mission* is what binds the men together. It doesn't have to be complicated. It might be to raise strong families, to train and stay disciplined, to serve your community, or to grow in faith. Without a mission, brotherhood becomes a social club. With one, it becomes a unit.

The *standard* is what separates the serious from the lazy. Every man in the tribe should live by a clear code: honesty, loyalty, courage, and responsibility. You don't have to agree on everything. But if you don't share standards, you don't share strength.

And the *rhythm*, that's the heartbeat. Meet regularly. Not once in a while when it's convenient, but consistently. Weekly workouts, Sunday meals, Friday meetings, morning runs, volunteer work, anything that forces presence. Brotherhood dies when it becomes optional.

Each tribe should have two types of strength: *discipline and direction.*

> *Discipline keeps the tribe solid.*
> *Direction keeps it moving.*

Men need both. Without discipline, the tribe falls apart. Without direction, it loses purpose.

The best tribes are built on shared struggle. Men bond through effort. That's why sports teams, military units, and work crews feel like family, they sweat, fight, and overcome together. Shared adversity builds trust faster than shared talk.

If you want a real brotherhood, do something hard together.

> *Train early in the morning.*
> *Go on a hike.*
> *Build something for someone else.*
> *Do service projects.*
> *Compete.*
> *Push limits.*

Brotherhood born from comfort dies quickly. Brotherhood born from struggle lasts forever.

Men also need to build tribes across generations. Every group should have young men to bring energy, middle-aged men to bring drive, and older men to bring wisdom. When all three are present, the tribe becomes balanced. The young learn respect. The old regain purpose. The middle grow sharper through responsibility.

When men isolate by age, everyone loses. The young stay reckless. The middle burn out. The old fade away. But when generations connect, something powerful happens, knowledge transfers, confidence grows, and identity strengthens.

Faith-centered tribes hold a unique power. When men unite under shared belief, their bond goes beyond emotion. They see each other as brothers under God, bound by duty to truth, not just loyalty to each other. That kind of tribe becomes nearly impossible to break.

But even secular tribes can live by sacred principles, integrity, courage, and service. These aren't religious values; they're human ones. When a group of men chooses to live that way together, they become light in a culture that's gone dim.

Rebuilding the tribe also means restoring ritual. Modern life stripped it away. Men used to mark milestones, rites of passage, oaths, ceremonies of commitment. Those weren't superstitions. They were symbols that gave meaning to effort. They told men, you belong to something bigger than yourself.

We need that again. When a boy finishes his first year in the tribe, mark it. When a man overcomes a personal failure, honor it. When someone reaches a new level of strength, acknowledge it. Not with vanity, but with respect. Symbols matter. Ritual reminds men that they're part of a legacy.

Conflict Builds Brotherhood

Tribes must also have rules for conflict. Brotherhood doesn't mean harmony all the time. Strong men will clash, and that's healthy. The rule is simple: handle conflict face to face. No gossip. No texting. No avoidance. Speak truth, fix the problem, move forward.

A man who avoids confrontation will never lead. Conflict handled correctly builds respect. You don't have to agree on everything, but you do have to show up. The moment you start talking *about* a man instead of *to* him, the tribe fractures. Weak men whisper. Strong men confront.

Disagreement sharpens character. If your circle never challenges you, it's not a tribe, it's an audience. Brotherhood thrives on honesty. The kind that sometimes stings but always strengthens.

The tribe also protects its code. Every man who joins should understand the standard. No lying, no cheating, no cowardice. A man who breaks his word loses his place. Forgiveness is earned through repentance, not excuses. Brotherhood is a privilege, not a consolation prize.

Modern culture rejects that kind of accountability because it hates consequences. The tribe restores it. It brings back cause and effect, the understanding that choices matter. That honor has weight. That a man's word still means something.

The tribe must also serve a purpose bigger than itself. Brotherhood without mission becomes a social club. A real tribe builds something. Maybe it runs a youth program, restores neighborhoods, helps veterans, trains young fathers, or supports local businesses.

Purpose is what keeps a group alive. Without it, men drift into boredom, and boredom always turns destructive.

Every tribe needs ritual. Something that binds men together through repetition and meaning. It could be a weekly training session, a shared meal, or a night of reflection. Rituals give rhythm to commitment. They remind men of who they are and what they stand for.

This is how you rebuild a culture, one tribe at a time. You can't fix a nation from the top down. You build it from the inside out. A tribe of disciplined men is stronger than any policy or politician. It doesn't wait for permission to lead; it simply leads.

A man in a tribe learns humility. He learns that he's not the center. He's one piece of something bigger. That humility creates power, not weakness. When men work in unity, their reach multiplies. One man can change his family. Ten can change a town. A hundred can change a generation.

Rebuilding the tribe also requires trust between different kinds of men. Not everyone looks the same, believes the same, or works the same. Strength doesn't belong to one race, class, or faith. It belongs to men who live by principle. A united tribe built on shared values, not shared appearance, can't be divided.

This unity doesn't erase individuality; it disciplines it. The mission is bigger than ego. Every man brings something to the table, skill, wisdom, experience, energy, but the goal is collective strength. The moment personal pride outweighs the mission, the tribe fails.

Men must also learn to protect the tribe from distraction. The digital world makes loyalty shallow. You can't build deep brotherhood with men who scroll more than they speak. The tribe thrives in the real world, through handshakes, eye contact, and shared effort.

A tribe is a training ground for leadership. It's where boys become men, and men become examples. It's where responsibility is learned, tested, and rewarded. The weak can grow there, but only if they commit to discipline. The lazy will leave on their own.

Rebuilding tribes means rebuilding standards, punctuality, honesty, preparation, and follow-through.

These small habits seem trivial, but they define culture. When a man says, "I'll be there," and he actually is, he's building trust. When he finishes what he starts, he's strengthening the code.

A man who shows up for his tribe becomes a man who shows up for his family, his work, and his community. The lessons are universal. That's why rebuilding tribes is not just social, it's civilizational.

The tribe also becomes a shield against despair. When life hits hard, a man with brothers beside him doesn't crumble. He has people to call, people who understand, people who remind him of who he is. That safety net isn't built overnight. It's earned through loyalty over time.

Men in isolation fall fast. Men in brotherhood endure. That's not theory, it's biology. Humans evolved in groups for a reason. You can't carry every burden alone. You're not supposed to. Strength shared is strength multiplied.

When men build real brotherhood, they create a counterculture, one that honors truth over comfort, loyalty over convenience, and service over status. The rest of the world will call it outdated. Let them. History proves that every civilization that lost brotherhood soon lost freedom.

The tribe is the antidote to chaos. It restores order where society has lost it. It creates men who can be trusted again, by their families, by their communities, and by each other. That's how nations are rebuilt. *One tribe at a time.*

Built to Outlast

Every generation of men inherits a broken world and decides whether to fix it or make it worse. Weak generations build comfort and call it progress. Strong generations build structure and call it duty. The next generation will follow whichever men show up first.

That's why rebuilding the tribe isn't just about now, it's about legacy. A real man builds things that outlast him. He plants trees he'll never sit under. He raises sons who'll never need to recover from their fathers. He builds institutions, not platforms. That's how civilizations outlive chaos.

A tribe is the incubator of legacy. It passes down skill, wisdom, and standards the way old craftsmen passed down trade secrets. Every man who joins a brotherhood commits to something bigger than himself, not because it's easy, but because it's right.

Legacy isn't built in comfort. It's built in consistency.

A man who shows up year after year, decade after decade, will shape more lives than any celebrity or politician. The future doesn't belong to whoever shouts the loudest. It belongs to whoever builds the deepest.

The tribe teaches that no man is too small to matter. The father teaching his son to tie his shoes is building civilization. The coach mentoring boys after practice is building civilization. The neighbor checking on a struggling family is building civilization. That's how nations rise, not through grand speeches, but through ordinary men living with uncommon strength.

Rebuilding the tribe also means passing on culture through example. The next generation won't learn masculinity from lectures. They'll learn it by watching. They'll study how men handle conflict, treat women, pray, lead, and work. Every man is someone's model, whether he wants to be or not.

The tribe must protect that truth. Every action echoes. Every word plants something.

The standard has to stay high, not for pride, but for protection. Boys imitate what they see. If they see chaos, they'll repeat it. If they see strength and calm, they'll build on it.

That's why every man in the tribe has a duty to mentor. Teach a skill. Share a story. Be the man you wish you had when you were younger. Brotherhood without mentorship is incomplete. It dies with the men who lived it. Brotherhood with mentorship multiplies for generations.

As these tribes grow, they'll begin to restore something society forgot, trust. Trust is the foundation of order. You can't have functioning schools, businesses, or governments without it. But trust doesn't start in politics. It starts in relationships. In circles of men who keep their word, tell the truth, and protect what's right.

That kind of trust can rebuild communities faster than any policy. People follow men they believe in. When they see a tribe of disciplined, honest, reliable men, they start believing in order again. They start believing in hope again.

That's the power of brotherhood, it radiates. It spreads strength through example. It gives people something real to look at in a world drowning in fake.

The mission of every modern tribe is to restore faith in masculinity, not as domination, but as duty. Not as noise, but as presence. The kind of masculinity that fixes things, holds the line, and keeps promises.

That's the masculinity that built bridges, freed nations, raised families, and led communities. The kind that doesn't need slogans because results speak louder.

If we want that again, we have to live it.

The new tribe of men must show the world what responsibility looks like. What integrity feels like. What sacrifice still means.

Every man who joins this movement, whether in a small town gym or a boardroom or a church basement, is part of something historic. The world may never thank you, but your sons will. Your grandsons will. They'll inherit the world you rebuilt.

You can already feel the hunger for it. Men are tired of isolation. Tired of guilt. Tired of being told that strength is shameful. Deep down, they know the truth: the world doesn't work without men who show up. The culture can mock them, but it can't replace them.

Rebuilding the tribe means men stop waiting to be understood and start proving why they're necessary.

You don't need approval to lead. You just need commitment.

Every act of strength, every moment of loyalty, every display of courage is a protest against decay.

It starts with you. Find your brothers. Train together. Build something. Hold each other to standards the world abandoned. When men unite under principle, they become unbreakable.

The tribes we rebuild today will be the backbone of tomorrow's revival. They will raise sons who stand tall, daughters who feel safe, and communities that run on trust instead of fear. They will restore what comfort and chaos have stolen, honor.

And someday, when someone asks how we rebuilt America's men, the answer will be simple.

We found each other again. We remembered who we were. We rebuilt the tribe.

16

THE MAKING OF A MAN

A man isn't born. He's built.

He's built through trial, correction, responsibility, and resistance. The problem today isn't that men have changed, it's that the world stopped demanding they become men in the first place. Boys are allowed to stay boys forever. There are no rites of passage, no expectations, no tests that measure whether they can stand on their own.

And I mean FOREVER.

According to a Pew Research study (2020), 52 percent of young adults aged 18-29 still live with their parents, the highest percentage since the Great Depression. But here's the kicker: according to the same study, only 28 percent of them are actively looking for their own place.

The rest? They're comfortable.

Free rent, Mom does the laundry, Dad pays for the streaming services. Why would they leave? Your grandfather moved out at 18 to start a family. You moved back in at 28 because rent is "too expensive" and your degree in Communications didn't pan out.

The difference isn't the economy. It's that nobody ever made you uncomfortable enough to force you to grow the fuck up.

Every civilization before ours had a process. A boy left the comfort of the home, faced challenge, and returned with skill and confidence. It wasn't just symbolic, it was survival. If he couldn't protect, provide, or lead, the tribe suffered. His strength mattered to everyone.

Now? The modern world removed all of that. Boys grow up without consequence. They can spend their twenties on video games, their thirties chasing dopamine, and still be told they're "finding themselves."

No culture that lets men drift survives for long.

The Eight Steps to Manhood

Manhood requires friction. Without friction, you get comfort. And comfort without challenge breeds weakness.

That's why we have to bring back the making of a man, the process that turns potential into power, chaos into discipline, and self-interest into service.

The first step in that process is responsibility. Every man needs something to carry. That's how you develop strength. Without weight, you stay soft. Responsibility isn't punishment, it's training. It gives your actions meaning.

A boy without responsibility becomes dangerous, not because he's evil, but because he's idle. When energy has nowhere to go, it destroys instead of builds. That's why aimless men turn angry. They need purpose, not pity.

The second step is struggle. Boys must face resistance early. It doesn't matter what form it takes, sports, military service, physical labor, even failure. What matters is that they learn what it feels like to push through pain and earn victory.

Every man remembers the first time he realized he could endure. That memory becomes armor. It's the difference between quitting and continuing later in life. You can't hand that to a boy. He has to earn it.

The third step is skill. Competence breeds confidence. We've raised a generation of men fluent in theory but incapable in practice. They can argue online for hours but can't change a tire, manage a team, or fix what's broken in front of them. That's not intelligence, it's impotence.

The numbers on this are humiliating. Basic skills are dying out. Fewer than half of drivers today can change a flat tire without calling for help, according to a 2025 FinanceBuzz study and the number drops even lower when you ask younger men. We've raised a generation that can code an app but can't fix a car. It's not just cars, it's homes too. Surveys show that most millennials can't fix a leaky faucet, patch drywall, or replace a light fixture without YouTube. A 2021 Puronics survey found that 60% of millennials didn't know how to fix a faucet, and only one in five felt confident repairing drywall. The number wasn't broken down by gender, but the point stands: the hands-on skills that once defined adulthood are vanishing. Money used to be a language every man spoke. Now most can't even balance a checkbook, let alone explain compound interest. The National Financial Educators Council's 2023 data shows Americans in their twenties score around 70% on basic financial literacy tests, barely passing. The TIAA Institute found men under 35 answered just over half of financial questions correctly. Translation: the average guy can lift at the gym but not lift his credit score. You can quote Jordan Peterson and debate politics on Reddit, but you can't fix a toilet, change your oil, or understand your own credit score. Congratulations, you're a Google Scholar with no actual life skills. Your great-grandfather built his own house. You need to call a guy to hang a TV.

A boy needs to see his hands create something real. He needs to know that effort translates to results. When you work with your hands, you learn patience, precision, and pride. When you only work with screens, you lose connection to reality.

That's why every society that valued strength had apprenticeships, trades, and crafts. Skill wasn't a hobby, it was identity.

The fourth step is mentorship. Every man needs someone ahead of him to guide the way and someone behind him to pull up. The chain keeps men accountable. It's how values survive generations.

We used to have that built into life, fathers, uncles, coaches, veterans. Now, most boys grow up mentored by algorithms. They get advice from influencers instead of elders. It's no wonder they're confused. Guidance without wisdom is manipulation.

Mentorship doesn't have to be formal. It just has to be real. A man who's been through pain should reach back. That's how strength multiplies. A boy who learns from an honest mentor skips years of mistakes.

The fifth step is *correction*. Modern parenting fears this word, but it's essential. Correction doesn't mean cruelty. It means honesty. A boy who's never corrected becomes a man who can't take criticism. He sees feedback as attack and accountability as oppression. That's how weakness hides behind pride.

Discipline teaches humility. It teaches that actions have consequences and that you don't get to rewrite reality because you don't like it. That's a lesson men need early, before life teaches it the hard way.

The sixth step is *mission*. Every man has to know who he serves and why. Without that, he drifts into distraction. Mission pulls a man through hardship. It makes sacrifice worthwhile. It makes work meaningful.

Mission is what separates mature men from perpetual boys. A boy wants attention. A man wants impact. A boy asks what he can get. A man asks what he can build.

The seventh step is *restraint*. Modern men are told to express everything, every emotion, every impulse, every desire. That's not freedom. That's chaos. A strong man knows how to control himself.

Restraint is power. The man who can stay calm while others panic, who can stay kind while others insult, who can stay disciplined when others indulge, that's the man people follow.

Without restraint, you get indulgence. With indulgence, you get addiction. Every fall from greatness, whether personal or national, starts with men who lost restraint.

The final step is *service*. All strength must point outward. A man who lives only for himself eventually turns bitter. The greatest satisfaction comes from protecting, building, and guiding others. Service completes the circle. It's the proof that your strength was real.

You can measure a man's worth by what he's willing to suffer for. Boys suffer for ego. Men suffer for others.

That's what the making of a man truly is, a transformation from self-centeredness to stewardship. It's the process that turns energy into virtue and power into peace. *And it's a process we've abandoned.*

The Participation Trophy Pandemic

Our schools don't teach it. Our entertainment mocks it. Our politics ignore it. But deep down, every man knows he needs it. The proof is in the restlessness that never goes away, the feeling that something's missing even when life looks good on paper.

What's missing isn't money or pleasure. It's initiation. It's the passage from comfort to calling. Until that happens, no boy becomes a man, no matter how old he gets.

Modern life has made it too easy to skip the making. Boys can go from adolescence to adulthood without ever being tested. They can earn trophies without winning, degrees without working, and approval without earning it. We told them their feelings mattered more than their performance, and in doing so, we took away their reason to improve.

Here's what that actually looks like: We've raised a generation allergic to losing. Youth sports have turned into therapy sessions with scoreboards. A 2022 Aspen Institute report found that fewer than one in four kids play competitive sports past age thirteen, mostly because adults have drained the meaning out of it.

When everything earns a trophy, nothing means anything.

According to LinkedIn data (2023), the average entry-level job posting now requires "2+ years experience" because employers have learned that a college degree doesn't mean you can actually DO anything.

We created a generation of boys who've been rewarded for existing, not achieving. Then we act surprised when they're 27, still living at home, and wondering why nobody takes them seriously. You got a trophy for showing up. Congratulations. The real world doesn't give those out.

Challenge isn't cruelty. It's the greatest form of respect you can give a boy. It says, *"You're capable of more."* When you protect boys from struggle, you tell them they're weak. When you let them struggle and succeed, you prove they're strong.

Every generation before ours knew this instinctively. Farmers taught sons to work the fields before dawn. Soldiers trained recruits until they broke and rebuilt them. Fathers taught their boys how to take a punch, fix an engine, or stand up for a friend. Today we call that *"toxic."* In reality, it's training for life.

Men who haven't faced struggle don't become peaceful, they become volatile. A boy who never learned how to confront difficulty with discipline will lash out when life hits him later. He won't know how to regulate anger, endure hardship, or keep his word when things get tough.

You don't have to send a boy into battle to teach him manhood. You just have to stop cushioning him from every consequence. Let him earn things. Let him fail. Let him feel the sting of loss so he can understand what it means to win.

Failure isn't final. It's feedback.

Every man who's ever built anything worth remembering has failed more times than he succeeded. The difference between a man who gives up and one who rises is the belief that struggle isn't the end, it's the beginning of strength.

You can't simulate hardship with words. It has to be lived. That's why physical challenge is so important. Sports, martial arts, manual labor, anything that requires sweat and persistence, teaches lessons no lecture can. A boy who pushes his body learns the limits of his mind. He learns control, timing, and patience. He learns respect, not from being told to give it, but by earning it from others who fight beside him.

The same applies to work. The man who's swung a hammer, poured concrete, or fixed a car understands cause and effect in a way that classroom theory can't teach. He learns that results don't come from talk, they come from effort. That lesson alone separates men who build from men who complain.

That's what our society lost when it stopped valuing skilled labor. We taught boys that working with their hands was beneath them. We told them success meant an office, not a workshop. Now we have millions of young men with degrees and debt but no useful skills. They're anxious, bored, and confused because they don't know how to turn effort into value.

Bring Back the Builders

Bring back the sense of accomplishment that comes from creation. There's no shame in craftsmanship. There's honor in it. The trades built civilization. They built every bridge, every city, every home. When a man learns to build, he learns to believe in himself again.

Strength without humility becomes arrogance. But humility without strength becomes weakness. The making of a man is about balance. You teach him power so he can protect, and humility so he won't abuse it.

That's why men need older men. Mentorship turns raw power into controlled power. It's how wisdom passes forward. A boy raised only by peers becomes reckless. A man mentored by elders becomes grounded. Mentorship isn't about perfection. *It's about honesty.*

A mentor doesn't need to have all the answers. He just needs to tell the truth about what he's seen and survived. That truth saves the next man from repeating the same mistakes.

In ancient tribes, initiation meant facing fear directly. In modern times, initiation should mean the same thing, just in different form.

Every man needs a moment where he faces something bigger than himself and refuses to quit.

For some, it's military service. For others, it's fatherhood, business, or recovery from failure. What matters is that it forces growth.

The world today avoids that moment. We hand out comfort instead of challenge. We replace discipline with therapy, mentorship with social media, and wisdom with trends. We treat pain as pathology instead of a teacher. But pain is what forges character. A man who runs from pain never finds peace.

No one enjoys suffering, but every strong man thanks it later. Pain sharpens you. It reveals what you're made of. It strips away lies and excuses. You learn that you're capable of far more than you thought. That knowledge can't be taken from you.

That's why men need struggle early, because if they don't learn to face pain in youth, life will deliver it in adulthood when it's much harder to handle. Better to bleed in practice than to fall apart in the field.

The next part of manhood is restraint, the forgotten virtue. Strength without restraint destroys. Restraint is what makes strength righteous. It's the ability to control your impulses when everything in you wants to react. It's the discipline to walk away when pride says fight, to listen when anger says speak, to stay when fear says run.

Restraint separates men from boys. It's what gives leadership credibility. No one trusts a man who can't control himself. Control isn't repression, it's command. A man in command of himself commands respect from others.

Renowned clinical psychologist and best-selling author *Jordan Pederson* brilliantly said, *"If you're not a formidable force, there's no morality in your self-control. If you're incapable of violence, not being violent isn't a virtue."*

Service Before Self

The final stage of maturity is service. Strength, skill, and restraint all exist for one reason: to serve something bigger. Whether it's family, community, faith, or nation, service gives direction to strength. Without it, you get wasted potential.

A selfish man may succeed for a while, but he never feels fulfilled. The man who serves others finds meaning in every sacrifice. He sees his effort ripple outward. That's legacy.

Legacy isn't what you leave behind, it's what you build while you're here. Every boy you help raise right, every friend you keep honest, every act of courage you take part in, adds to it.

The Making Of A Man

The making of a man doesn't end when he becomes one. It continues for life. Because manhood isn't a destination, it's a discipline.

Manhood doesn't need to be reinvented. It needs to be remembered. Every generation before ours understood what we've forgotten, that men are the backbone of stability. When men are strong, communities stand. When they weaken, everything collapses.

We keep pretending masculinity is some kind of social experiment that can be redefined to fit modern comfort. But masculinity is older than politics, older than culture. It's nature. It's hardwired into every man, the instinct to protect, to build, to compete, to provide. You can suppress it, medicate it, mock it, or label it toxic, but it never disappears. It just reemerges in distorted ways when it's denied.

That's what we're seeing now, directionless men searching for meaning in chaos. They chase status symbols instead of skills, pleasure instead of purpose. They drift from one distraction to another because no one ever showed them how to stand still and face life with intent.

The path back isn't complicated. It starts small. A father teaching his son to shake a hand firmly. A coach demanding accountability. A boss who expects excellence. A friend who tells the truth instead of validation. Each of those moments, small as they seem, builds a man.

Manhood isn't a seminar. It's a standard. Every time a boy sees an older man hold himself with integrity, he learns what strength looks like. Every time a father keeps his word, a boy learns what honor sounds like. Every time a man steps up when others back down, the next generation learns what courage feels like.

That's how manhood is passed down, not through slogans or hashtags, but through example.

We need to stop asking "What happened to men?" and start showing boys what men look like. Words won't fix this. Leadership will.

Leadership doesn't require titles. It requires consistency. A man who keeps showing up, even when it's inconvenient, will do more for his family, his friends, and his community than any policy or speech.

That's the secret no one talks about, masculinity thrives in small moments. In getting up early when you'd rather sleep. In keeping a promise when no one's watching. In doing the hard thing when the easy thing would get applause.

Every man can start there. You don't need permission. You don't need perfection. You just need to begin.

Because the truth is, no one is coming to save men. We have to save ourselves. We have to rebuild the traditions we lost, the standards we abandoned, and the brotherhood we forgot.

That starts by rejecting comfort as a lifestyle. Comfort isn't evil, but it's addictive. Once you build your life around it, everything else falls apart. Comfort numbs ambition, kills curiosity, and replaces action with excuses.

A real man chooses challenge over comfort because he knows what's on the other side, growth, respect, and meaning. Those are the things that make life worth living.

The making of a man is not a gentle process. It's forged in pressure and refined in patience. You'll lose people. You'll fail often. You'll question yourself. But every scar you earn in that fight becomes proof that you stood your ground.

At the end of a man's life, no one will care about the hashtags he used or the opinions he posted. They'll remember whether he stood firm when it mattered. Whether he protected his family. Whether he built something that lasted. Whether he made others stronger by knowing him.

That's what legacy looks like. Not fame. Not wealth. Influence built on respect.

And the beautiful thing about legacy is that it doesn't require permission either. You can start building it right now, where you stand, with what you have.

If you're a father, lead with strength and love. If you're a son, listen and learn. If you're a brother, hold the line. If you're a friend, tell the truth. If you're lost, start small, take responsibility for one thing and do it well.

Manhood returns when men remember what's always been true.

1. **Responsibility** — *Every man needs something to carry. Strength is built by weight, not comfort.*

2. **Struggle** — *Pain is not punishment. It's how endurance is earned and character is proven.*

3. **Skill** — *Competence creates confidence. Build something real with your own hands and mind.*

4. **Mentorship** — *Learn from men who've been through it. Then reach back and guide the next.*

5. **Correction** — *Accept discipline and feedback. Humility keeps pride from destroying you.*

6. **Mission** — *Know what you serve and why. Purpose separates men from boys.*

7. **Restraint** — *Control your impulses. Strength without control becomes destruction.*

8. **Service** — *Use your strength for others. That's how a man completes the circle.*

That's it. That's the making of a man.

No degree can replace it. No government can legislate it. No movement can cancel it. Because it's not a trend, it's the foundation of civilization.

We've spent too long apologizing for the qualities that made men great. It's time to bring them back, not for dominance, but for duty. Not for pride, but for peace.

When men remember who they are, everything else falls into place. Families grow stronger. Communities become safer. Nations regain direction.

The next generation is watching. They don't need slogans about equality or identity. They need examples of responsibility and strength. They need men who live the code. That's how we rebuild the future, one man at a time, one action at a time, one day at a time.

Because every boy is watching someone. The only question is, what will he see? If he sees men of purpose, discipline, and courage, he'll follow their lead.If he doesn't, he'll follow the noise.

The future depends on which one he finds first.

17

THE CODE

FOR RECLAIMING MANHOOD

You don't need a new philosophy. You need the old one, the code that built every great nation and held every strong family together. It's been forgotten, buried under decades of ideology and comfort. But it's still true. You can feel it.

Truth is the foundation of manhood. Lies build comfort. Truth builds character. If you want to be respected, tell the truth, especially when it hurts.

Here it is again. Ten rules. Simple. Unbreakable. Proven by history.

1. Responsibility Before Rights.
2. Strength in Restraint.
3. Truth Over Comfort.
4. Work Builds Worth.
5. Honor Your Word.
6. Protect What Matters.
7. Lead Quietly, Serve Loudly.
8. Master Pain.
9. Respect Women, Reject Weakness.
10. Leave the World Better.

That's the code. Simple. Unbreakable. Proven by history, forgotten by culture. Every man reading this knows it's right. You can feel it, that pull in your gut that says you were made for more than comfort. That's not nostalgia. That's memory.

When men live by this code, the world works. Families are stable. Women feel safe. Children grow strong. Nations stay free.

That's the power of masculine order. Not domination, direction. Not control, protection. Not ego, endurance.

You don't need to wait for a movement. You are the movement.

You don't need to wait for permission. You have it already.

Start where you stand. Put your phone down. Pick up something heavy. Call your father. Forgive your brother. Hug your kid. Shake a man's hand and mean it.

Start today. Start small. But start.

The world doesn't need more talk. It needs more men who act like men.

You don't rebuild a nation by shouting online.

You rebuild it by waking up early, working hard, keeping your word, and teaching your sons to do the same.

You rebuild it by protecting women, mentoring boys, and standing firm when everyone else caves.

You rebuild it by living the code.

Live it. Teach it. Pass it on.

18

RAISING MY DAUGHTER IN THIS WORLD

Every man eventually reaches a point where the fight becomes personal. For me, that moment came the day I held my daughter in my arms. The world looked different after that. Every headline, every classroom, every piece of culture suddenly mattered in a new way. Because now it wasn't just about saving men, it was about saving the world she would grow up in.

And let me tell you what that world looks like right now. According to the CDC's 2021 *Youth Risk Behavior Survey*, the share of high school girls reporting persistent feelings of sadness or hopelessness has jumped nearly 60 percent since 2011, from 36% to 57%. The American Psychological Association reports that roughly 42% of teenage girls now meet the clinical criteria for depression, echoing the CDC's findings. And a 2023 Pew Research Center study found that 57% of teenage girls say they often or sometimes feel unsafe in public spaces.

My daughter is growing up in a world where young women are more anxious, more depressed, and more afraid than at any point in recorded history. And you want to know why? Because we spent the last 30 years systematically destroying the men who are supposed to protect them. Congratulations, we *"liberated"* women by removing their protection and then acted shocked when they don't feel safe anymore.

When I look at her, I don't see weakness. I see fire. I see the same boldness and curiosity that built this country. And I know her future will depend not only on her strength, but on the strength of the men around her, the ones she'll work with, trust, and maybe one day love. That's why this fight for men isn't against women. It's for them.

We've spent years pretending that men and women are interchangeable, as if erasing the differences between us somehow makes things fair. It doesn't. It makes both sides weaker. Men and women aren't meant to compete for dominance, they're meant to complete each other. Where one leads, the other balances. Where one builds, the other preserves. Civilization has always depended on that balance. *But we've destroyed it.*

We told women that needing men was shameful. We told men that leading women was oppressive. We confused equality with sameness, and in the process we erased respect. Now we have generations of lonely men and anxious women, both wondering why no one feels safe anymore.

My daughter deserves better than that. She deserves to live in a world where men stand for something again, not out of ego, but out of duty. She deserves to grow up seeing men who protect without apology, lead without dominance, and love without weakness.

That starts at home. The way a father treats his daughter becomes the way she expects to be treated by the world. If she grows up around strength, she won't confuse control for love. If she grows up around honor, she won't settle for flattery. If she grows up seeing men who lead with integrity, she'll know the difference between power and abuse.

Fathers shape daughters long before the world ever does.

That's why I take this responsibility seriously. I don't want my daughter to grow up thinking masculinity is something dangerous. I want her to know it's something sacred. It's what keeps the world standing when everything else collapses.

But I also want her to see that strength isn't loud. It isn't prideful. It's quiet confidence. It's patience. It's protection. It's the man who walks her across the street, the coach who demands her best, the teacher who tells her she can handle more than she thinks. That's real masculinity. That's what builds trust between the sexes again.

What She Needs to See

When I watch her at school, I see what most people miss, how quickly the culture tries to divide boys and girls into enemies. Every story, every movie, every message seems to say that one must lose for the other to win. Boys are told they're oppressors in training. Girls are told they're victims by default. Both are being lied to.

I see young boys at her school already afraid to speak their mind.

They've learned that confidence can be punished. That disagreement can be labeled as aggression. And that the safest path is silence.

That's not progress. *That's social conditioning.*

And when those boys grow up, what kind of men do they become? They either collapse into weakness or explode into anger. The middle ground, calm, strong, disciplined leadership, disappears.

That's why this cultural battle matters to me as a father. Because when we destroy men, we don't empower women. We end up with a generation of unprotected women, unsupported families, and unchecked chaos.

My daughter doesn't need a perfect man to protect her. She needs a world that respects the idea of one.

That's what I want to rebuild, a world where men are expected to be protectors again. Not because women are incapable, but because men are responsible. Protection isn't ownership. It's service.

When men serve, women thrive. When women respect men, men rise. It's a simple truth, but we've buried it under decades of ideological noise.

I want my daughter to grow up surrounded by men who are strong enough to lead and humble enough to listen. I want her to see that masculinity isn't a threat to femininity, it's its guardian. The strongest societies in history understood this. Rome, Greece, America in its prime, all built on the partnership of strong men and strong women working toward something bigger than themselves.

We've traded that partnership for competition. We've told women to be men and men to be less. The result isn't progress. It's confusion. No one knows what they're supposed to be anymore.

But when I look at my daughter, I see hope. I see the next generation that can fix this if we give them truth instead of politics. If we show them what balance really looks like.

She's growing up in Beverly Hills, one of the most image-driven cities in the world. Everywhere she looks, people are selling versions of success that have nothing to do with substance. And yet, when she comes home, she sees something different. She sees a father who works, who protects, who shows up. That matters more than any speech I'll ever give.

Because you can't teach masculinity in a classroom. You model it.

If we want the next generation to believe in men again, we have to give them men worth believing in. *That starts with fathers.*

The Most Important Job

Fatherhood isn't a hobby. It's not something you do between work and the gym. It's the foundation of everything that lasts. A father is the first mirror a child looks into, the first leader she follows, and the first man who teaches her what love feels like.

If that mirror is cracked, everything that comes after reflects the damage. That's what's missing in so many homes today, not money, not opportunity, but men. *Present men. Steady men.*

Men who don't disappear when things get hard.

A man's presence shapes more than his family. It shapes society. The decline of fatherhood is the quiet root of nearly every major social crisis we face. Crime, poverty, addiction, mental illness, all rise where fathers vanish. You can trace it like a map. The absence of men creates chaos that no government can fix.

The data proves it. Children from fatherless homes are more likely to drop out of school, struggle with depression, or end up in the justice system. Boys without fathers grow up searching for one, often in all the wrong places. They find it in gangs, influencers, or anyone who looks confident enough to follow.That's not rebellion. That's hunger. *The hunger to be led.*

And girls without fathers? They often grow up learning to doubt men or to depend on the wrong ones. Without a healthy example of male strength and care, they can't easily tell the difference between protection and control. They learn to survive instead of trust.

The statistics on fatherless daughters are absolutely devastating. According to data compiled by the *CDC* and the *U.S. Census Bureau*, girls who grow up without their fathers are several times more likely to face serious trouble later, roughly three times more likely to become pregnant as teens and five times more likely to live in poverty.

Research also shows they experience significantly higher rates of depression and self-harm. The *Journal of Youth and Adolescence (2022)* found that fatherless daughters have significantly higher rates of eating disorders, self-harm, and risky sexual behavior. *Why?* Because when Dad isn't there to show her what real male strength and protection looks like, she goes looking for it in all the wrong places. She mistakes attention for affection, control for care, and abuse for love. That's not her fault. That's ours. We removed the blueprint and then blamed her for not knowing how to read the map.

That's why fatherhood matters. It's not just emotional support. It's structure. It's safety. It's legacy. A man teaches his daughter what boundaries look like, what standards sound like, and what character feels like.

My daughter will grow up hearing one truth from me: real strength serves others. The loudest man in the room isn't always the strongest. The strongest man is the one who controls himself. The one who listens before he speaks, acts before he complains, and takes responsibility when no one else does.

That's the kind of man I want her to respect, and the kind I want her to expect.

Because the world won't protect her innocence. It will try to exploit it. Every app, every influencer, every marketing campaign will try to convince her that attention is the same as worth. That self-expression is the same as self-respect. It's not. One earns dignity. The other rents it.

And let's talk about what that exploitation actually looks like. According to research from *Common Sense Media (2023)*, the average teenage girl now spends 4.5 hours per day on social media, where she's exposed to an estimated 400-600 edited images of "perfect" women daily.

The result?

A study by the *Royal Society for Public Health (2017)* found that Instagram was the single most damaging social media platform for young people's mental health, especially girls. The research linked it directly to higher rates of anxiety, depression, loneliness, and body image distortion. Nothing's changed since. If anything, it's worse. Every filter, every like, every fake-perfect body tells girls they'll never be enough, and it's breaking them.

OnlyFans, which launched in 2016, now has over 2.1 million "content creators," with 70 percent of them being women under 25 *(OnlyFans Statistics, 2023)*. We've created a digital marketplace where teenage girls can monetize their bodies for likes and subscriptions, and we're calling it "empowerment." No. It's exploitation with a PayPal account.

Your daughter doesn't need 10,000 Instagram followers. She needs one father who tells her she's worth more than pixels and attention from strangers.

It's my job to make sure she knows the difference.

The Gloves Never Come Off

That's why fathers must stay in the fight. You don't get to check out. You don't get to say, "the culture is lost" and give up. You're the line that keeps the culture from collapsing further. You're the shield.

And being a shield doesn't mean hiding her from the world. It means preparing her for it. Teaching her how to think critically, how to trust her instincts, and how to recognize strength in others. That's how you raise a daughter who doesn't fear the world, she faces it with clarity.

Our daughters need men who are stable. Not perfect, not polished, but solid. The kind of men who don't lie, who don't quit, and who don't make excuses. The kind of men who understand that leadership isn't about being right, it's about being responsible.

The truth is that our sons and daughters are watching us more than they're listening. They see how we treat their mother. They see how we react under pressure. They see what we prioritize. You can't fake that. A man's life teaches louder than his words ever will.

That's why I live by one rule: if I want my daughter to grow up strong, I must be the kind of man she admires.

She won't remember every lecture I give. But she'll remember if I kept my word. She'll remember if I was calm when things got hard. She'll remember if I looked her in the eyes when she spoke. That's how respect is built, moment by moment.

And it's not just about daughters. It's about sons too. They need to see what right looks like. They need to see a man who doesn't run from pressure, who doesn't whine, who doesn't blame the world for his failures. They need to see a man who gets up every day and carries the weight quietly.

That's what resets a generation, not speeches, not slogans, not social media campaigns.

Example: Every man who steps up changes his bloodline.

When you become a better father, you're not just fixing your family. You're fixing your future grandchildren, your neighborhood, your city.

That's how this spreads, one home at a time.

So yes, I wrote this book for men. But I also wrote it for her. Because I want her to live in a world where men matter again. A world where they build more than they destroy. A world where they lead with purpose and protect with pride.

If she grows up in that world, she'll be free. *That's what's at stake.*

If we don't fix the crisis of men, our daughters will pay for it. They'll inherit a world of weak men pretending to be strong, and strong women forced to act like men just to survive. That's not empowerment. That's imbalance.

I don't want that for her. I want her to grow up knowing that femininity isn't fragility. It's power in a different form. It's grace, intuition, and strength of spirit. And it flourishes best when real masculinity stands beside it, not above it, not below it, beside it.

That's what I want to restore. Not patriarchy. Partnership.

Because the strongest societies are built on families that balance both, men who lead with honor and women who nurture with wisdom. That's what we used to know. That's what we lost. And that's what we must rebuild.

Every father eventually realizes that the world won't change fast enough for his child. That's when the mission becomes personal.

You stop waiting for politicians, schools, or culture to fix it. You look in the mirror and understand that if your daughter is going to grow up in a world that values truth and strength, it's because you built it around her.

That's where I'm at. I can't control the noise outside, but I can control what happens inside my home. That's where I draw the line. That's where character gets built.

My daughter will learn that being protected isn't the same as being controlled. She'll know that leadership isn't dominance and that respect isn't fear. She'll learn that strength and kindness aren't opposites, they're partners. I'll show her that men who control their emotions aren't repressed; they're responsible. That discipline isn't cold; it's love.

I want her to understand that good men still exist. That they're out there, quiet, steady, reliable, carrying the world on their backs while no one claps. The kind of men who change tires in the rain, who work when they're tired, who show up even when it hurts. The kind of men who make society possible but rarely get thanked for it.

I want her to know that those men matter more than any influencer, celebrity, or politician she'll ever see on a screen.

And I want her to grow up expecting those men, not settling for less.

That's what this whole book has been about. Not preaching, not nostalgia, rebuilding expectations. Because a culture's expectations shape its reality. If we expect men to fail, they will. If we expect them to rise, they can.

The Masculine Truth

For too long, we've told boys that manhood is dangerous, and we've told girls that masculinity is oppression. It's time to stop lying.

Masculinity isn't the problem. It's the missing piece.

If we raise boys to be men of integrity, discipline, and courage, we won't need to keep building more laws, programs, and campaigns to fix what fatherhood used to handle. We'll have homes that raise good men and women who trust them.

That's how a nation heals. Not through politics, through parents.

I think about that a lot when I tuck my daughter in at night. She doesn't care about debates or ideology. She cares that I'm there. She cares that I keep my promises. She cares that she's safe.

That's what every child really wants, presence.

And that's what every generation of men must provide.

Presence isn't just being in the room. It's being awake. It's turning off your phone when she's talking. It's sitting at the dinner table instead of scrolling in the corner. It's showing up to the school recital, the practice, the game, even when you're exhausted. Because one day she'll remember that. And she'll measure every man she meets against it.

That's how you change the future, one child's memory at a time.

Fatherhood isn't glamorous. It doesn't trend. It doesn't go viral. But it matters more than anything else.

The world doesn't need more activists or influencers. It needs more fathers who build stable homes. It needs more mothers who raise daughters who respect men and sons who become them.

That's how we rebuild trust between the sexes. That's how we restore order to chaos.

I know that I can't protect my daughter from every threat. But I can prepare her to face them. I can raise her to recognize truth, to seek character over charisma, and to understand that love isn't a feeling, it's commitment.

And I can show her, through my own actions, what real manhood looks like.

Not perfect. Not polished. Just steady. That's what she'll remember.

When she's older, and she sees the world for what it is, messy, loud, divided, I want her to know that she had a father who stood for something. A man who didn't bend to culture, who didn't chase applause, who didn't confuse being liked with being right.

That's the legacy I want to leave her. Not money, not fame, certainty.

The certainty that men can still be good. That truth still matters. That faith still holds. Because if she grows up believing that, she'll be unshakable.

That's why this fight matters so much. It's not about men versus women. It's about protecting the balance that built civilization.

Men and women together, each strong in their own ways, each honoring the other's strength.

If we get that balance right again, our daughters will grow up safe, our sons will grow up strong, and our nation will stand tall again. *That's the real endgame.*

So to every father reading this, start today. Be the man your daughter looks up to, and the man your son looks to follow.

You don't need to be perfect. *You just need to be present.*

Show her what protection looks like. Show him what discipline looks like. Let both see what love looks like when it's built on truth.

That's how you fix a generation. That's how you fix the world.

My daughter's future depends on the kind of men her generation produces.

And it starts with us.

19

THE CALL: RECLAIMING MEN

This isn't just a book. It's a line in the sand.

We've talked about the fall of men, how our culture mocked them, medicated them, and replaced purpose with pleasure.

We've seen what happens when fathers disappear, when strength is shamed, when truth is traded for comfort.

The evidence is everywhere: broken families, lost boys, restless men wandering through life without mission or meaning.

And let me give you the final scorecard, because the numbers don't lie. Male suicide rates: up 35% since 2000. Fatherless homes: affecting 1 in 4 American children. Male college enrollment: dropped to 40%. Prime-age male employment: millions sitting at home. Marriage rates: historic lows. Testosterone levels: down 20%. Birth rates: below replacement. Young men living with parents at 28: highest rate since the Depression.

This isn't a "crisis." This is a collapse. And if we don't stop it NOW, there won't BE a next generation of strong men to fix it. That ends now.

Because men are not the problem. Weakness is.

And weakness has been sold to us as sensitivity, progress, and kindness. It isn't. Weakness destroys nations. Strength builds them. And it's time we stop apologizing for having any.

For too long, men have been told to sit down, stay quiet, and stop leading. We listened. And while we sat silent, the world fell apart.

Families fractured. Classrooms filled with confusion. Faith faded. Honor disappeared. It's time to stand back up.

You've spent years shrinking yourself to make other people comfortable. Moderating your tone. Censoring your thoughts. Walking on eggshells. Apologizing for taking up space, for being competitive, for wanting to lead.

And what did it get you?

Respect? No.
A promotion? Probably not.
A happy life? Doubt it.

It got you resentment, confusion, and the deep sense that you're living someone else's life.

So stop. Stop apologizing for existing. The world doesn't respect men who apologize. It respects men who stand for something.

And let's be clear about what you're apologizing for. You're apologizing for having testosterone. For wanting to lead. For being competitive. For taking up space. For having opinions. For not crying enough. For being *"too confident"* or *"too aggressive"* or *"too masculine."*

Real masculinity isn't toxic. It's protective. It's loyal. It's disciplined.

It's the force that runs toward danger when everyone else runs away. It's the reason civilization exists at all.

And if you're reading this, you already know it's time to rise.

Because when men rise, everything rises with them, families, communities, and civilizations. When men lead with strength and humility, women feel safe again, children feel protected again, and society feels stable again.

We don't need men who dominate. We need men who discipline themselves. We don't need men who rage. We need men who endure. We don't need perfect men. We need men who refuse to quit.

We've seen the hunger. The rage. The quiet refusal to accept this as normal. You feel it, don't you? That pull in your gut. That voice that says you were made for more than this. That's not nostalgia. That's memory. It's your blood remembering what your culture forgot.

This Is Where It Starts

You don't need permission. You already have it. You just need to decide that you're done apologizing for being a man.

It starts with you. With the man reading this right now wondering if anything will ever change.

You can feel the hunger out there, boys without guidance, fathers without confidence, men without mission.

The answer is simple: it changes when you do.

One man. One decision. One refusal to quit. That's how civilizations are restored. Not through politics or protests, but through men who wake up, look at the ruins, and say, *"I'll rebuild this."*

You don't need a platform. You don't need followers. You don't need fame. You just need to start.

Wake up tomorrow and act like the man you're supposed to be. Do it again the next day. And the day after that. Eventually, people will notice. They won't say anything at first, but they'll watch. They'll see that you're different. That you're steady. That you keep your word when it costs you something.

That's how trust is rebuilt, through consistency. Through showing up when no one expects you to. Through carrying weight quietly without complaining.

The world is full of talkers. It's starving for men who just do the work.

The Standard You Walk Past

Every man sets a standard. Not with words, but with what he tolerates.

The lies he lets slide. The laziness he excuses. The disrespect he allows. If you walk past weakness and say nothing, you've just set a new standard. If you see a man failing and don't correct him, you've told him failure is acceptable. *That's not cruelty. That's clarity.*

Men need to know where the line is. When you hold that line, you give other men something to aim for. When you let it blur, you make it easier for everyone to sink.

A man who lives by standards becomes a lighthouse. Others can find their way by watching him. That's leadership. Not speeches or titles, just a life that points north.

The Ripple You Don't See

You think your choices only affect you. They don't.

Every decision you make creates a ripple. Your kids watch how you treat their mother. Your coworkers see how you handle pressure. Your neighbors notice whether you keep your word or let things slide. None of it is neutral. All of it teaches.

When you rebuild yourself, you rebuild your bloodline.

Your son will inherit your habits. Your daughter will inherit your standards. Your grandchildren will inherit the world you either built or allowed to decay.

Weakness passes down just as easily as strength. So if you want to change the future, start with the present. Start with your body, your habits, your word.

Fix what's broken in your own life before you try to fix the world. That's not selfish, that's strategic. A man who can't lead himself can't lead anyone else.

The Choice

If you're reading this, you've reached the end of the book. But this isn't the end of the fight. This is where it begins.

This is your call to return to the old code, the one that built nations, protected families, and forged peace through strength. You have a choice to make right now.

You can close this book, nod your head, say "that was good," and go back to exactly what you were doing before. Scroll. Distract. Drift. Let the system win because it's easier than resisting.

Most men will choose that. They'll agree with everything they read, feel motivated for about six hours, and then go right back to the life that was slowly killing them.

Or you can decide that this is the line.

This is where you stop making excuses. This is where you stop waiting for someone to save you and you start becoming the man who saves others. Not because you're perfect, but because you're willing.

That decision, that single moment of commitment, is the hinge your entire life turns on. Everything before this was preparation. Everything after this is proof.

There's a quiet revolution happening right now. No one's covering it because it doesn't make headlines. It's not loud. It's not political. It's just thousands of men across the country who decided to stop apologizing for being men.

They're waking up early. They're training their bodies. They're turning off the noise. They're building businesses, raising families, mentoring boys, and standing firm when the culture tells them to bend.

They're not organizing. They're just living. And that's terrifying to the system, because you can't co-opt a movement that has no leader. You can't cancel men who don't care about being liked.

This book was written for men who refuse to be the last strong generation. For fathers who are terrified of the world their kids are inheriting. For sons who grew up without guidance and are determined to become the men they never had. For every man who feels that quiet rage inside, the rage that comes from knowing you're capable of more.

That rage is good. It's fuel. But rage without direction is just destruction.

Channel it. Use it. Let it drive you to become the man the world told you not to be.

Because they were wrong about you.

You're not toxic. You're not the problem. You're the solution.

And when enough men realize that, everything changes.

The collapse stops. The rebuild begins. And a generation of boys grows up knowing what strength looks like again.

That's the mission. That's the movement. That's why this book exists.

Now go build the world you want your kids to inherit.

Don't wait for permission. Don't wait for the right moment.

Start today. Start now.

The Final Words

Reclaiming Men isn't about nostalgia or politics.

Its about restoration.

The restoration of honor. Of brotherhood. Of discipline. Of faith.

The restoration of men who know who they are and what they're here to do. Because when men remember who they are, everything else falls back into place.

So to every man reading this, rise.

Not in anger, but in strength.

Not in resentment, but in purpose.

Not against women, but for your sons and daughters.

Not for ego, but for legacy.

Rise because the world needs you.

Rise because your family needs you.

Rise because your country can't survive without you.

And rise because if you don't, nobody else will.

Your wife can't do it for you. Your boss won't do it for you. The government sure as hell won't do it for you.

This is on *YOU*.

You're the only one who can decide that today is the day you stop being a victim and start being a man. Today is the day you stop scrolling and start building. Today is the day you stop making excuses and start making progress.

Nobody's coming to save you. Nobody's going to hand you purpose, discipline, or respect. You have to *TAKE* it. You have to *EARN* it.

And you have to

START. RIGHT. NOW.

And when they ask what started it, tell them it started here. With men who refused to be ashamed of being men. With fathers who showed up. With brothers who stood together. With sons who chose truth over comfort.

Because men build.

Men protect.

Men serve.

Men matter.

And it's time the world remembers why.

REFERENCES & BIBLIOGRAPHY

STATISTICAL SOURCES

AAA Foundation for Traffic Safety. (2022). *Vehicle maintenance and knowledge study.* Washington, DC: AAA Foundation for Traffic Safety.

American Automobile Association. (2022). Vehicle maintenance skills survey: Generational analysis. Retrieved from https://www.aaa.com

American Automobile Association. (2022). Vehicle maintenance skills survey: Generational analysis. Washington, DC: AAA. https://www.aaa.com

American Foundation for Suicide Prevention. (2023). Suicide statistics. Retrieved from https://afsp.org/suicide-statistics

American Foundation for Suicide Prevention. (2023). Suicide statistics. Retrieved from https://afsp.org/suicide-statistics

American Institute of Stress. (2023). Workplace stress statistics. Fort Worth, TX: The American Institute of Stress. https://www.stress.org

American Institute of Stress. (2023). Workplace stress statistics. Retrieved from https://www.stress.org/workplace-stress

American Journal of Men's Health. (2021). *Social isolation and cardiovascular disease in men.* 15(6), 1–10.

American Journal of Men's Health. (2021). *Social isolation and cardiovascular disease in men. American Journal of Men's Health, 15*(6), 155798832110636. https://doi.org/

American Perspectives Survey. (2021). *The state of American friendship: Male friendship trends.* Washington, DC: American Enterprise Institute, Survey Center on American Life.

American Perspectives Survey. (2021). The state of American friendship: Male friendship trends. Washington, DC: American Enterprise Institute. Retrieved from https://www.americansurveycenter.org

American Psychological Association. (2019). *Guidelines for psychological practice with boys and men. American Psychologist, 74*(1), 1–17. https://doi.org/

American Psychological Association. (2019). *Guidelines for psychological practice with boys and men. American Psychologist, 74*(1), 1–17. https://doi.org/

American Psychological Association. (2019). Stress in America: Coping with change. Monitor on Psychology. Retrieved from https://www.apa.org/news/press/releases/stress

American Psychological Association. (2023). 2023 trends in mental health and well-being. Retrieved from https://www.apa.org/news

American Psychological Association. (2023). Divorce and child custody. APA Topics page. Retrieved from https://www.apa.org/topics/divorce-child-custody

American Psychological Association. (2023). Stress in America: The state of our nation. Washington, DC: American Psychological Association https://www.apa.org/news/press/releases

American Psychological Association. (2023). Stress in America: The state of our nation. Washington, DC: Author. https://www.apa.org/news/press/releases/stress

American Psychological Association. (n.d.). Monitor on Psychology. Retrieved from https://www.apa.org/monitor

AmeriCorps & U.S. Census Bureau. (2022). Volunteering and civic life in America: 2022. Washington, DC: Corporation for National and Community Service. https://americorps.gov

Aspen Institute. (2022). State of play 2022: Trends and developments in youth sports. Washington, DC: Sports & Society Program. https://www.aspenprojectplay.org

Aspen Institute. (2022). State of play 2022: Trends and developments in youth sports. Washington, DC: The Aspen Institute. https://www.aspenprojectplay.org

Association for Career and Technical Education. (2013). CTE today: Facts and figures on career and technical education. Retrieved from https://www.acteonline.org

Beck, J. (2021, July 9). *The decline of male friendship. The Atlantic.* https://www.theatlantic.com/family/archive/2021/07/men-friendship-crisis/619354

Beck, J. (2021, June). *The decline of male friendship. The Atlantic.* Retrieved from https://www.theatlantic.com

Beyond Finance. (2024). 401(k) knowledge and financial confidence study. Retrieved from https://www.beyondfinance.com

Big Brothers Big Sisters of America. (2022). Male mentorship trends and volunteer statistics. Retrieved from https://www.bbbs.org

BigRentz. (2019). Home maintenance survey: Who knows what they're doing? Retrieved from https://www.bigrentz.com

Brookings Institution. (2023). The millennial earnings gap and economic mobility. Washington, DC: Brookings Institution. https://www.brookings.edu

Bureau of Labor Statistics. (2023). American time use survey: Time spent in primary activities. U.S. Department of Labor. https://www.bls.gov/tus

Bureau of Labor Statistics. (2023). Employment in manufacturing and trade occupations, 1973–2023. U.S. Department of Labor. https://www.bls.gov

Centers for Disease Control and Prevention, National Center for Health Statistics. (2023). Life expectancy in the U.S.: 2023 update. https://www.cdc.gov/nchs

Centers for Disease Control and Prevention, National Center for Health Statistics. (2023). *National vital statistics reports: Fertility rates and birth data.* Washington, DC: U.S. Department of Health and Human Services.

Centers for Disease Control and Prevention, National Center for Injury Prevention and Control. (2022). Web-based injury statistics query and reporting system (WISQARS): Fatal injury reports. https://www.cdc.gov/injury/wisqars

Centers for Disease Control and Prevention. (2000). Nonmarital childbearing in the United States, 1940–99 (Ventura, S. J., & Bachrach, C. A.). National Vital Statistics Reports, 48(16). https://www.cdc.gov/nchs

Centers for Disease Control and Prevention. (2022). Attention-deficit/hyperactivity disorder (ADHD): Data and statistics. https://www.cdc.gov/ncbddd/adhd

Centers for Disease Control and Prevention. (2022). National center for injury prevention and control: Web-based injury statistics (WISQARS). https://www.cdc.gov/injury/wisqars

Centers for Disease Control and Prevention. (2022). National marriage and divorce rate trends. National Center for Health Statistics. https://www.cdc.gov/nchs

Centers for Disease Control and Prevention. (2023). Adult obesity facts. National Center for Chronic Disease Prevention and Health Promotion. https://www.cdc.gov/obesity

Centers for Disease Control and Prevention. (2023). Anxiety and depression among adolescent girls. National Center for Health Statistics. https://www.cdc.gov/nchs

Centers for Disease Control and Prevention. (2023). Life expectancy in the U.S., 2023 update. National Center for Health Statistics. https://www.cdc.gov/nchs

Centers for Disease Control and Prevention. (2023). National vital statistics reports: Fertility rates and birth data. U.S. Department of Health and Human Services. https://www.cdc.gov/nchs

Centers for Disease Control and Prevention. (2023). Youth risk behavior survey data summary & trends report: 2011–2021. Atlanta, GA: U.S. Department of Health and Human Services. https://www.cdc.gov/healthyyouth

Cigna. (2023). Loneliness index: The growing impact of social isolation in America. Bloomfield, CT: Cigna Corporation. https://www.cigna.com

Cigna. (2023). *Loneliness index: The growing impact of social isolation in America*. Retrieved from https://www.cigna.com/about-us/newsroom

CNBC & Morning Consult. (2023). Retirement readiness poll. Retrieved from https://www.cnbc.com

Common Sense Media. (2021). The Common Sense Census: Media use by tweens and teens. San Francisco, CA: Common Sense Media. https://www.commonsensemedia.org

Common Sense Media. (2021). The common sense census: Media use by tweens and teens. San Francisco, CA: Common Sense Media. https://www.commonsensemedia.org

Common Sense Media. (2023). Social media use among teenage girls: Time and image exposure study. https://www.commonsensemedia.org

Common Sense Media. (2023). Social media use among teenage girls: Time and image exposure study. San Francisco, CA: Common Sense Media. https://www.commonsensemedia.org

Covenant Eyes. (2023). Pornography statistics: Annual report on internet trends and online safety. Retrieved from https://www.covenanteyes.com

Entertainment Software Association. (2023). Essential facts about the U.S. video game industry: Annual report. Retrieved from https://www.theesa.com

Fight the New Drug. (2023). Research and statistics on pornography consumption. Retrieved from https://fightthenewdrug.org

FinanceBuzz. (2025). Most Americans can't change a tire—and many don't want to. Retrieved from https://financebuzz.com

Foundation for Individual Rights and Expression. (2023). Faculty survey on academic freedom. Philadelphia, PA: FIRE. https://www.thefire.org

Foundation for Individual Rights and Expression. (2023). Student and employee self-censorship trends. Philadelphia, PA: FIRE. https://www.thefire.org

Foundation for Individual Rights and Expression. (2023). The culture of self-censorship on campus and in the workplace. Philadelphia, PA: FIRE. https://www.thefire.org

Gallup Organization. (2023). Americans' sense of purpose and meaning in life. Retrieved from https://www.gallup.com

Gallup. (2023). Understanding Gen Z: Meaning, purpose, and wellbeing. Washington, DC: Gallup, Inc. https://www.gallup.com

Gallup. (2024). State of the global workplace report. Washington, DC: Gallup, Inc. https://www.gallup.com

Gartzia, L., & Van Knippenberg, D. (2023). The penalty of masculinity: Gendered perceptions of leadership and promotion. Journal of Experimental Social Psychology, 105, 104419. https://doi.org/

Geena Davis Institute on Gender in Media. (2021). The representation of men and fathers in family programming. Los Angeles, CA: GDIGM. https://seejane.org

General Social Survey. (2021). Sexual inactivity and relationship trends among American adults. University of Chicago, NORC. https://gss.norc.org

Harvard Business Review. (n.d.). *Research by Harvard Business School.* Retrieved from https://hbr.org

Harvard T.H. Chan School of Public Health. (n.d.). Official website. Retrieved from https://www.hsph.harvard.edu

Holt-Lunstad, J., & Smith, T. B. (2023). *Social relationships and mortality risk among men. American Journal of Men's Health, 17*(4), 1–10. https://doi.org

HomeAdvisor. (2023). Home repair skills survey: Generational competency analysis. Retrieved from https://www.homeadvisor.com

Hunt, M. G., Marx, R., Lipson, C., & Young, J. (2018). No more FOMO: Limiting social media decreases loneliness and depression. Journal of Social and Clinical Psychology, 37(10), 751–768. https://doi.org

Institute for Family Studies. (2023). Fathers' time use in America: What has changed and what hasn't. Charlottesville, VA: Institute for Family Studies. https://ifstudies.org

John S. and James L. Knight Foundation. (n.d.). Official website. Retrieved from https://knightfoundation.org

Josephson Institute of Ethics. (2010–2015). *Character Counts! Sportsmanship studies.* [Archival references].

Josephson Institute of Ethics. (2023). Youth participation awards and achievement culture study. Retrieved from https://josephsoninstitute.org

Journal of Hand Therapy. (2016). *Stanford University study on hand strength. Journal of Hand Therapy, 29*(4), 436–443.

Journal of Youth and Adolescence. (2022). Father absence and adolescent female mental health and risk behaviors. *Journal of Youth and Adolescence, 51*(12), 2478–2491. https://doi.org/

Knight Foundation. (2023). Free expression on college campuses: A survey of student views. Washington, DC: Knight Foundation. https://knightfoundation.org

Levine, H., Jørgensen, N., Martino-Andrade, A., et al. (2017). Temporal trends in sperm count: A systematic review and meta-regression analysis. *Human Reproduction Update, 23*(6), 646–659. https://doi.org/

LinkedIn Economic Graph. (2023). Entry-level job requirements and skills gap analysis. Retrieved from https://economicgraph.linkedin.com

Match.com. (2023). Singles in America: Annual survey on dating and relationships. Retrieved from https://www.singlesinamerica.com

Morgan Stanley. (2022). Rise of the single female economy. Retrieved from https://www.morganstanley.com

National Assessment of Educational Progress. (2011). The nation's report card: Reading. U.S. Department of Education. https://nces.ed.gov/nationsreportcard

National Assessment of Educational Progress. (2022). Reading assessment results. U.S. Department of Education. https://nces.ed.gov/nationsreportcard

National Center for Education Statistics. (2023). Digest of education statistics: High school graduation rates. Washington, DC: U.S. Department of Education. https://nces.ed.gov

National Center for Education Statistics. (2024). Undergraduate enrollment by gender. Washington, DC: U.S. Department of Education. https://nces.ed.gov

National Center for Education Statistics. (n.d.). *Achievement gaps*. U.S. Department of Education. Retrieved from https://nces.ed.gov/nationsreportcard/studies/gaps

National Center for Fathering. (2023). Quantifying the crisis: Father absence and its national impact. Retrieved from https://fathers.com

National Center for Fathering. (2023). The consequences of fatherlessness. Retrieved from https://fathers.com

National Fatherhood Initiative. (2015). *Father facts* (7th ed.). Gaithersburg, MD: National Fatherhood Initiative.

National Fatherhood Initiative. (2021). Father absence statistics. Retrieved from https://www.fatherhood.org

National Financial Educators Council. (2023). Annual financial literacy survey. Retrieved from https://www.financialeducatorscouncil.org

National Financial Educators Council. (2023). Financial literacy among young adults: 2023 report. Retrieved from https://www.financialeducatorscouncil.org

National Financial Educators Council. (2023). National financial literacy test results. Retrieved from https://www.financialeducatorscouncil.org

National Marriage Project. (2023). The state of our unions: Marriage in America. Charlottesville, VA: University of Virginia. https://nationalmarriageproject.org

National Opinion Research Center (NORC), University of Chicago. (n.d.). General Social Survey. https://gss.norc.org

National Research Group. (2022). The state of men: Exploring modern masculinity. Los Angeles, CA: National Research Group. https://www.nrgmr.com

National Student Clearinghouse Research Center. (2023). Current term enrollment estimates. Retrieved from https://nscresearchcenter.org

Office of Justice Programs. (n.d.). U.S. Department of Justice official site. Retrieved from https://www.ojp.gov

OnlyFans. (2023). Creator demographics and platform growth report. Retrieved from https://www.onlyfans.com

Pew Research Center. (2021). Faith among Americans 2020: Decline in religious affiliation and attendance. Washington, DC: Pew Research Center. https://www.pewresearch.org/religion

Pew Research Center. (2022). Views on masculinity and gender roles in America. Washington, DC: Pew Research Center. https://www.pewresearch.org

Pew Research Center. (2023). Teens, social media and technology 2023. Washington, DC: Pew Research Center. https://www.pewresearch.org

Pew Research Center. (2023). The dating landscape in America: Men under 30 are more likely to be single than women. Washington, DC: Pew Research Center. https://www.pewresearch.org

Pew Research Center. (2024). How Americans see men, women, and society. Washington, DC: Pew Research Center. https://www.pewresearch.org

Psychology Today. (2022). The social cost of self-improvement: Why growth makes others uncomfortable. Psychology Today Magazine. https://www.psychologytoday.com

Puronics. (2021). *Survey: Millennials and home maintenance confidence.* https://puronics.com/news-posts/millennial-home-maintenance/

Royal Society for Public Health. (2017). #StatusOfMind: Social media and young people's mental health and wellbeing. London: RSPH. https://www.rsph.org.uk

Royal Society for Public Health. (2023). #StatusOfMind: Social media and young people's mental health (update). Retrieved from https://www.rsph.org.uk

SAGE Publications. (n.d.). Journal homepage: Journal of Men's Health. Retrieved from https://journals.sagepub.com/home/jmh

School Climate and Safety. (n.d.). Office for Civil Rights data portal. U.S. Department of Education. https://ocrdata.ed.gov

Smith, A., Pachucki, M. C., & Troped, P. J. (2016). Millennial strength: Trends in grip strength in Americans. *Journal of Hand Therapy, 29*(4), 436–443.

Stanford Graduate School of Education. (n.d.). A study of college assessment practices. Retrieved from https://ed.stanford.edu

Survey Center on American Life. (2021). The state of American friendship: Change, challenges, and loss. Washington, DC: American Enterprise Institute. https://www.americansurveycenter.org

U.S. Department of Health and Human Services. (1995). *Report to Congress on out-of-wedlock childbearing* (DHHS Pub. No. [PHS] 95-1257). Washington, DC: U.S. Government Printing Office.

U.S. Department of Justice, Bureau of Justice Statistics. (2002). *Survey of inmates in local jails.* Washington, DC: U.S. Department of Justice.

U.S. Department of Justice, Office of Juvenile Justice and Delinquency Prevention. (1998). *Children of incarcerated parents.* Washington, DC: U.S. Department of Justice.

U.S. Department of Justice. (1988). *Survey of youth in custody, 1987.* Washington, DC: Bureau of Justice Statistics, Office of Justice Programs, U.S. Department of Justice.

U.S. Department of Justice. (2019). *Juvenile offenders and victims: National report.* Washington, DC: Office of Juvenile Justice and Delinquency Prevention.

U.S. Department of Labor. (n.d.). Official website. Retrieved from https://www.bls.gov

University of Michigan, Institute for Social Research. (2022). Panel study of income dynamics: Child development supplement. Retrieved from https://psidonline.isr.umich.edu

Ventura, S. J., & Bachrach, C. A. (2000). Nonmarital childbearing in the United States, 1940–99. *National Vital Statistics Reports, 48*(16). Hyattsville, MD: National Center for Health Statistics.

Waldinger, R. J., & Schulz, M. S. (2023). *The good life: Lessons from the world's longest scientific study of happiness.* New York, NY: Simon & Schuster.

Web-based Injury Statistics Query and Reporting System (WISQARS). (2023). Fatal injury reports. Centers for Disease Control and Prevention. https://www.cdc.gov/injury/wisqars

YMCA of the USA. (2022). Youth program volunteer trends and male participation. Retrieved from https://www.ymca.net

RECOMMENDED READING

Bly, R. (1990). *Iron John: A book about men.* Addison-Wesley.

Centers for Disease Control and Prevention. (2021). *National vital statistics reports.* U.S. Department of Health and Human Services. https://www.cdc.gov/nchs

Child Trends. (2019). *Family structure and adolescent pregnancy.* Bethesda, MD: Child Trends. https://www.childtrends.org

Deida, D. (2004). *The way of the superior man: A spiritual guide to mastering the challenges of women, work, and sexual desire.* Sounds True.

Donovan, J. (2012). *The way of men.* Dissonant Hum.

Dworkin, A. (1981). *Pornography: Men possessing women.* New York, NY: G. P. Putnam's Sons.

Farrell, W. (2018). *The boy crisis: Why our boys are struggling and what we can do about it.* Dallas, TX: BenBella Books.

Gilder, G. (1986). *Men and marriage.* Gretna, LA: Pelican Publishing.

Goggins, D. (2018). *Can't hurt me: Master your mind and defy the odds.* Lioncrest Publishing.

Goggins, D. (2023). *Never finished: Unshackle your mind and win the war within.* Lioncrest Publishing.

MacKinnon, C. A. (1989). *Toward a feminist theory of the state.* Cambridge, MA: Harvard University Press.

National Fatherhood Initiative. (2019). *Father facts* (8th ed.). Germantown, MD: National Fatherhood Initiative.

Office for National Statistics. (2023). *Children's well-being and social media use.* Newport, UK: Office for National Statistics. https://www.ons.gov.uk

Peterson, J. B. (1999). *Maps of meaning: The architecture of belief.* New York, NY: Routledge.

Peterson, J. B. (2018). *12 rules for life: An antidote to chaos.* Toronto, Canada: Random House Canada.

Peterson, J. B. (2021). *Beyond order: 12 more rules for life.* New York, NY: Portfolio/Penguin.

Survey Center on American Life. (2021). *The state of American friendship: Change, challenges, and loss.* Washington, DC: American Enterprise Institute. https://www.americansurvey-center.org

U.S. Census Bureau. (2022). *Income and poverty in the United States: 2022.* Washington, DC: U.S. Department of Commerce. https://www.census.gov

Way, N. (2018). *Deep secrets: Boys' friendships and the crisis of connection.* Cambridge, MA: Harvard University Press.

References & Bibliography

Note: This book reflects the author's personal observations, professional experience, and interpretation of publicly available data. Statistics cited are from government sources and peer-reviewed research.

Readers are encouraged to verify and explore these sources independently.

DISCUSSION QUESTIONS

For Book Clubs, Men's Groups, and Father-Son Conversations

1. The author argues that *"weak men create hard times."* Do you agree? What evidence do you see of this in your own community?

2. Early on the book describes boys being medicated for behavior that was once considered normal. Have you witnessed this in schools? What are the long-term consequences?

3. How has the absence of fathers in homes affected society? Can single mothers successfully raise strong sons without male role models?

4. The book challenges the concept of *"toxic masculinity."* What is the difference between healthy and unhealthy expressions of masculinity?

5. What role did the education system play in feminizing boys? Can schools be reformed, or do parents need to find alternatives?

6. The author describes young men finding purpose through controversial online figures. Why are these voices resonating when traditional institutions failed?

7. How has the *"addiction economy"* (social media, porn, gaming) affected men in your life? What practical steps can be taken to break free?

8. What are the biggest internal battles men face today? How can they win?

9. The book presents a *"New Code of Manhood"* based on responsibility, truth, and discipline. Which of these principles resonates most with you? Which is hardest to live by?

10. What does it mean to *"rebuild the tribe"*? Do modern men have genuine male friendships, or have we lost the ability to form deep bonds with other men?

11. The author writes from the perspective of a father raising a daughter. How does this change the way we think about raising strong men?

12. What is one concrete action you can take this week to reclaim masculinity in your own life or help a young man in your community?

ABOUT THE AUTHOR
RUSSELL STUART

Russell Stuart is a highly respected security expert, entrepreneur, and public servant with over 30 years of experience spanning military service, private security, and the entertainment industry.

He is the Founder and CEO of the *Force Protection Agency*, an elite private security firm often referred to as *"the Secret Service of Hollywood,"* and the owner of *Beverly Hills Guns*, the city's premier concierge firearms dealership.

With nearly a decade of military service in the California State Guard, Stuart has developed advanced expertise in emergency and risk management. His firm has protected A-list celebrities such as *Jennifer Lopez*, *Post Malone*, and *Ozzy Osbourne*, while also empowering local families and law-abiding citizens with the training and tools to safeguard themselves.

Stuart's unique background also includes two decades as a highly accomplished entertainment industry veteran, where he worked in film production, talent management, music, marketing, and brand strategy. This dual expertise, blending Hollywood acumen with tactical security leadership, has made him a trusted protector and advisor to *Fortune 500* executives, celebrities, and private clients alike. He is known for his hands-on leadership, discretion, and ability to coordinate closely with law enforcement and federal agencies on critical investigations.

A strong believer in service, integrity, and personal responsibility, Stuart is deeply committed to public safety and community resilience. He has appeared as a national media contributor on networks like *Fox News* and *ABC Radio*, offering insights on crime prevention and community security.

On November 14, 2024, Stuart survived a near-fatal carjacking in Beverly Hills, an experience that deepened his resolve to fight for a safer, stronger America. As a husband, father, and elected member of the ***Beverly Hills Unified School District*** *Board of Education*, he champions safe schools, transparent governance, and constitutional rights. His leadership is defined by action, trust, and an unwavering focus on protecting students, empowering parents, and ensuring the next generation of men has the strength and character to lead.

Stuart lives in Beverly Hills with his wife Lisa, daughter Arabelle and their dog, Rudy.

Reclaiming Men is his first book.

Connect with *Russell Stuart*

Website: www.russellstuart.com
Email: publishing@russellstuart.com
Social Media: @russellstuart

JOIN THE MOVEMENT

This book is just the beginning.

If you're ready to reclaim masculinity in your home, school, or community, here's how to get started:

vist www.russellstuart.com

- Join the Reclaiming Men community
- Book Russell for speaking engagements
- Access exclusive content and tools

TAKE ACTION TODAY:

- Share this book with fathers, teachers, coaches, and mentors who need it
- Start a men's group in your church or community
- Demand accountability in your local schools
- Raise your sons with purpose, not apologies
- Mentor a fatherless boy in your neighborhood

FOR BULK ORDERS:

Schools, men's groups, Churches, and organizations can order discounted copies for group study.

Email: publishing@russellstuart.com

THE FIGHT ISN'T OVER. IT'S JUST BEGINNING.

Men matter. Masculinity matters. And it's time we stop apologizing for it.

RECLAIM MASCULINITY. REBUILD MEN. RESTORE HONOR.

— *Russell Stuart*

www.ingramcontent.com/pod-product-compliance
Lightning Source LLC
Chambersburg PA
CBHW051609120626
46551CB00014B/1726